The Politics of Economic Restructuring in India

State rescaling is the central concept mobilized in this book to interpret the political processes that are producing new economic spaces in India. In the quarter century since economic reforms were introduced, the Indian economy has experienced strong growth accompanied by extensive sectoral and spatial restructuring. This book argues that in this reformed institutional context, where both state spaces and economic geographies are being rescaled, subnational states play an increasingly critical role in coordinating socioeconomic activities.

The core thesis that the book defends is that the reform process has profoundly reconfigured the Indian state's rapport with its territory at all spatial scales, and these processes of state spatial rescaling are crucial for comprehending emerging patterns of economic governance and growth. It demonstrates that the outcomes of India's new policy regime are not only the product of impersonal market forces, but that they are also the result of endogenous political strategies, acting in conjunction with the territorial reorganisation of economic activities at various scales, ranging from local to global.

Extensive empirical case material, primarily from field-based research, is used to support these theoretical assertions. Scholars of political economy, political and economic geography, industrial development, development studies and Asian Studies will find this a stimulating and innovative contribution to the study of political economy in developing countries.

Loraine Kennedy is a Research Director at the French National Centre for Scientific Research (CNRS) in Paris, France. Her current research focuses on subnational political economy in India.

Routledge Contemporary South Asia Series

The Politics of Economic Restructuring in India

Economic governance and
state spatial rescaling

Loraine Kennedy

Routledge
Taylor & Francis Group

LONDON AND NEW YORK

First published 2014
by Routledge

2 Park Square, Milton Park, Abingdon, Oxfordshire OX14 4RN
711 Third Avenue, New York, NY 10017

Routledge is an imprint of the Taylor & Francis Group, an informa business

First issued in paperback 2017

British Library Cataloguing in Publication Data
A catalogue record for this book is available from the British Library

Library of Congress Cataloging in Publication Data
Kennedy, Loraine.
The politics of economic restructuring in India : economic governance and
state spatial rescaling / Loraine Kennedy.
  pages cm. -- (Routledge contemporary South Asia series ; 75)
Includes bibliographical references and index.
   1. Structural adjustment (Economic policy)--India. 2. Income
distribution--India. 3. India--Economic conditions--1991- I. Title.
   HC435.3.K42 2014
   338.954--dc23
      2013021549

ISBN: 978-0-415-82282-4 (hbk)
ISBN: 978-0-8153-6911-0 (pbk)

Typeset in Times New Roman
by Taylor & Francis Books

Dedicated to the
memory of
Jos E. Mooij (1959–2013)

Contents

List of maps and tables

Maps

Tables

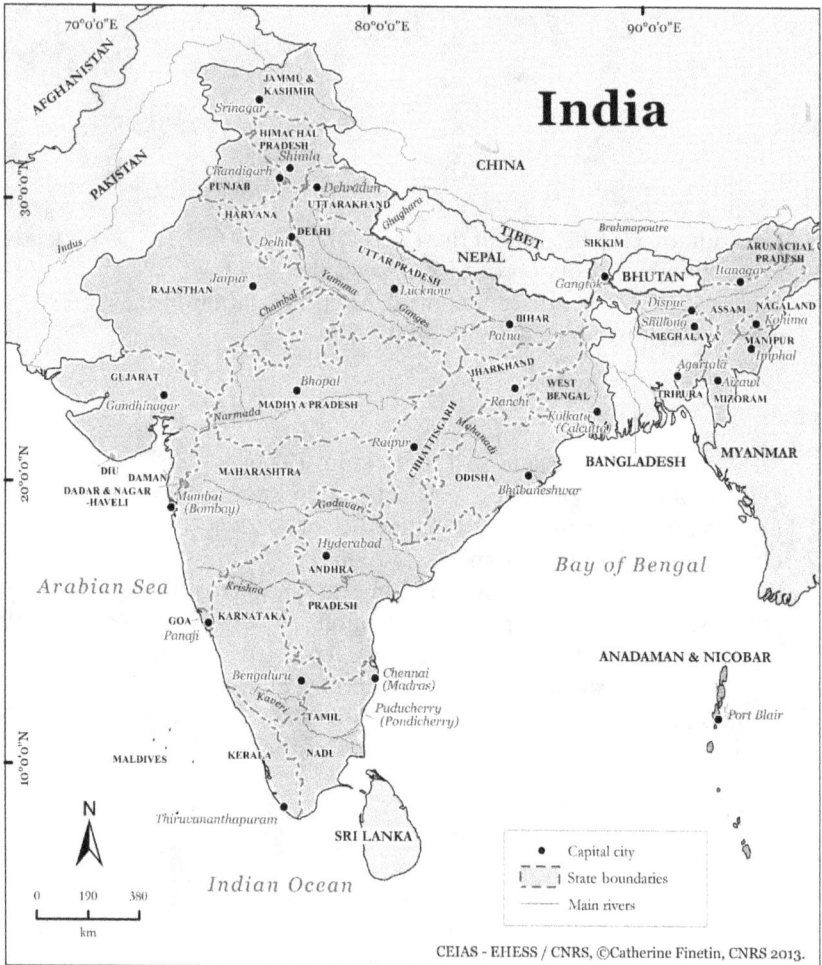

Map of India

Acknowledgements

The research material discussed in this book was generated over a long period of time, a period over which I have contracted many debts. Although it would be impossible to acknowledge all of the individuals—colleagues, friends, countless people interviewed in Kerala, Tamil Nadu, Andhra Pradesh, Haryana, Orissa and Delhi—who contributed to my understanding of India's political economy, I would like to mention here some key figures.

It is appropriate for a book on state spatial rescaling to start by acknowledging my debt to the geographers with whom I have been fortunate to interact since joining the CNRS in 1998. For first clueing me in to the critical relevance of space and scale for social science research, at REGARDS/ADES in Bordeaux, my thanks go to Xavier Amelot, Jean-Paul Deler, Guy Di Méo, Kamala Marius-Gnanou and to two colleagues no longer with us, Doryane Kermel-Torres and Philippe Schar.

My growing interest in space and territory, and the finer distinctions between the two, was considerably enhanced through collaboration with an international research group, starting in 2005, that sought to compare and contrast various types and degrees of territorialisation in metropolitan cities (*Territorialisation des espaces urbanisés dans les grandes villes: une confrontation Nord–Sud*). It was then I started a systematic exploration of rescaling theory and its relevance for interpreting the Indian case. My personal research greatly benefited from discussions held within that group and I am grateful to Sylvy Jaglin for that opportunity. Special thanks to C. Ramachandraiah for many joint fieldwork outings in Hyderabad, to M. Sitamma for her able assistance and pleasant company and to K. Srinivasulu, whose deep understanding of the political economy of Andhra Pradesh has been a source of inspiration over the years, for many thoughtful discussions.

Another research programme, "Urban Actors, Policies and Governance", provided a timely opportunity to study in some depth the impact of liberalisation and decentralisation reforms on governance in India's metropolitan cities, and examine in a comparative perspective rescaling processes in urban spaces. Under Stéphanie Tawa Lama-Rewal's competent leadership, this lively research group debated how the reforms observed in service delivery systems were indicative of broader changes underway.

A two-year stay at the Centre de Sciences Humaines (CSH) in Delhi between 2007 and 2009 allowed me to pursue the study of subnational economic processes and compare the varying responses of India's States to the national reform agenda. Through their dedicated research, Kim Robin and Diego Zamuner contributed in significant ways to furthering that project, and I am thankful for their collaboration. I am grateful to the colleagues and staff at the CSH whose camaraderie and good cheer made my stay in Delhi (and subsequent visits) very enjoyable. Special thanks to Basudeb Chaudhuri for his constant support and natural enthusiasm and to Mallika Hanif, whose peerless efficiency always went along with a smile and a kind word.

Equally important for sharpening arguments on the articulation of state scales was a research project on the politics of India's Special Economic Zones. The idea for this project took shape in discussions with Rob Jenkins, with whom I have had the delight and good fortune to collaborate over the years on our many common research interests. The idea transformed into a full-fledged project, which Rob and I coordinated with Partha Mukho-padhyay, starting in 2008 at the CSH and the Centre for Policy Research. I express my gratitude to the participants of that eleven-State study for their dedicated and careful research and for many stimulating discussions over the years.

A word of appreciation goes to my employer of the last fifteen years, the CNRS, where I have enjoyed tremendous freedom to pursue my research interests. At a time when budgets for public research are under growing pressure, I gratefully acknowledge support from the French ministry of research and higher education, which funded most of the projects mentioned above.

The first draft of this book was publicly defended as a *habilitation* thesis in 2012 at the Université Paris Ouest Nanterre. Alain Dubresson was the perfect 'tuteur' for this exercise, combining with graceful ease scientific rigour and good humour at every stage of the process and I am grateful to him. We had the occasion, when meeting hard deadlines, to reiterate our mutual appreciation of how informal institutions allow formal institutions to function! Warm thanks also to the members of the jury: Isa Baud, Frédéric Landy and Jean-Luc Racine, for instructive inputs based on their deep understanding of the Indian case, and Jean-François Huchet, for his insightful comparisons of state restructuring and economic governance in India and China.

Finishing the habilitation thesis on schedule would not have been possible without the encouragement and support of my co-directors at the Centre d'Études de l'Inde et de l'Asie du Sud (CEIAS, CNRS-EHESS) in Paris: Aminah Mohammad-Arif, Blandine Ripert and Stéphanie Tawa Lama-Rewal, who willingly took over my share of the work so I could finish writing up. Sharing the burdens and joys of administration over the last few years with such excellent colleagues, now friends, has been a rich and satisfying experience.

The manuscript also benefited from stimulating discussions which took place in a series of workshops on 'State Restructuring and Rescaling in Comparative Perspective' held in Paris and Leiden in 2012, with support from the CEIAS and the International Institute of Asian Studies. Special thanks to my co-coordinators Véronique Dupont, Tak-Wing Ngo and Aurélie Varrel and to the participants: Jean-François Huchet, Hein A.M. Klemann, Damien Krichewsky, Frédéric Landy, Darel E. Paul, Xuefei Ren, Nikita Sud, M. Vijayabaskar and Ben Wubs.

Through their incisive questions and feedback, my students at the EHESS also contributed to shaping this volume and I record here my appreciation and best wishes.

For helping to turn the manuscript into a book, I wish to thank Kelly Keeler for copy-editing (and renewed friendship), and at Routledge Dorothea Schaefter, the Senior Editor for Asian Studies, as well as Jillian Morrison and Ruth Bradley, who have been most helpful every step of the way.

Lastly, special thanks are in order for my dear friends who have accompanied me in my research over the years by offering critical and constructive comments, through joint fieldwork or just taking time to discuss over countless hours Indian society, politics and economy: Zarin Ahmad, Amitabha Bagchi, Keshab Das, Hélène Guétat-Bernard, Christophe Guilmoto, Rob Jenkins, Ratika Kapur, K.N. Kumar, Kamal Lodaya, Jos Mooij, Madhavan Mukund, Blandine Ripert, Sunanda Sen, Meenakshi Thapan, G. Venkatasubramanian, Gilles Verniers, M. Vijayabaskar, Marie-Héléne Zérah, Ines Zupanov.

Jos E. Mooij, to whom this book is dedicated, deserves particular mention. Her friendship and intellectual company were a tremendous source of pleasure and inspiration over the ten years we knew each other. She is sorely missed by her friends and colleagues and the field of Indian studies has lost a dedicated scholar.

1 The politics of economic restructuring in India

1.1 Introducing the core topics

In the quarter century since India introduced economic reforms, its economy has experienced remarkable change: strong growth accompanied by extensive economic restructuring, both sectoral and spatial. Although largely driven by market forces, I argue here that these economic changes can only be understood in relation to *state restructuring*, which has come about as a result of political strategy, territorial reorganisation of economic activities within and without India, and institutional change. Not only has the Indian state's role in the economy been significantly redefined through the reform process, the state's relation to national territory has been distinctly reconfigured in recent decades. In particular, the concomitance between national state and national space *in the definition of its economic development policies*, which was carefully constructed during the nationalist movement for independence and further strengthened in the following decades through institutions, policies and discourse, has been re-examined and reconfigured. The core objective of this study is to understand this unfolding process and explore its consequences for *economic governance*, defined as the institutions and actors shaping the economic and political processes that coordinate economic activities. In my analysis, I assume that economic governance, as it is exercised at different territorial scales, is a key determinant of the spatial organisation of economic activities.

I undertake here to study three sets of interrelated processes: (1) the reconfiguration of state spatial scales; (2) economic policy-making at subnational scales; and the (3) interactions between rescaling and economic governance.

Changes in the economic policy regime at the national level in the context of gradual but deep-seated economic reforms provide the departure point for this study. I will argue that these reforms have put into motion processes of state spatial restructuring, which reposition the state with regard to economic governance. This research consists in analysing the modalities of state restructuring, with particular attention to processes of territorial rescaling, defined as the reordering of jurisdictional spaces in a polity. Although rescaling can occur as a consequence of administrative reforms in the shape of decentralisation or devolution, it will be argued here that more significant processes are underway, which are contributing to the construction of new 'state spaces' (Brenner 2004), occurring largely as a result of uncoordinated processes. These include strategies on the part of national and subnational political elites as well as initiatives of individuals and social groups, private firms, and associations located at various spatial scales.

This study will examine examples of emerging governance mechanisms such as new rules and policies for industrial investment, regulatory tools for promoting new clusters of activity that largely target transnational corporations, and public–private partnerships for large-scale infrastructure projects on the basis of locally negotiated arrangements. As these examples indicate, local and regional dynamics bring together players as well as rules and regulations from different scales. It is within this fluid and sometimes legally ambiguous context that state actors pursue goals, which are not limited to predefined political objectives such as economic efficiency or social justice. As Campbell *et al.* have observed: 'struggles over *strategic control and power within economic exchange* (…) provide the principal dynamic for governance transformations' (1991: 5, emphasis added).

My central argument is that in India's reworked institutional context, subnational scales are crucial for understanding emerging patterns of economic governance. However, the emergence of subnational state spaces is not a necessary outcome, nor does it follow a predetermined template. It is a historical process originating from territorially embedded institutions and dynamics – the mobilisation of social groups through political processes as well as the activation of territorially embedded socio-economic resources (entrepreneurship, regional economic specialisations, socioeconomic configurations) – in conjunction with state actors and structures. Furthermore, I consider that these new state spaces are increasingly penetrated by dynamics occurring at other scales, and influenced by their interactions with transnational actors (e.g., international development agencies, multinational corporations, global NGOs, organised diasporic groups) and that the latter are contributing directly and indirectly to building these scales.

Finally, this research is concerned with the consequences of state spatial restructuring on everyday economic governance at various spatial scales in India, notably on the conditions affecting collective action.

As these points underscore, this research is primarily concerned with the consequences of economic reforms, not on economic performance directly.[1] I am interested in the process of institutional change, how the 'rules of the game' are being rewritten, with special attention to state actors and to the spatial dimension of the state. These processes involve multiple scales and the conceptual framework I adopt is designed to favour a multiscalar approach.

One of the broad objectives of this study is to counter macro-scale structuralist narratives about India's growth story with a more fine-grained account of political processes that are constructing new political economic spaces. One such structuralist narrative contends that India's decision to undergo reforms and its subsequent policy regime were imposed from outside the country, suggesting that India's leadership has not acted of its own volition. Another such narrative interprets increasing social and spatial disparities across national territory and within States[2] as a mechanical consequence of India's more liberal policy regime thereby neglecting to consider outcomes as the result of deliberate policy choices. Both of these suggest helplessness and both remove responsibility from India's elected leaders. The argument advanced here is that India's political elites exercise agency and they are contributing in significant ways to shaping economic governance, along with other actors. Recognising these processes as part of politics opens the possibility that they can be contested within the political process.

1.2 Theoretical foundations

State spatial restructuring, or state rescaling, is the main theoretical concept mobilised in this study. This spatially sensitive approach to the study of state power and political economy is combined with an institutional perspective of social change to form a hybrid conceptual framework (see below).

The rescaling literature was built up over the 1980s and 1990s to explain how the economic slowdown of the 1970s (1960s for the US), analysed as a crisis of capitalism, was shaking up the welfare-state model in advanced industrialised economies. It focused on how national states were responding to increasing competition at all spatial scales and to the changing geographical organisation of economic activities (internationalisation then outsourcing). Policies adopted at that time, most explicitly under Margaret Thatcher in the UK and Ronald Reagan in the US, focused on downsizing the state through privatisation and deregulation. Backed by powerful interest groups, these countries pushed a neo-liberal policy agenda in international fora aimed at easing restrictions on trade and capital movement. Although fundamentally an ideological project, global economic integration was facilitated by the development of information and communication technologies that accelerated capital movement. As trade barriers were dismantled and markets became more integrated, states responded by adopting strategies aimed at producing competitive spaces at subnational scales, primarily in urban areas. These were termed 'rescaling' strategies because they involved shifting the policy focus from the national scale to subnational scales and to specific spaces deemed more capable of competing in global markets.

David Harvey, one of the key theorists working in this stream, analysed these processes as a shift of capitalist reproduction from national to subnational scales (1989). Continuing in the same broad theoretical path, subsequent scholarship elaborated the concepts of 'glocal states' (Swyngedouw 1996) and 'glocal fixes' (Brenner 1998), referring to the specific ways states seek to equip local spaces to better engage with global markets. Such strategies attract capital through space-based interventions, such as specialised infrastructure, in well-connected places, usually urban regions. One of the central hypotheses of this neo-Marxist perspective is that each phase of capitalism is rooted in particular forms of territorial organisation, socially produced geographical *infrastructures* intended to facilitate capital investment and accumulation (Brenner 1998: 13).

Similar observations about spatial economic restructuring, framed differently and using different terminology, emerged simultaneously in other branches of scholarship, notably on competitive regions. Throughout the 1980s and 1990s, there was increasing scientific interest in subnational regions among scholars studying global economic restructuring as well as the dynamics of urban and regional economies (Benko and Lipietz 1992). The idea that regions were becoming the engines of the global economy gained ground progressively (Scott 1998, 2001). A common pattern emerging from various fields was the growing tendency for economic activities to concentrate in space, such as in industrial clusters or metropolitan regions (Veltz 1996; Sassen 1991).

These various bodies of research shared a common concern with the changing role of the national state in the context of globalisation and with the emergence of new regulatory spaces – regional, urban, global. The world cities research project was also engaged with this question to the extent that it undertook to analyse the spatial organisation of the new international division of labour (Friedmann 1986, cited by Brenner 1998: 4)

The 'new competition' emblematic of the emerging economic order was based on more flexible production and emphasised cooperation and connectivity (Piore and Sabel 1984; Best 1990). Economic performance depended increasingly on the density and the quality of cooperative relations among economic agents (Veltz 1996). The contribution of the literature on industrial districts in the Third Italy, for instance, was extremely important for elucidating socioeconomic processes at the meso and local scales, which were rooted in social institutions and dynamics, such as the social regulation of the market (Brusco 1982; Trigilia 1986). This scholarship inspired research on small firm clusters in developing economies as well (Schmitz 1995; Nadvi and Schmitz 1999), including India.[3] French economists and economic geographers built on these theoretical developments and a school of 'proximity' economics arose in the early 1990s, emphasising the importance of territorial moorings as well as local and regional institutions.[4] The idea was that the adaptation of firms to more stringent competition compelled them to redefine their relation to space, and to consider the advantages of a territory-based strategy. For Bernard Pecqueur, a 'territoire' is not a spatial entity, although situated in space, but rather the result of a unique process of coordination among different actors which creates a modality for capital accumulation and for valorising new types of resources, including latent ones (2001: 243). A *territoire* emerges from the constitution of a group or competing groups and hence from collective action, at least partially structured around spatially based resources.

During this same period, the role of institutions in economic performance started receiving more serious attention, including from mainstream economists, thanks chiefly to the theoretical contribution of Douglas North (1990).

Although not explicitly his project, the Nobel Prize winner's work bridged a gap between the 'old' American institutionalist school[5] and the mainstream economics establishment. This provided a theoretical foundation for integrating social and historical factors into the performance equation providing a better understanding about why growth happens in some places and not in others. Dani Rodrik in particular has been at the forefront of research mobilising an institutional framework to examine developing economies (Rodrik 2007), including India (Rodrik and Subramanian 2004). This research underscores the pre-eminence of institutions, compared to other factors such as free trade, as explanatory variables for economic development.[6]

Institutions are the foundations of social organisation, or to use a popular analogy, the 'rules of the game', and as such they organise the behaviour of political and economic actors. It is important to emphasise that while institutions reflect deeply held social and cultural values, they also emerge as a result of social compromises. Bruno Amable (2003) defines social compromise as a 'political economy equilibrium' between social groups with conflicting interests. Institutions prevailing at a particular point in time express this compromise, and must be constantly renegotiated:

> the institutional configuration of an economy depends on the political support provided by a dominant socio-political coalition or 'social bloc'. Institutional change is the outcome of strategies aimed at improving the situation of some or all components of the dominant bloc. The bloc itself being heterogeneous, institutions are always the result of compromises between actors who do not generally have perfect vision of all inter-dependencies and complementarities between institutions. With changes in agents' options and strategies, the social compromise has to be continuously re-established.
>
> (Crouch *et al.* 2005)

As previously stated, the goal here is to analyse changes in economic governance, including institutional change brought about through policy reform, which I assume to have direct consequences for growth and development. Economic reforms, which are fundamentally a political process, consist in changing the rules of the game. At the same time, reforms are mediated through *existing* institutions. This is an important point and supports the argument that India's current economic performance is rooted in pre-existing institutions, and is not a result of a *tabula rasa*; there is continuity along with rapid change. A second important theoretical principle is that while policies are mediated through institutions, policies also shape action via incentives or penalties, and contribute to forging new institutional arrangements. This is illustrated for instance, when policy-makers revise a policy as a result of its reception on the ground, particularly in cases of mobilised contestation (see Chapter 5). The revisions then modify the incentive structure.

Broadly defined, economic governance refers to the institutions and actors who shape the economic and political processes that coordinate economic activities; governance mechanisms include markets, bureaucracies, associations and informal networks of various kinds (Campbell *et al.* 1991: 3). As with the concept of 'governance' the idea is that multiple actors, state and non-state, local and supra-local, participate in political outcomes (policy statements, rules, regulations) and shape their implementation. Governance, as it is used here, incorporates power, and can accommodate institutionalised unequal power relations, which must be established empirically for each case. In the Indian context, it is particularly important to underscore the tendency for institutions to reflect the beliefs and values of dominant social groups, and to reproduce the social order. In the process of institutional change, differential power relations affect outcomes. Institutional change can be conceptualised as a *political compromise* expressing the expectations and power relations of the social actors involved (Amable and Palombarini, 2005: 208). It follows that emerging institutional arrangements do not correspond to one unique purpose, regardless of the stated purpose that prompted their elaboration.

In this study of India, I proceed on the assumption that state actors and structures play a predominant role in shaping the new economic governance arrangements; even in the presence of other powerful actors and 'market forces', they dispose of a degree of agency, although this degree is variable across time and space and contingent on other factors. Economic reforms have provided tremendous opportunities for political elites in India, both elected officials and bureaucrats, to reap economic gains, through licit and illicit means, and this incentive structure is shaping emerging economic governance arrangements. This position is not based on rational choice (utility maximising) assumptions but rather on the *contingent rationality* of social actors 'where the political, economic, ideological, and other institutional conditions prevalent at the moment constrain the range of choices available in the first place. Indeed, a variety of values or ideologies, including but not limited to opportunism and avariciousness, motivates economic activity and is conditioned by all of these contingencies, not just markets' (Campbell *et al.* 1991: 6; see also Hall 1986). This approach to agency is not incompatible with one that places emphasis on collective social action. Indeed the two can be fruitfully combined in a multiscalar approach.

To study the support bases of subnational political regimes and seek insights into the social compromises over which they preside and give expression, I mobilise a qualitative political economy framework. This framework does not assume the state to be 'captured' by specific social classes; indeed class categories are not necessarily the most useful for understanding social mobilisation in India, where identity (caste, religion, regional) plays a pre-eminent role. In this book, the use of the term class (e.g., middle class, working class) is descriptive and not analytical; it does not assume mobilisation on the part of the group.

Within this overarching theoretical framework, the key components are not only institutions and actors, but also space and territory. The rescaling concept is the tool through which I propose to apprehend the emergence of new state spaces as well as the spatial dimension of specific economic policies.

1.3 A hybrid conceptual framework

The rich research emerging from the rescaling field of inquiry provides a powerful theoretical framework for engaging with processes of federalism, decentralisation and multilevel governance that are at the core of this study. It constitutes a major source of inspiration for the hybrid conceptual framework I will be using here.

Compared to the traditional field of government science and policy studies the value-added of the rescaling literature is that it gives full attention to the geographical dimensions of the state. A fundamental contribution of this literature has been to show that geographical dimensions of state power are not fixed once and for all: 'the scalar organisation of state space (...) is liable to recurrent redesign, restructuring and reorientation' (Brenner *et al.* 2003: 5). Scales are conceptualised in such a way that they have political and social texture; they do not correspond to generic *levels* nor are they defined *a priori*. In this approach, the emphasis shifts to the 'scalar dimensions of political and social practices' rather than focusing on phenomena occurring at various ready-made scales (e.g., local, national, global, etc.) (Moisio 2011). In this way, the literature on political rescaling builds on existing conceptions of scale, elaborated mainly by political geographers, wherein spatial scales are understood as an outcome of struggles for influence and power.

Although geography has long been interested in scales, including the links between capitalist development and the production of scale, much current interest in scales in social science scholarship has come about as a result of a revisit by political geographers, sociologists, and political scientists – a movement sometimes referred to as 'the spatial turn'.[7] In their efforts to understand how globalisation is affecting state power and the spatial deployment of reconfigured states, social scientists are confronted with the spatial dimension of power.[8] As Bernard Jouve noted, work on political rescaling has flourished because this concept addresses the issue of new regulatory spaces (regional, urban, global) seen as 'alternative' or capable of replacing the nation-state (2007: 48).

Another compelling aspect of the rescaling concept is its capacity to bridge the fields of political economy and political geography. A core feature of this scholarship is its conception of how scales are constructed or what is sometimes called the 'political economy of scale': new state spaces are produced via a contested process by socio-political forces emanating from various geographical scales. In terms of method, this is critically important because it allows the analytical focus to shift from a level/scale to a process. Moreover, it introduces a distinction between state space and territoriality, as the latter is understood to represent 'only one dimension within the complex geographical architectures of modern state spatiality' (Brenner *et al.* 2003: 9).

Territorial organisation is understood here to mean the administration by the state of its territory, the manner in which space is subdivided into smaller units and responsibilities and finances distributed. Among other things, it refers to the correspondence, the 'fit', between state and space. Often such a function is exercised simultaneously by several levels of government, wherein each agency formulates policy for a particular territorial unit, giving way to overlap (e.g., national, provincial or local economic development agencies). In India's particular case, analysed in the next chapter, central government agencies were unambiguously the predominant actors of industrial development until the 1990s. Since then, the economic reform process has set in motion a process of territorial reorganisation and state spatial rescaling affecting many aspects of state action.

There is a tendency in some strands of the literature to conceive of rescaling as a deliberate instrument. This is the case, for instance, in a study by Jones on the Regional Development Agencies created in England by New Labour in the 1990s, which he interpreted as a rescaling initiative on the part of the British state aimed at enhancing the country's competitiveness. 'New policies and forms of representation are then sought to unify this process, which is *scaled* (in this case, to the region) according to political strategy' (2001: 1204, emphasis in the original). By using this term in a way that is nearly synonymous with devolution, there is a risk of reducing *scale* to *level*. This book endeavours to sharply distinguish these two concepts (see below).

Brenner *et al.* (2003) propose distinguishing between a 'narrow' conception of state space, such as Jones uses here, and an 'integral' sense.[9] State space in the narrow sense is grounded in the territorialisation of political power; when used in this sense, rescaling refers to 'the changing organization of state territoriality in the modern inter-state system; the evolving role of borders, boundaries, and frontiers; and the changing intra-national geographies of state territorial organization and internal administrative differentiation' (Brenner *et al.* 2003: 6). On the other hand, the 'integral' sense of state space takes into account the full range of state spatial strategies that attempt to influence the geographies of socioeconomic activities. It refers to 'the territory-, place-, and scale-specific ways in which state institutions are mobilized strategically *to regulate and reorganize social and economic relations* and, more generally, to the changing geographies of state intervention into social and economic processes' (Brenner *et al.* 2003: 6, italics added).

A closely related concept, whose definition tends to vary, however, across disciplines and even academic traditions, is territorialisation. Inspired by French scholarship, it refers here to a process of appropriating space with an intention to organise or control activities therein.[10] It is a social process that is not restricted to state actors. In a similar vein Robert Sack defines human territoriality as 'the attempt by an individual or a group to affect, influence, or control people, phenomena, and relationships, by delimiting and asserting control over a geographic area' (1986: 19). Alain Dubresson and Sylvy Jaglin (2005) propose an important theoretical contribution to the concept of territorialisation, which they conceive as a *continuum*, by contrasting lower degrees, indicating a *delegation of authority* (e.g., from national state authorities to subnational state levels), which they call *spatialisation*, and upper degrees, a process that creates an autonomous system of collective action, with its own mode of governance, called *territorialisation*. They argue that these processes should be clearly distinguished because they have very different consequences in terms of governance. In the discussion of the Indian case here, these analytical distinctions will be useful for qualifying the processes underway. I am particularly interested in exploring the conditions under which subnational state territoriality is expressed.

I will not employ the concept of rescaling in a normative sense, as either a positive or negative evolution. Rescaling has been used in a normative sense in some studies of applied policy, for instance, to argue why subnational regions or metropolitan regions are the most appropriate scale for economic development. One of the most egregious examples of this kind of applied research is Kenichi Ohmae, who triumphantly heralded the end of the nation-state and the rise of the regional state (1996). But even among more academically inclined writers, the regional scale has often been presented in a somewhat utilitarian way, i.e., as a lever to be activated for achieving broad (national) goals, for instance, as the crucial basis for knowledge creation and innovation, both of which are considered essential for fostering competitiveness in an era of globalisation (Storper 1997, cited by Jones 2001: 1186).

1.4 Positioning this research

The rescaling literature provides important conceptual inputs for this study, but I seek to engage critically with this scholarship, questioning its capacity to explain the Indian case.

Grounded in a Marxian tradition, rescaling theory is posited on the inherent internal contradictions of capitalism, which inevitably lead to crises and shifts as capital seeks new sources of accumulation. This theoretical underpinning explains a certain degree of determinism evident in the writings of some authors working in this vein with regard to the evolution of economic phenomenon. However, among the forefront theorists, notably Neil Brenner, the perspective gives central importance to local politics and culture. Even though this distancing from the structuralist origins is not always explicit, most contemporary rescaling theory does *not* postulate the subordination of the political sphere to the economic sphere, and leaves considerable space for politics (Jouve 2005: 2). Rescaling theory has been deeply inspired by French regulation theory and borrows many of its central concepts, such as regulation and 'accumulation regime', although they tend to be less rigorously defined than in the theoretical works of the regulation school.[11]

What has made the rescaling literature so attractive is its ability to offer a convincing explanatory framework, supported with abundant empirical analyses, for the current patterns of restructuring in Europe and North America following the slowdown in the 1970s. It identifies as a fundamental feature of post-Fordist capitalism: 'the reorientation of state spatial strategies from nationally redistributive modalities towards urban-centric, competitiveness-oriented forms of locational policy' (Brenner 2009: 129). Indeed, so convincing are these accounts that there is a temptation to transpose them on other contexts where 'Fordism' was never the dominant form of capital accumulation, but where one can observe nonetheless a similar strategic reorientation of economic development policies. The risk then is that the understanding of state power be predicated on assumptions about the nature of the dominant 'nationally redistributive' regulatory mode, elaborated in Western societies in the post-Second Word War period. Although the theory leaves room for varieties of capitalism in the broad context of 'worldwide capitalist restructuring', I would argue that advanced economies have much more in common among themselves, with regard to the reach of formal institutions, the normalisation of work practices, the spread of the welfare state – to name just a few aspects, than compared to developing societies. A similar problem is encountered when using regulation theory to approach developing economies, since finding regular features across the national economy is problematic; in many of these cases, there are arguably several varieties of capitalism coexisting *within* a given national economy, perhaps all the more in large diverse societies like India and China.[12]

Thus, there is a need for caution when handling the concept of rescaling, and mobilising its related theoretical propositions. The Indian case is very different from European cases not least because it is not and was never a Keynesian welfare state. Rescaling processes emerged in Europe as a result of the crisis of 'North Atlantic Fordism'. Their occurrence in the Indian case, a country on the periphery of global capitalism until very recently, requires attention in relation to its specific institutions and to its political economic trajectory. Another crucial reason that the hypotheses and especially the conclusions of the state rescaling literature cannot be applied blindly to the Indian case is that the emergence and evolution of the 'territorial state' have followed fundamentally different patterns in Europe and South Asia. The modern territorial state in Europe gradually emerged over several centuries steadily replacing 'the plurality of hierarchical bonds with an exclusive identity based upon membership in the common juridical space defined by the writ of the state. In other words, "the principle of hierarchical subordination gradually gave way to the principle of spatial exclusion"' (Walker 1990: 10, cited by Agnew and Corbridge 1995: 85).[13] The reality of territorial boundaries of the contemporary Indian state, dating from 1947, and the nature of its sovereignty, presents radically different characteristics, with repercussions for state action. But I hasten to clarify that the nation-state model and its concomitant territorial sovereignty, were fully appropriated by independent India. And it is assumed, following Jean-François Bayart, that this complex process of appropriation conferred on the Indian nation-state its own specific social and cultural foundations (2004: 53).

In the period since independence (1947), India's economic development policies have indeed been resolutely based on the national scale (see Chapter 2), but the associated institutional characteristics with regard to regulating the economy, based on the European model and implicit in most of the rescaling literature, do not apply. Nowhere is this more evident than with regard to labour. Whereas the welfare state model was based on the notion of full, salaried employment, approximately 90 per cent of India's active population works in the informal sector (i.e., without a legally binding contract or any guaranteed benefits). In India, there are national redistributive policies, and recently a large-scale employment programme (NREGS), but fundamentally these represent a small portion of the economy and are to be viewed more as an important safety net than a 'regulation mode' in the régulationniste sense of the term. One exception to this may be the Public Distribution System, which has over the last fifty years made available subsidised staples to households (rice, wheat, sugar, sometimes kerosene), via mandatory procurement of grain from farmers and a state monopoly on wholesale trade.[14] The state effectively redistributed food and resources to a large proportion of the population, although this policy reflects a top-down developmental state mode, rather than a social compromise won through mobilisation and political struggle.

In addition to limited reach of the organised labour market, mentioned above, the relatively non-integrated nature of the domestic market, despite the country's 'single market', is another indicator of the non-normalised nature of the Indian economy. There are large income gaps between regions, labour migration remains quite limited and both price and tax disparities are considerable (Melchior 2010). This fundamental caveat probably applies to all but the advanced industrial economies.

Another critical remark is linked to method. Starting from a global scale, i.e., the crisis of capitalism, rescaling theory often posits regionalisation and/or new localisms as concomitant processes of globalisation, most colourfully illustrated by the concept of 'glocalization' (Swyngedouw 1992). In this conception, globalisation and localisation are 'particular scalar manifestations of *one broad restructuring process*' (Paul 2005: 7–8, emphasis added). But, as Darel Paul points out, this characterisation tends to portray a restricted view of the 'rich geographical transformation that includes both the refashioning of existing scales as well as the creation of new ones' (2005: 7). It explicitly or implicitly tends to neglect the national scale *and* to see local processes as by-products rather than production. In other words, this view of globalisation as one broad restructuring process tends to automatically place national and subnational scales in a *secondary* position and to implicitly postulate their subordination to processes at the global scale. Paul suggests rather incorporating into the analytical framework subnational scales, structures and agents as critical elements that contribute to forging the global political economy:

By thinking of rescaling rather than simply globalization, one makes visible the invisible, finally seeing the subnational and its contributions, both to the recapitulation of the global in conventional ways as well as to efforts to alter it, through practices that contradict established patterns. One also

> sees subnational institutions, including subnational sates, in a new light,
> as sites in and through which actors defined at any scale interact with
> global structures to produce and reproduce the global political economy.
>
> (Paul 2005: 8)

Notwithstanding these critiques, I argue that the rescaling framework represents a potent conceptual tool for interpreting processes underway in India. I consider that it will allow me to engage meaningfully with several key hypotheses:

- India's recent but increasingly intense engagement with the global economy and its political project of realising market reform have catalysed a restructuring process that is reconfiguring the Indian state and its relation to the economy.
- Current processes involve not only redefining state–market and state–society relations, but a political reordering whereby new state spaces are emerging.
- This reordering is *not* primarily about decentralisation or the delegation of functions per se, but rather the spatial implications of new regulatory arrangements deployed at various scales. Strategies elaborated by national and subnational political elites are shaping the emerging scales of socio-economic activities in conjunction with other actors, within governance networks.

Finally, an additional advantage to using the state rescaling framework is that it favours international comparisons, although until now these have mainly dealt with industrially advanced countries.[15] I consider that the Indian case can contribute important theoretical insights to the international literature by engaging with the rescaling concept in a context radically different than the one from which it emerged: India has a fast growing economy; the state is not 'retrenching', there is not a 'rolling back of the welfare state', rather there is major restructuring of a developmental state. To date, this framework has not been mobilised in an extensive way in scholarship on India.[16] It is my contention here that it can contribute in meaningful ways to understanding the current spatial transformations of state power taking place in India and the implications for economic governance at various scales, offering a fresh alternative to the sterile dichotomy between decentralisation and (re)centralisation.

Decentralisation debates in India

At this juncture, it is no doubt necessary to situate the rescaling framework in relation to the main strands of literature that engage with multilevel governance in India, framed for the most part around *decentralisation* and *federalism*. It is particularly important to avoid from the outset confusion between rescaling and decentralisation (or recentralisation), all the more since both types of processes can and do occur concurrently. The term decentralisation has been extensively employed and debated in India since the 1960s to question critically the power-sharing arrangements in the Indian polity, between the national state (or Centre) and the States, and also between the States and local governments. To a degree, the literature has evolved over the years to reflect political developments as well as the various reforms undertaken, with the last two decades in particular witnessing significant events including: the advent of coalition government in New Delhi, the adoption of economic reforms, and the ratification of constitutional amendments to empower rural and urban local governments.

The vast literature on India's federal system, more commonly referred to as Centre–State relations, has embraced a wide range of issues, starting with the provisions of the 'quasi-federal' Constitution of 1950. However, the main issue of debate until at least the 1990s was the actual functioning of the federal system, i.e., the degree of sharing of political power and resources between New Delhi and the State capitals. In an often-repeated pattern, studies of Centre–State relations cited *over-centralisation* as the reason for the malfunction of India's federal institutions. The Congress party in particular, was accused of abusing its position to concentrate power in all branches of the central government, through both constitutional and extra-constitutional means, at the expense of the States. Indeed much of this literature gave expression to the frustration of regional political forces *vis-à-vis* the national ruling party: encroachment on their policy space, subordinate fiscal relations, political interference in internal affairs. These academic studies generally concluded with a call for reforms to India's centralised political institutions to introduce more 'balance', echoing the appeals made by other sections of society such as political parties, NGOs and activists. Whether in the name of greater democracy e.g., through empowering local governments and enhancing participation, or greater efficiency in promoting socio-economic development, the solution was believed to lie in political reform, a greater devolution of power and resources. To some extent, this reformist view was encouraged by the central government, which occasionally appointed high-powered committees to make recommendations (e.g., administrative reforms commission, commission on Centre–State relations) – a view that, in retrospect, appears somewhat naïve. A top-down decree, no matter how well designed, still has to square with political realities.

The rescaling processes analysed in this study are not primarily the result of political or administrative reforms. They are rather an outcome of a combination of uncoordinated actions, which include gradual political change, new policy frameworks and strategies pursued by various types of actors situated at various spatial scales. In the conceptual framework adopted here, these processes are indicative of a change of scales that are not limited to a 'downward' movement in favour of regional or locale scales. In that sense, rescaling is essentially an open-ended process – we will examine examples of both upscaling and downscaling – and is usually not driven by any single actor.

Although rescaling may produce *decentralising effects*,[17] for example, by reordering policy jurisdictions, the process by which this happens is fundamentally different than 'decentralisation', which generally refers to a deliberate reform.

Conversely, it should be noted that formal political or administrative decentralisation, when it effectively leads to the devolution of decision-making powers or resources, can produce *rescaling effects* to the extent that new political jurisdictions become (usually over time) relevant arenas for collective action. In Chapter 6, several different examples of territorial reorganisation are examined, with attention to the manner in which they reorder political and economic geographies.

Because of the propinquity of the concepts of rescaling and decentralisation, I insist here on the distinctions although some of the rescaling literature adopts a less rigorous definition, as mentioned above. I am primarily interested in state spatial rescaling in the *integral sense* following Brenner *et al.* (2003) i.e., when it refers to way that state institutions are mobilised strategically to regulate economic and social relations and influence their locational geographies, and will use it in that sense here unless otherwise indicated.

1.5 Presenting the volume

Chapter 2 sets the stage for the subsequent chapters of the book by providing essential background on India's core political institutions. These include the constitutional division of powers and responsibilities between the national (or central) government and the States of the Union, and some indications about how the federal system has functioned in practice. The main focus of the analysis is on India's development strategies in the first few decades following independence, roughly 1950–1980, and economic policy-making in a system of multilevel government. Using a scale sensitive perspective to revisit Centre–State economic relations in the pre-reform period, the aim is to understand the processes that contributed to the construction of state scales as well as economic geographies. The analysis moves beyond formal levels of government to examine specific examples of political society and the factors that condition collective action. Of particular interest for subsequent chapters is the discussion of territorialisation processes and regional political economy.

The politics and scales of economic reforms are the core topics examined in Chapter 3. It traces the reform process, starting in the 1980s, discussing the context, contents and actors. Based largely on a critical review of the literature, the discussion centres on the multiscalar context in which state actors operate, examining how reforms were implemented and managed. I analyse the internal political factors that motivated reforms, and situate them within a larger context of political restructuring occurring in India. I garner evidence to develop one of my key arguments, i.e., that rescaling processes in India express above all a political strategy on the part of state actors, and not a compulsion imposed by exogenous forces. As a result of this process, the central state's carefully constructed frame of reference between industrial development and national territory has been disconnected, and new state spaces are being forged.

Chapter 4 sets out to demonstrate on the basis of concrete examples how economic reforms have put into motion rescaling processes, with regard both to economic activities and state space, and to examine the modalities. The objective is to analyse what has changed at the regional scale, how different State governments are redefining their economic development policies and the factors conditioning these changes. Case material from several States will be used to compare reform agendas and specific policies and to situate them within their respective political economic environments. I will engage with the theoretical literature on questions relating to the agency of subnational states in the realm of economic governance and with regard to globalisation processes.

The national Special Economic Zone policy is the focus of Chapter 5, chosen as an emblematic example of current rescaling processes. By offering attractive tax incentives, simplified investment procedures and a deregulated environment for export-oriented production, this policy aims to redefine India's engagement with global capitalism and put it on a fast track. Although the policy's frame of reference is the national scale, it does not apply uniformly across national territory but only to strictly delineated zones, creating spaces of exception to the regulatory regime prevailing at the national scale. Thus, the policy rescales economic growth, shaping the geographies of industrial agglomeration and infrastructure investment, and rescales geographies of statehood. Case material from Andhra Pradesh and Haryana demonstrates how State-level SEZ strategies converge or diverge with those emanating from the central state, and also explain interstate variations in relation to the wider political economic context of each State.

Chapter 6 examines state spatial strategies in India that are currently constructing or redefining urban scales, such as regulatory instruments and direct investments in physical infrastructure. This allows a critical comparison with the international literature on rescaling, the empirical basis of which rests largely on cities in advanced industrialised countries. With case material from Hyderabad, four distinct state spatial strategies are analysed and discussed: the constitution of sub-municipal political entities, reforms in delivery mechanisms for urban services, the establishment of Greater Hyderabad, and the promotion of a premium space for the IT sector (Cyberabad). A core objective is to explore to what extent such state-led strategies are contributing alongside actions originating from other actors, e.g., business groups, residents' associations, civil society organisations, to the construction of new urban scales. A secondary aim involves evaluating the consequences of such strategies on the scope and scale of public action, as well as on other forms of collective action.

Chapter 7 concludes the monograph. Retracing the book's itinerary, it reiterates the main research questions, the conceptual framework and the findings. A series of theoretical propositions are discussed relating to: (1) the subnational state as a territorial reference for organising social and economic activities; (2) the increasingly significant role of subnational scales in coordinating socioeconomic activities; and (3) state rescaling as a contested political process. Finally, drawing on the theoretical insights generated by this study, the discussion explores ways to take the rescaling concept further.

Notes

1 On the consequences of reforms on economic geographies in India see Chakravorty (2000) and Chakravorty and Lall (2007).
2 To avoid confusion, I capitalise State to designate the constituent members of the Indian Union.
3 See for example Holmström (1998), Cadène and Holmström (1998), Kennedy (1999, 2004c), Knorringa (1999), Tewari (1999), Das (2005).
4 See for instance Gilly and Torre (2000), Pecqueur and Zimmermann (2004).
5 See for instance the scholarship published in the *Journal of Economic Issues* (ISSN 0021–3624), the official journal of the Association for Evolutionary Economics.
6 See also Rodrik *et al.* (2002).
7 See for instance Warf and Arias (2009).
8 Henri Lefebvre, a French sociologist, has been a major source of inspiration for current theories of scale. Neil Brenner, a major theorist, has a project 'to revisit and reappropriate some of Lefebvre's key ideas in light of our own specific theoretical and political concerns' (2001: 764). A chapter of the fourth volume of Lefebvre's opus *De l'État*, was included in *State/Space: A Reader* (Brenner *et al.* 2003).
9 A third dimension of state space, not explored here, is a representational sense referring to 'competing spatial imaginaries that represent state and political spaces in different ways as a basis for demarcating states from each other, demarcating the state from the wider political system, and demarcating the wider political system from the rest of society' (Brenner *et al.* 2003: 6).
10 It should be noted that within French scholarship, there is considerable debate about the meaning of the term. See Dubresson and Jaglin (2005).
11 See Boyer (1990) and Boyer and Saillard (2002), for an introduction.
12 This argument is made with regard to India in Kennedy *et al.* (2013).
13 A central issue is the sovereignty of the state over its territory. As Agnew and Corbridge point out 'The total sovereignty of the state over it territorial space in a world fragmented into territorial states gives the state its most powerful justification. Without this a state would be just another organization. *Its claim to sovereignty is what distinguishes the state*' (1995: 84, emphasis added).
14 In one exceptional year, 2000–1, it was estimated that 80 per cent of the wheat available in the market was procured by the state (Landy 2009: 197). In the past decade, the scope of PDS has been considerably reduced (Landy 2009).
15 Notwithstanding the assertion by a key proponent of the field that: '[It] has so far provided a relatively coherent, unifying conceptual rubric within which to interpret these otherwise disparate patterns of *worldwide sociospatial restructuring and territory-specific institutional reorganisation*' (Brenner 2009: 131, italics added).
16 An exception is Grant and Nijman (2004). References to this literature also appear in Shaw and Satish (2007), and in some of the studies brought together in Banerjee-Guha (2010).
17 See for instance the introduction of the special issue of *Publius* on India's federal system (Singh and Verney 2003). See also the incisive introduction in Gupta and Sivaramakrishnan (2011), which explores the relation between decentralisation and liberalisation.

2 Nation-building and scale in India's federal polity

This chapter sets the stage for the analyses elaborated in the remainder of the book by providing critical background on the institutions that organise India's federal governance. By reviewing the arrangements in place before the adoption of economic reforms it is possible to establish a baseline for understanding the far-reaching changes of the last two decades. Federal institutions and practices are revisited using a spatially sensitive lens that sheds light on the predominant patterns of territorial organisation of the Indian state. Examining articulations between the national state and subnational state spaces and their evolution over time is of particular importance to understand how power has been distributed across various levels of government, and the scope for agency within a centralised state apparatus.

In addition to territorial organisation of state institutions, attention is given to the spatial organisation of collective action, and to socially produced scales.

2.1 Institutional infrastructure of India's federal system

Before turning our attention to reforms, it is necessary to provide a brief account of how state scales were constructed in the 1950s and 1960s in the immediate period following independence as background for the core discussion of transformations in the current period. This involves reviewing the institutional infrastructure inasmuch as transformations are mediated through existing institutions, which are then reshaped in the process. The focus will be on analysing how institutions have contributed to defining the territorial dimensions of state power at different scales. Two sets of institutions are particularly relevant for this purpose: federal institutions and institutions for promoting economic development.

The 1950 Constitution outlines the basic principles defining India's federal democracy, although interestingly the document does not actually contain the word 'federal'. This ambiguous posture reflects the tensions within the Constituent Assembly between a federal and unitary state; tensions stoked by the partition of British India and the ensuing violence, which provoked one of the largest displacements of people in human history. In the first decades of the twentieth century, as the independence movement gained strength, its proponents were largely favourable to strong federalism. In other words, a system characterised by a relatively weak central state and strong federal units – a formula justified by India's tremendous cultural diversity, and a reaction against a highly centralised and powerful colonial state. However, as the partition took place and communal violence engulfed the country, attitudes changed quickly.[1]

In its final form, the outcome of three years of deliberation, the Constitution reflects overall a concern with unity: 'Unity and integrity are mentioned in the Constitution's Preamble, which establishes India as a "Union of States" and the Constitution's *highly centralised federalism had unity and integrity as its purpose*' (Austin 1999: 7, emphasis added). Apart from dealing with the aftermath of the partition, India's new leaders were preoccupied with nation-building and territorial integration. The colonial administration had left a fragmented territory, further complicated by a large number of Princely States, more than 500, with heterogeneous political and administrative regimes.

India's Constitution was inspired by the model of cooperative federalism like other later systems (e.g., Germany) based on greater interdependence of the constitutive elements, i.e., the national and regional governments. It contrasts with the so-called classic federal system, which exists in the United States and Australia, where the central or federal government and the States each have their own prerogatives. Moreover, in the United States the federal government has separate agencies in charge of implementing its policies and programmes. In India national programmes are channelled through the administrative apparatus at the State level and from there to the *districts*, a territorial unit inherited from the colonial period, and then to the local bodies. In this way central policies and programme specifications (staffing patterns, selection of beneficiaries) channel 'down' through the administration, through line departments, into local space and society, in a perfect illustration of a vertically nested state model. This was and continues to be the manner in which state space is represented and, to a large degree, practiced at subnational scales, notwithstanding the lower bureaucracy's relative autonomy to resist or divert directives from its administrative hierarchy.

The Constitution establishes the authority of the central and State governments and the relations between them. It outlines the territorial organisation of the federal state: national representatives are directly elected to the lower house of Parliament, the *Lok Sabha*, and indirectly to the upper house, the *Rajya Sabha*. The government is formed on the basis of elections to the Lok Sabha under the leadership of a Prime Minister and a Council of Ministers. At the regional level, twenty-eight States, many of which have very large territories and populations,[2] also have elected Assemblies (*Vidhan Sabha*), presided over by a 'Chief Minister' in the top executive position, selected by the party or coalition that secures a majority. Each of the twenty-eight States is a discrete political space with it own executive, deliberative and judicial branches of government, mirroring the national-level institutions. In this respect, '[i]t is two constitutions in one: a constitution for the nation and central government, and one uniform constitution for all the [S]tate governments. The two constitutions are consistent, for both are parliamentary systems based on the Westminster Model. The President is the Head of State and a presidentially appointed governor fill the analogous function in each [S]tate' (Austin 1999: 6–7).

State Assemblies are empowered to pass legislation on the subjects assigned to them by the Constitution. Schedule VII delineates in separate Lists the respective legislative jurisdictions of the Union and the States, as well as shared powers, which appear in the Concurrent List. *A priori*, there is nothing in the distribution of legislative jurisdictions that indicates an overcentralisation in favour of the Union.[3] It is rather the interpretation of the Constitution and the decision to use certain provisions dispersed throughout the Constitution pertaining to specific situations that have reinforced the powers of the Centre. Two such examples are article 246, which asserts the supremacy of the Parliament over the State assemblies in case of an 'irreconcilable overlap' between Lists I and II, and article 248, which grants the Centre 'residual powers' or the power to legislate in all areas not explicitly mentioned in the Lists. The latter underscores the centralising tendencies of Indian federalism since other federal systems grant these powers to the constituent parts. Finally, and here the scope for discretionary decisions is very broad, the upper chamber of Parliament has special powers to declare that Parliament promulgate laws in areas contained in the State List if the Parliament considers it to serve the national interest.

Industry, for example, figures in the State List, but the national government was able to appropriate this subject and pass important laws in Parliament, particularly the Industries (Development and Regulation) Act (1951) and the Mines and Minerals Act (1957), because of such constitutional provisions. Similarly, using an article in the Concurrent List, the Union was able to regulate trade and commerce in a large number of products, including agricultural products (via the 1955 Essential Commodities Act), which are assigned to the States. This constitutional design, including the special provisions, was justified by the need to empower the national state to drive the development process, and enable the new nation to meet its three main objectives: economic growth, social justice and self-reliance. Section 2.2 further elaborates on this process of constructing the national scale.

As mentioned previously, in India's cooperative federalism most of the laws promulgated by the Centre are implemented by the States (except for some specific areas, e.g., external affairs, treasury, postal services, telecommunications, rail and air transport, and customs and taxes). Anticipating differences in interpretation, the architects of the Constitution authorised the Centre to give directives to the States (Arts. 256 and 257), a provision that underscores the supremacy of the former with respect to the latter.[4] Two other aspects of the Constitution that underscore the States' subordinate position *vis-à-vis* the Centre also deserve mention: the 'special powers' attributed to the Centre and the division of fiscal powers. As guarantor of the Constitution, the central government acting through the Governor, can invoke special powers to supersede elected State governments and declare direct rule of the State by the Centre (Art. 356), referred to as *President's Rule*. Designed for exceptional use only, e.g., when no government can be formed due to a lack of majority in the Assembly or when civil order is threatened, in practice it was quite blatantly abused by the central ruling party for political ends starting in the 1960s and lasting until the mid-1990s.[5] A 1994 Supreme Court ruling effectively put an end to this pattern,[6] although the deeper causes are linked to changes in the political dynamics of the country (see below).

Regarding fiscal federalism, the Constitution empowers the Union to collect the major share of the country's fiscal resources (income tax, except on agricultural revenue, indirect taxes, customs duties), which it then shares with the States. This highly unequal division of fiscal powers has no doubt aggravated the tension between the two levels since independence with the States claiming that inadequate resources have prevented them from assuming their responsibilities. They argue that although their tax sources tend to stagnate, unlike those of the Union, they are required to incur heavy expenditure on education, health and infrastructure, which do not yield returns in the short term. The unequal division of fiscal powers was justified by the need to create a single unified economic space, a national market, and to avoid the erection of tax barriers around States (Vithal and Sastry 2001: 24). Greater efficiency in tax collection was a second argument in favour of fiscal centralisation.

An independent Finance Commission, whose mandate is five years, determines the distribution of fiscal revenue between the Union and the States on one hand, and among the States, on the other, and recommends grants to make up for the shortfall between revenue and expenditure of each State. It is important to specify that most of the transfers recommended by the Finance Commission can be used by State governments as they choose. Another central body, the Planning Commission, also plays an important role in distributing resources to the States, approximately 30 per cent of total transfers on average between 1950–2010. This extra-constitutional body, which works closely with the central government and is chaired by the Prime Minister, is considered less neutral by State governments than the Finance Commission and its transfers more 'discretionary'. The preponderance of centrally sponsored schemes in particular have been criticised as an infringement of States' prerogatives[7] because the Union spends a large amount of money in policy areas attributed to the States by the Constitution. For instance, during the Sixth Five-Year Plan (1980–5), 40 per cent of the total outlay for agriculture and rural development came from the budget of the central government, more than 50 per cent for the small-scale cottage industries, and about 90 per cent for the medium and large-scale industries.[8]

Before concluding this section, whose objective was to briefly introduce the formal institutional framework that define the relations between the Centre and the States in India's federal system, it is necessary to say a word about the bureaucracy. The present-day administrative set-up is to a large extent the heritage of the British colonial regime. At independence, the nation's new leaders decided to maintain in place the elite corps of civil servants, which became the Indian Administrative Service (IAS), to act as a unifying force. Indeed IAS officers, assigned to States, work together with a regional corps of administrative officers, and occupy the highest-ranking positions in State-level bureaucracy, notably the 'Secretary' post in each ministry, who interacts with the Minister. District magistrates or 'Collectors' as they are still called in parts of the country, are recruited from within the IAS and represent the central state at the local level. This corps grew rapidly from 800 members in 1948 to 1,900 in 1962 and by 1985 the number was 4,284; current figures are approximately 5,500.

It can be recalled also that IAS officers are often posted (or 'seconded') to the central government in New Delhi at some point in their career. This intergovernmental mobility of key actors in the system contributes no doubt to smoothening relations between central and State bureaucracies and ensuring a certain degree of coherence in the implementation of policies and programmes, notably the ubiquitous 'centrally sponsored schemes' or vertical programmes.

Political relations between New Delhi and the States are sometimes played out through the administration, bypassing elected officials at the State and local levels, with implications for governance. For instance, one can observe problems of communication and delays in allocation of credit, particularly when different political parties are in power at these two levels. Conversely, when the same party or alliance is running the government at both levels, the political network reinforces the administrative network, adds oil to the machine, as was the case when the Congress dominated for many years both in New Delhi and in a majority of the States. Still today, it can be observed that State governments closely connected to the ruling coalition in New Delhi obtain a bailout more easily when they default on their loans.[9]

2.2 State scaling in the service of a national development strategy

In the period immediately following independence, India's national leadership, led by Jawaharlal Nehru, was strongly committed to pursuing a state-led development process. This is a familiar episode of India's economic and political history and only the broad outlines will be recalled here. The aim is to discuss the link between this development strategy, characterised by a strong reference to the national scale, and the territorial organisation of the Indian state. I argue that formal and informal institutions of economic governance forged in those early years served to consolidate the national scale, and anchor territorially the national economy. It is useful to recall here that the territorial state formed in 1947 encompassed spaces that had never before been united, politically speaking. In addition to British-administered provinces there were more than 500 'Princely' or 'Native' States, which accounted for about 40 per cent of the new territory! Each of these States had their historical specificities, which were reflected in their political institutions, as well as in their socio-economic indicators.

From the mid-1950s onward, industrialisation came to occupy the centre stage of the national development strategy, largely inspired by the Soviet model. Import-substitution industrialisation was the policy chosen to build up and diversify the country's industrial base in a planned manner, and ensure its economic independence. Indeed the goals of industrialisation and growth cannot be distinguished from the larger political project, i.e., nation-building, but also the grounding of national state power for ensuring national security and buttressing military might (Nayar 2005: 222). In this mixed economy model, within the framework of a private property regime, state entrepreneurialism coexisted side by side with private sector initiatives. New investments in a number of areas were 'reserved' for the public sector (heavy industry, mining, telecommunications) or were to be shared with the private sector (machine tools, chemical, pharmaceutical, automobile, textile, transport).

In this set-up, it was the state and not the market that occupied the 'commanding heights' of the economy, and the national scale was the point of reference. One of the most striking illustrations of this guiding principle was with regard to industrial policy. In addition to being directly involved in industrial production via public sector enterprises[10] and via direct investments in infrastructure projects throughout the country, the central state closely regulated *all private industrial investments*: what was produced, how much, with which capital-labour mix, and where. All new investments in medium and large-scale industries, as well as projects to increase capacity in existing plants, required permission and approval from the central government ministries. The idea was to be able to channel scarce capital, public *and* private, to those sectors deemed most essential by central government planners, as well as to selected regions.

In practice, this was accomplished by putting in place a complex system of licences, disparagingly called 'licence-permit raj' (rule by licence), whereby high-level commissions evaluated private industrial projects and proposed geographical locations with regard to national planning priorities (and not only investors' preferences).[11] In theory, this framework, in which subnational state boundaries effectively disappeared, ensured that decisions could be taken rationally *at the national scale*, on the basis of objective criteria (inputs, final markets, etc.), the primary goal being to increase industrial output *at the national scale*.

An example of another powerful policy instrument, illustrative of the pre-eminence of the national scale in policy-making, was the freight equalisation policy, which regulated the costs of transporting mineral resources throughout the country. It was intended to create an even playing field for industrial growth by equalling out transport costs in the national economy. Consequently, mineral rich States like Bihar and Odisha (formerly Orissa),[12] which are industrially underdeveloped States, were not in a position to benefit from their comparative advantage. The aim here is not to evaluate this policy, however, but to underscore how central government policies constructed state scales in the first decades following independence. Political elites and bureaucrats in New Delhi mobilised a wide range of policies and regulatory instruments, like licensing and freight equalisation, for pursuing their political and economic objectives. In the process they put in place a system of economic governance that concentrated power firmly in the hands of bureaucrats and politicians in the central government, which did not preclude agency at other levels, as will be discussed below.

In addition to diversifying and increasing industrial output, planning was the tool by which the state could attempt to correct regional imbalances, which had been exacerbated under colonial rule, and curb capital's tendency to concentrate in space. Fiscal measures and other incentives were put in place to attract investments to 'backward areas'.[13]

A planned national approach was intended to build up a national economy based on a common market in what was an extremely heterogeneous space.[14] Markets in India are still quite highly segmented, e.g., for retail prices and wages, but they are no doubt more integrated than in the immediate aftermath of independence. At that time only a fraction of national territory was linked up to markets via networked infrastructure in the form of roads and railways built by the colonial state to facilitate the transport of commodities or manufactured goods to urban centres or seaports for export, in a configuration that François Durand-Dastès (1995) coined a 'trading post economy'.[15]

So how did these institutions function in practice in India's complex, vertically nested federal state? Did regional governments, situated on the receiving end of economic development policies e.g., industrial and infrastructure investments, come into the picture at all? To what extent could they influence the process and how did political factors come into play? How were other social groups involved in this process of scale building? In the next section the focus shifts to the subnational state and to intergovernmental relations.

2.3 Policy space at the State level

There has been remarkably little research on economic policy-making at the subnational level or multilevel economic policy-making in the first decades after independence.[16] This research gap is in itself revealing of the predominant view in the literature on Centre–State relations, namely that State governments had very little scope for developing distinct economic policies, and because of their dependency on central government resources were resigned to passively implementing central state directives. Two studies counter that view and propose slightly different interpretations of the nature of federal relations and more specifically the scope for economic policy-making by subnational States.

In her comparative study of Gujarat, West Bengal and Tamil Nadu, Aseema Sinha makes a significant contribution to filling this research gap (2005). She argues that, although highly centralised, the regulatory regime left ample scope for regional political elites to engage with the Centre and thereby influence investment outcomes in their respective territories. State-level politicians could influence licensing decisions, for instance, by bargaining for industrial projects, either through formal bureaucratic channels or through parallel informal channels, most notably through the Congress party. In Gujarat, the political leadership consistently chose to bargain with central institutions through intense lobbying, mainly through bureaucratic channels, and was proactive in putting in place arrangements for following up investment proposals in a systematic way, all of which, she argues, resulted in a higher rate of success in bagging industrial projects (Sinha 2005: 92–8). In contrast, West Bengal, under both Congress and communist rule, chose a confrontational strategy towards the Centre and constantly mobilised regionalist sentiment around the idea that New Delhi was discriminating against the State (ibid.: 99–105). Tamil Nadu pursued a mixed strategy that alternated between intensive lobbying in the early period (1950–67), mainly through informal party channels, and opportunistic bargaining at key electoral moments combined with anti-Centre rhetoric at other times (ibid.: 105–8).

According to Sinha, the level of centrally managed investments that States were able to capture can be explained by examining the strategies deployed by the States (ibid.: 91).[17] Although I fully agree that States' actions and reactions to the national regulatory regime were strategic and intentional, I am more doubtful about a direct causal relationship between those actions and the investment flows mediated through the central state. Numerous factors necessarily came into this equation and I believe that national policy elites, benefiting from their vantage point at the summit of the regulatory machine and centralising information from various quarters, exercised a considerable degree of autonomy. Likewise, political calculations on the part of central government elites should not to be entirely discounted.[18]

Indeed, a study using disaggregated data for fifteen major States of India, over the period 1972–95, showed that State governments that are politically affiliated with the central government receive significantly greater plan grants and loans, via the Planning Commission, than States not aligned with the central government (Khemani 2003, cited by Nooruddin and Chhibber 2008: 1077).[19] This indicates there is a degree of discretion in the central government's dealings with State governments and that political leverage can explain why some States receive more resources (Nooruddin and Chhibber 2008).

Nevertheless, Sinha's empirically rich study goes a long way in rectifying an erroneous conception of economic development as a purely top-down process that leaves no room for State-level agency. Her thesis is that 'national economic policy is the aggregate product of regional political strategies and institutions given a certain set of centrally imposed constraints' (2005: 115). Yet it is important to critically qualify Sinha's thesis by underscoring the fact that not all States participated equally in this process. Her focus on large industrially advanced States may suggest general lessons that do not apply to other States; for instance, as Sinha herself remarks, 'most provincial [S]tates follow what I call "passive dependence" strategy, one that depends upon the center for transfers and licenses but does not actively engage with the opportunities or constraints provided by its rules of the game' (ibid.: 296, note 2). If this is the case, it is important to try to understand why this is so. From a theoretical point of view, it suggests that not all subnational state scales are equally 'salient', a proposition I will discuss further in the next section.

My research in Kerala, in the late 1980s and early 1990s, reached conclusions similar to Sinha's regarding the existence of a distinct developmental strategy on the part of regional States.[20] I did not focus on bargaining with central authorities for industrial investments, but rather addressed more broadly the issue of multilevel policy-making for economic development and State-level capacity for garnering support from the Centre for particular policies, even when these were the expression of fundamentally different approaches to development (i.e., redistribution vs. growth).

2.4 Political economy of multilevel policy-making

My study of Kerala, a political economy of multilevel policy-making, was specifically focused on industrial development. In the early 1990s, Kerala's regional economy was characterised by the preponderance of labour intensive traditional industries: the three most important being coir manufacturing (coconut fibre), cotton handloom weaving and cashew-nut processing. At the time of the study, 60 per cent of organised industrial employment (i.e., in registered factories) was supplied by these industries, as well as many more jobs in the informal sector. Hence, the State government's concern with traditional industries was explained to some extent by their objective weight in the regional economy, but equally, if not more important, was the capacity of various social actors in those industries to make their claims heard by the State government (workers, unions, small business owners, exporters, etc.). Trade unions are particularly strong in Kerala and are present in practically all activities, including agriculture,[21] and have managed to institutionalise numerous rights for workers, including minimum wages.[22] Kerala was the first State to elect a communist government in 1957, and communist parties continue to lead within governing coalitions, alternating with Congress-led coalitions.

Political mobilisation, over the long term, is largely responsible for the high level of public services in Kerala and these have contributed to the State's remarkable performance in terms of human development. However, Kerala suffered until recently from low growth and from high unemployment, including among educated youth; its economy relies heavily on remittances from migrants. The selection of Kerala, an 'extreme' case, was deliberate, my assumption being that a politically independent regional State would be more likely to assert its policy preferences *vis-à-vis* the central state, here in the area of economic development, and to confront it in case of divergent positions.

In addition to analysing both State-level policies and central government policies implemented in Kerala, as well as the modalities of their application on the ground, it was necessary to unpack the complex relationship between economic policy-making and planning institutions at the State and central levels, which involved examining both bureaucratic procedures and less visible political practices mainly via informal channels. The findings confirmed that political factors do indeed condition intergovernmental relations. At the time of the study, a communist-led coalition had been elected to office in 1987, the Left Democratic Front (LDF), whereas in New Delhi, Rajiv Gandhi's Congress government had been in office since late 1984. Although relations were confrontational in political discourse, it was observed that planning institutions, which involved mainly bureaucrats, e.g., working groups from the State Planning Board and the central Planning Commission, appeared to function relatively smoothly.

I found that Kerala's State government took full advantage of those central government programmes that were coherent with its own broad objectives and served to strengthen its own capacity for action. Of particular importance were the numerous schemes designed to promote and lend support to small-scale industries and cooperative societies. Although by the late 1980s and early 1990s the central government was no longer giving strategic importance to these policies, they continued to exist in the form of centrally sponsored schemes. Through them, central funds were channelled to the State where they contributed significantly to overall spending on economic development policies. For the LDF government, these two policies continued to have crucial importance well into the 1990s: its primary preoccupation with regard to its economy was maintaining employment. Assistance to coir and handloom cooperative societies (inputs of working capital, buying and marketing stock, etc.) allowed them to continue providing some degree of employment, and to assure the payment of minimum wages. To understand this approach, it should be recalled that the ruling coalition's social bases were in the trade unions and the cooperative societies, and they were expected to deliver to their constituencies in the form of employment. Because the working class in Kerala has managed to institutionalise its power through laws and political practices it could act as a 'politically hegemonic force' (Heller 1995).[23]

However, conflicts arose between regional and national state spaces in relation to programmes designed to mechanise the coir industry and also diversify its production by developing products made with brown fibre, which is cheaper to produce than traditional white fibre. Kerala chose to 'opt out' of these programmes, but was nonetheless confronted with the fact that the national coir promotion agency, the Coir Board, implemented them in neighbouring States through the head office situated in Kochi (ex Cochin), in the heart of Kerala, creating direct competition for its own production. Admittedly, the central agency was exercising its 'national' mandate to develop and promote the coir industry across national territory, and although Kerala was the Indian State most concerned by the coir industry, its government was not in a position to shape national policies, at least not in the political configuration prevailing at the time of the study. It can be recalled that central government policies were increasingly responsive at this point in time (1980–90) to pressures from business groups, including coir exporters from Kerala. This fundamental difference in the territorial scale of reference is a defining feature of India multilevel state and structures inter-governmental relationships in a hierarchical fashion.

In different ways, this example and Sinha's three cases demonstrate that there was indeed scope for State governments to 'work the system', as long as they played within the rules of the games made in New Delhi. An important theoretical finding coming out of both studies is that States responded differently to incentives produced by central institutions and policies depending on their political objectives, which were defined in relation to regional mobilisation patterns. More importantly for the purposes of the thesis put forward here, it shows that there were competing conceptions of economic space coexisting among political elites situated at various scales, one scaled to national territory, the other to subnational state territory. The tension in the federal system was situated, at this stage in India's history, i.e., 1950–90, between the central state and the subnational state in an exclusive vertical relationship. The elaborate institutional set-up for managing the economy was instrumental in shaping federal relations and in structuring the actions of subnational politicians and officials. As Sinha observes:

> Given the dominance of the central regime, all competitive strategies were formulated with a view to get crucial resources (economic or political) from the center. Given the regulatory licensing regime that allocated both public- and private-sector 'goodies', there was competition between the [S]tates for these allocations, but the competition was mediated through the central government.
>
> (2005: 109)

Private economic actors were the third point in the triangle, and they deployed various strategies, depending on their resources (financial and social capital, political contacts), to try and influence decision making. These included both direct lobbying to central ministries and officials, and indirect lobbying via State government officials. In the same way that the licence-permit raj created incentives for regional elites, it also generated it own incentives within the bureaucracy for bribes and others rents. As numerous studies have shown, Indian bureaucracy was porous to 'lobbying' and offering bribes for pushing files was an institutionalised practice, although the amount varied depending on the ministry or the point in time.

Inevitably, political factors came into the equation, notwithstanding the rigorous deployment of rational models for economic planning and the pre-eminence of the national scale as a basis for economic decision making. Investments are realised in space, in particular places, and these are never politically neutral. The central leadership, elected from the Congress party without interruption until 1977, was constantly under pressure from MPs and other political elites at the State-level to intervene in favour of their constituencies. Relations between New Delhi and State capitals were competitive or cooperative, depending on various political considerations, including but not limited to whether ruling parties at both levels were the same. Factional equations were equally important, and factional politics continue to be a characteristic feature of India's political parties.

This points to another critical feature of India's political institutions: the concentration of power in individuals. Individual party or faction leaders have tremendous power that they exert through informal networks, encompassing party and non-party organisational arenas (Jenkins 1999). Their capacity to wield influence may be rooted in ascribed or acquired qualities (caste or clan leader, patron, landowner), but access to power allows them to further con-solidate their networks of influence. As Kohli reminds us, 'Since the state structures the life chances of many, power in Indian democracy is contested vigorously, from the top to the bottom. The winners in turn use their positions and power just as vigorously, at times in the interest of the general good, but just as often for narrow, self-serving ends' (2012: 5). Such indivi-duals serve as nodal points, or brokers, in the political system and ensure its functioning. In this system, formal and informal political institutions dovetail with each other and work in tandem to produce outcomes on the ground. These distinctions are important because they remind us of the necessity to think beyond 'levels' of governance; the point is that geographies of state power *do not obey predefined scalar units*. The Congress party, its function-aries and faction leaders operated across various scales as a key political matrix for many decades and still today, although they have lost their monopoly. Even when Congress was in the opposition in a particular State, its leaders could still access national decision-makers, unlike regional party lea-ders for instance, and make claims for resources to benefit their constituencies or special interests.

Accusations of favouritism are a regular feature in all political systems, and one that became more pronounced in India over the years. Under Indira Gandhi's leadership in the late 1960s and 1970s in particular, federal relations deteriorated, in a context of growing political competition. The central ruling party in its dealings with State-level leaders increasingly used national eco-nomic resources, such as infrastructure projects or public sector enterprises, as bargaining chips. This corruption of central authority, lending credence to accusations that national development goals were increasingly subordinate to the central leadership's political machinations, was deeply resented by State-level leaders and contributed to a deterioration of federal relations. For years, State governments and opposition party leaders called, in vain, for reforms. Finally, in 1983 New Delhi agreed to constitute a high-level task force, the Sarkaria Commission, to investigate Centre–State relations and recommend reforms. The two-volume report, compiled on the basis of large-scale consultations, offered a unique comparative picture of how various regions and political formations evaluated the functioning of the federal system at that point in time. However, the central government did not translate its recommendations into a reform programme.[24]

2.5 Scales for political society and collective action

It can be recalled that from a theoretical viewpoint, geographical scales are socially produced, and are 'simultaneously a platform and container of certain kinds of social activity' (Smith 2003: 228). In other words, scale is produced through human activities and relationships and provides 'a materially real frame' for such activity. But it is useful to make an additional distinction between space, which is socially produced, and territory, which introduces a political dimension.

Territory is defined here as appropriated space, the idea being that the tangibility of borders, their significance, is contingent on groups of people appropriating the space within and imbuing it with meaning. A more precise definition, which has been elaborated in literature in France for analysing territorialisation processes, considers that territory has a strong socio-political dimension and is based on particular power relations within a bounded geographical area; in that respect, it defines the conditions for collective action (Dubresson and Jaglin 2005). In his analysis of globalisation and the 'archipelago economy', Pierre Veltz asserts that *territoire* has become a fundamental element of economic calculation, 'an organisational matrix' for social interaction and not just a store of resources (1996: 10).[25]

In the state/space framework I am using here, the constitutionally created 'States', the territorial units at the regional scale, constitute fundamental elements of state space in federal India, even though this corresponds to a 'narrow sense' of the concept as opposed to the more integral sense, which does not rely on territoriality (Brenner *et al.* 2003: 9; see Chapter 1 in this volume). For this reason, it is necessary to establish empirically for any given State the relative salience of the territorial dimension as compared to other spatial strategies that include, for instance, 'historically specific strategies for parcellizing, regulating, monitoring, and representing social space' (Brenner *et al.* 2003: 9). Examples mobilized in the following chapters will illustrate such strategies.

At the time of independence, the territorial boundaries of India's States and other subdivisions, such as districts, were inherited to some degree from previous political regimes (British colonial state, Mughal empire, regional and local kingdoms). These delimitations did not always reflect historical formations and protests and claims from various regions led to the decision in 1956 to redraw States' boundaries. In the time since their creation, approximately fifty years for most States,[26] they have progressively developed distinct political systems based on specific historically grounded forms of political society and mobilisation.

However, and this is a crucial point, the tangibility of political boundaries, their significance to people, the density of the State's organisational matrix, the degree of spatial and social fragmentation, the nature of governance (and this list is not exhaustive) vary enormously across States. In other words, the salience of the subnational state scale depends on its specific social history. As the discussion on Kerala suggested, Kerala's political society is a somewhat exceptional case; its political space is fully invested, 'worked', by social forces. High levels of political mobilisation, especially but not exclusively among the working class, date back to the early decades of the twentieth century. Broad based social reform movements starting in the nineteenth century were instrumental in mobilising popular demand for education and healthcare even among traditionally stigmatised social groups on the lowest rungs of the ritual hierarchy. This specific social history is critical for explaining why Kerala's social indicators are the highest in India, on par with many high-income countries. As I argued in my doctoral thesis, Kerala's political leadership was able to effectively assert and defend its policy positions *vis-à-vis* an 'unfriendly' central government because of its solid social base (Kennedy 1994).

In many States including Kerala, contemporary political borders correspond *grosso modo* to linguistic boundaries; they may also encompass territorially based ethnic groups, notably caste or clan clusters. As a result, various aspects of identity (regional, linguistic, ethnic) overlap and reinforce each other within many of India's States, contributing to a sense of territorial appropriation. This was the rationale that ultimately prevailed in the 1950s when States' borders were reorganised on the basis of language after prolonged mobilisation on the ground, notably in Andhra Pradesh and Maharashtra. National leadership had been extremely reluctant to open the Pandora's box of internal political borders, not wishing to turn attention away from the national scale and fearing an upsurge in parochial or, worse yet, separatist sentiments. In a speech to the Parliament in 1955, Nehru exhorted the members of the Lok Sabha to 'take a total view of India':

> I recognize that the language of the people is a vital matter for their development, whether it is education, administration or any other matter. But there is a distinction between developing a language to the fullest extent, and this passion for building up a wall around a linguistic area and calling it a border.
>
> (Nehru 1968: vol. 3: 172)

And as Emma Mawdsley reminds us:

> The struggle for Independence was seen by Nehru and many other nationalists as a critical period of 'nation-in-the-making' through the forging of a modern national consciousness, and they were concerned that the reactionary forces of ethnicity, language, religion and regional culture would hinder this process, or even prevail.
>
> (2002: 39)

The fundamental argument for a reorganisation of States' boundaries on the basis of language was the conviction that a culturally grounded base would facilitate mobilisation and ensure the robust functioning of democratic political institutions. For the most part, this reorganisation satisfied the most vociferous claims, although contestation has continued in some places. Among ongoing claims for statehood that flare up from time to time, one can cite Telengana in Andhra Pradesh and Bodoland in Assam. Despite such territorial movements, no revisions took place for more than forty years. Then in 2000, three new States were formed in the Hindi-speaking belt of northern India: Chhattisgarh, Uttaranchal and Jharkhand. This time, the ruling BJP coalition in New Delhi justified the decision on the basis of governance and administrative efficiency, although analysts were quick to show the self-serving political logic at hand: the new territorial boundaries gave an electoral edge to the BJP.[27]

2.6 The emergence of regional parties

Of particular interest for the study of the territorial dimensions of political economy is the emergence of 'regional' parties capable of effectively competing with Congress. These parties appeared rather soon on the scene, initially on the geographical peripheries of continental India, such as Akali Dal in Punjab and Dravida Munnetra Kazhagam (DMK) in Tamil Nadu, in both cases expressing aspirations for greater autonomy within the federal set-up. Technically speaking, regional parties operate in a bounded geographic space as opposed to national parties, and they can only aspire to govern at the State level. However defining 'regional parties' or 'State parties' (as they are classified by the Electoral Commission) is highly problematic because of the tremendous variety and attempts to find one neat definition have failed.[28] Even regional parties who mobilise on the basis of regional pride demonstrate very different characteristics. Whereas the DMK in Tamil Nadu arose out of a social movement in the early part of the twentieth century opposing Brahmin social dominance (non-Brahmin movement), the Telugu Desam Party (TDP) in Andhra Pradesh was created in 1983 to oppose Congress dominance of the State and ostensibly to recover Telugu pride flouted by the domineering practices of the Congress party high command, especially the practice of designating and discharging at will the Chief Ministers of the State.

Interestingly, in practice even national parties have taken on distinctly regional characteristics. This is the case of the communist parties in Kerala and West Bengal, the two regions in the country where they regularly form governments.[29] Although sharing broad ideological positions, each has its own political programme, organisational structure, and electoral strategies.[30] Even the Congress party, which has a centralised structure, has always depended on regional branches, some of which are run in a largely autonomous fashion around a powerful leader. This was the case for instance with Sharad Pawar in Maharastra, who regularly renegotiated his support to Congress, leaving and rejoining the party on several occasions.[31] Electoral pragmatism, and not ideology, has always characterised the Congress, but the threat of the BJP has made it even more prepared to view its regional units as distinct parts, each with their particular strategic role in inter-party competition. In the 1990s some of the Congress State branches even circulated their own election manifestos.

According to one observer: 'Every political party today is, in fact, a coalition of several State or local units. Each State or local unit excises some autonomy – something that was unheard of in the earlier era' (Sarangi 2005: 85).

These are manifestations of a process of regionalisation of politics, arguably one of the most important trends in Indian politics today. The term also refers to the participation of regional parties in national coalition governments, which have become the norm since the 1990s because no single national party is capable of winning a majority in Parliament. Starting in 1996 all national governments have been formed with the support of regional parties. The latter have shown their capacity to leverage their seats in exchange for ministerial berths (Mitra 2007: 101) and other special treatment for their respective States. Chandrababu Naidu, the Chief Minister of Andhra Pradesh from 1995 to 2004, was one of the first to fully exploit this new opportunity, a case I will come back to in the next chapter.

The regional political system or 'regime' to use Kohli's term (1987), reflects at any given point in time the manner in which power and resources are shared among social groups, a kind of 'social compromise' organised at a more localised scale.[32] To explain political performance, for instance the inclination and capacity to address certain issues like poverty, Kohli identified the key political factors to be the ideology of the ruling party, its internal organisation (e.g., elections within the party), and its social bases. Territorialised political mobilisation is a key consideration in this model and patterns in a given place are the result of a historical process, which is more or less broad-based. As John Harriss remarks with regard to India, where hierarchical social relations are institutionalised, it is particularly crucial to understand the degree to which traditionally subordinate groups participate in political processes, and the links between caste/ethnicity and historical structures of dominance (1999). As we shall see in subsequent chapters, the sociology of India's subnational political societies vary tremendously, even between neighbouring regions such as Odisha and Andhra Pradesh, which are analysed comparatively in the next chapter.

2.7 Conclusion

The aim in this chapter was to provide essential background about India's political institutions for subsequent chapters, starting with constitutional provisions that define the federal system. Federal relations as they developed in the decades after independence and until the 1990s were, for the most part, exclusively vertical between central and subnational states.[33] However federal governance was not defined once and for all but evolved over time, a reflection of more profound changes in the polity arising through political development, inter-party competition and fragmentation, the advent of coalition governments, as well as national leadership styles.[34]

Attention was given to the territorial organisation of the Indian state and the effective emergence of state spaces and scales through the actions of the developmental state in the period following independence. We saw that economic policies were calibrated to the national scales, and various instruments ensured a centralised management of the allocation of resources for economic development.

Of particular significance for the next chapters was the discussion of the manner in which central and subnational state spaces interact with regard to economic development policy-making. Despite the pre-eminence of the national government with regard to economic development policies, regional elites, bureaucrats and politicians, have had some room to manoeuvre and could adapt central government programmes to their own conditions, and pursue to some degree their own policy agendas. However the scope for strategic engagement with the Centre was strongly conditioned on regional political systems, as specific examples helped to illustrate.

Subnational scales emerge from territorialisation processes that are not necessarily contingent on political boundaries, and hence do not always 'fit' the State's borders. These scales are both social and political, and correspond to spatial patterns of social organisation. It follows that not all Indian States constitute equally salient scales of collective action, which offers a compelling explanation for the variegated functioning of multilevel policy making, not just the outcomes, namely central government transfers or projects, but more fundamentally the social relations and the social compromise prevailing in a given political territory.

Notes

1 Other sources of tension surrounding the deliberations of the Constituent Assembly, as Paul Brass notes, were generated by the efforts to integrate the Princely States into the Union, which involved the use of armed forces in three cases (Junagadh, Hyderabad and Jammu and Kashmir), as well as the assassination of Gandhi (in January 1948) and the communist-led insurrection in Telengana (2000: 60–1).
2 Ten of India's twenty-eight States have populations exceeding 50 million.
3 The Union List (97 items) includes defence, external affairs, communications, currency and the main taxes. The State List (66 items) includes public order and police, local administration, education, health, agriculture, industry and local taxes. The Concurrent List consists of 47 items, including modalities for the application of the Penal Code, labour laws and family planning (a result of an amendment passed in 1976).
4 There is no such provision in the Australian or American Constitutions, and some Indian States have demanded the revocation of these articles.
5 Whereas President's Rule had been declared only ten times before 1967, it was implemented forty times between 1967 and 1977, a rough indicator of the deterioration of federal institutions during that period.
6 In March 1994, in *S. R. Bommai versus Union of India* the Supreme Court decided that the two houses of Parliament must approve of the use of Article 356 to dissolve an assembly, and that even in case of their approval the courts could restore the *status quo ante*. See Adeney (2005).
7 This came out clearly for instance in the Sarkaria Commission Report (Government of India 1987, 1988).
8 Government of India (1988 annexe X-4: 324).

9 See Govinda Rao and Singh 2003, cited by Bagchi (2003: 35). On favouritism in transfers, see Nooruddin and Chhibber (2008).

10 The public sector contributed 40 per cent of industrial output in 1981 compared to 8 per cent in 1961 (Landy 2010: 407).

11 For a detailed discussion of this set-up, see Sinha (2011).

12 Orissa was officially renamed Odisha in 2011.

13 In fact, the Five-Year Plans did not elaborate clear guidelines for territorial planning, with the exception of the Second Plan (1956–60), which mentions the necessity of balanced regional development (Landy 2006: 209).

14 Notwithstanding, the Centre allowed States to erect barriers to trade in order to retain what they deemed to be 'essential commodities' and to impose taxes on interstate trade (Bagchi 2003: 28–9).

15 It could hardly have been anticipated that such enclaves would foreshadow the SEZs of the 2000s, deemed 'foreign territory for the purposes of trade operations and duties and tariffs' (see www.indiainbusiness.nic.in/FAQ/sez.htm; and Chapter 5 in this volume).

16 Two exceptions are Sinha (2005) and Kennedy (1994).

17 Sinha states: 'In Gujarat, regional rulers attempted to mitigate the constraining effects of the central rules by bureaucratic pressure, lobbying, and monitoring internal to the regime. Investment flows were quite high *as a result*' (2005: 91, emphasis added). Later she states: 'In West Bengal, however, *political and public* channels were employed to evolve a rhetoric of conflict and confrontation. Tamil Nadu rulers, in an opportunistic vein, followed the swings of the electoral cycle; anti-center rhetoric and lobbying efforts were followed at different moments. *As a consequence*, investment flows under the control of the central machinery languished in West Bengal and oscillated over time in Tamil Nadu' (ibid., second set of italics added).

18 Sinha discounts as invalid the idea that the central state biased the flow of licences towards certain States (2005: 54–61), thereby suggesting that investment flows under the control of the central machinery can be explained entirely by the ability of State level elites to effectively bargain with the central state.

19 Interestingly, Khemani finds that these favoured States received significantly lower *statutory transfers*, those attributed by the Finance Commission. However, '[I]f the two sets of transfers are pooled, then the partisan effect on plan transfers dominates, that is, total general-purpose transfers from the center are greater when a state government is politically affiliated with the center' (Khemani 2003: 3).

20 The aim of my doctoral research was to understand to what extent a State government could define policy priorities for its regional economic development and translate them into action on the ground given the centralised regulatory regime at the Centre (Kennedy 1994).

21 In 1988 there were 8,662 registered trade unions in Kerala, which represented 19 per cent of all unions in the country (GoI 1988: 74, cited by Heller 1995: 655). To put this in context, Kerala's share of the total population was roughly 3.5 per cent at that time.

22 In practice, unions also operate as employment brokers: they are in charge of distributing work to paid union members. See Kennedy (1996).

23 Heller (1995) explains how this position allowed the working class to negotiate a new developmental strategy for the State in the 1990s.

24 There is a vast body of literature on Centre–State relations dating back to the 1960s covering political, economic and fiscal dimensions, almost all of which is critical in nature, i.e., denouncing the dysfunctional and constantly deteriorating federal relations. A cursory review indicates that since economic liberalisation, there is relatively less scholarship and its focus has changed considerably. In 2007 a national commission was nominated to review Centre–State relations and make

recommendations (see GoI 2010). The initiative came from the central government '(u)nlike the Sarkaria Commission which was constituted in the aftermath of consistent demands by some major political parties and opposition led State Governments' (ibid.: xxi).

25 'le territoire entre désormais dans le jeu économique comme matrice d'organisation et d'interactions sociales (...)' (Veltz 1996: 10).

26 In 2000, three new States were formed Chhattisgarh, Uttaranchal and Jharkhand.

27 See Mawdsley (2002).

28 See Verniers (2005).

29 With Tripura, a small State in the north-east.

30 It should be pointed out that tremendous geographical, historical and cultural differences separate Kerala and West Bengal located at two extremes of India's continental territory (south-west and north-east respectively; see Map of India).

31 In 1999, in sharp disagreement with the party's central command, he formed a break-away regional party, the NCP, which then formed a government with what remained of the State branch of Congress.

32 Social compromise is a concept used in regulation theory to designate the prevailing social relations between capital and labour in a particular accumulation regime, usually at a national scale. It is used here in a less restrictive way, referring broadly to the manner in which economic gains are shared in society between groups (see Kennedy *et al.* 2013).

33 Although mentioned in the Constitution, intergovernmental institutions intended to favour horizontal coordination and provide a forum where States could interact were either not formed or not maintained regularly (e.g., Inter-State council); de facto, the National Development Council and the Planning Commission served this function although they represented forms of 'executive federalism'. See Sáez (2002, especially Chapter 4).

34 Different phases of Centre–State relations have been distinguished. For an overview, see Kennedy (2011).

3   The politics and scales of economic reforms

This chapter discusses the various phases of economic policy reform starting in the 1980s. Literature on the politics of reforms is mobilised to explain the decision to adopt and pursue reforms, as well as to understand how reforms have been managed. I will argue here and in subsequent chapters that economic reforms are inextricably linked to political strategies that have emerged as a result of the wider political changes taking place in the last thirty to forty years. These are characterised by the gradual decline of Congress party dominance, the rise of Hindu nationalism and the regionalisation of politics.

The discussion here, largely based on the literature, sets the foundation for subsequent chapters that examine how economic reforms have put in motion a process of intense restructuring that is contributing to the construction of new state spaces at various scales.

3.1 The substance of India's economic reforms

The structural adjustment programme adopted in 1991 aimed both to attain macroeconomic stability in the short term and to modify the conditions for investment and trade in the longer term. Regarding the latter, a new trade policy started removing quantitative import restrictions and significantly reduced customs duties, among the highest in the world at the time, from maximal rates of 150 per cent to 110 per cent and then progressively lower.[1] Quotas and licenses for importing and exporting were lifted for most goods, although some items, mainly consumer goods, continued to require a license and some strategic goods were reserved for exclusive import by government agencies (e.g., petroleum, food grains). Incentives were devised for encouraging exports, including duty-free imports of inputs, marking an explicit shift in favour of a more trade-oriented economic development policy. Restrictions on foreign ownership were relaxed from a maximum of 40 per cent ownership share to 51 per cent in the case of joint ventures. In priority sectors, like energy, 100 per cent foreign ownership was allowed, and incentives such as tax holidays were proffered.

Gradually, over the course of the years, spanning several different governments and continuing till today, subsequent measures have been announced, duties further reduced, foreign ownership stakes increased, etc., moving more or less constantly toward less restricted markets. Although it continues to account for about 35 per cent of industrial value-added (Ahluwalia 2002: 83), the public sector has practically ceased making new investments in the productive sphere. It has experimented with disinvestment, withdrawing part of its capital from public and joint sector ventures while maintaining control over management, and to a lesser degree with privatising or closing state-owned enterprises. However, privatisation and the revision of labour laws are two areas where successive governments have been reluctant to undertake far-reaching reforms.

Of particular interest here is the dismantling of the centralised licence-raj apparatus, examined in the last chapter, which had been put in place to manage industrial investments. Its dismantling meant that private enterprises were no longer required to apply to the central government for a license to start or expand production, and the choice of industrial location was left up to the investor. As we will discuss in the next chapter, the deregulation of industrial investment had significant implications for the relative policy space of State and central governments. It will be seen that for the central state, the carefully constructed *frame of reference* between industrial development and national territory has been disconnected.

3.2 Sovereignty issues: the decision to reform in 1991

The standard account about *why* market reforms were adopted in 1991 centres around crisis and hence constraint, i.e., that the stabilisation package was adopted under duress. Two main factors, one internal and the other external, are usually cited: the liquidity crisis and threat of default on one hand, and international instability produced by the invasion of Kuwait by Iraq on the other. The Indian state had become deeply indebted in the 1980s, including borrowing in international capital markets at high (and variable) rates of interest, as part of Rajiv Gandhi's drive to modernise the economy. Debt was linked both to the liberalisation of imports, notably technology, from the mid-1980s and also to recurring annual fiscal deficits linked in part to the continuing policy of subsidies to various groups, mainly farmers (fertilisers, power, petroleum). Although India's financial situation was critical, especially its balance of payments (reserves covering only two weeks of imports), the 1990 Iraqi invasion of Kuwait and ensuing war exacerbated India's situation by creating a climate of instability in international markets. Sharp increases in world oil prices had an immediate impact on India's trade balance: petroleum products made up about one-quarter of India's import basket. The downgrading of India's credit rating in late 1990 made default look inevitable and pushed India to seek a loan from the IMF.[2]

There can be little doubt that the objective factors just mentioned – balance of payments crisis, external debt and international instability – precipitated India's decision to contract a loan from the IMF and commit to a structural adjustment programme. But the 'crisis' argument is not sufficient for explaining why reforms were pursued and intensified under successive regimes well after India's macroeconomic fundamentals were redressed. That decision expresses a political strategy on the part of India's policy-making elites in New Delhi. Viewed in that respect, the balance of payment crisis provided an opportunity for bringing about an overhaul of the Nehruvian model of state-led development whose day, they felt, had come.[3]

Endogenous factors are considered here to be the most relevant for understanding India's decision to pursue a reform agenda beyond the initial stabilisation package. This position does not discount the fact that the Indian government was subjected to strong pressure from international organisations to enact reform, but it contrasts sharply with those analyses that emphasise the predominant role of exogenous forces and the restricted autonomy of India's leadership. For proponents of that view, which include many critics in India, international organisations (mainly the IMF and the World Bank) working at the behest of international financial capital have hoisted the reform agenda onto India because those interests stand 'to gain the most from the removal of restrictions on capital flows and currency unification and convertibility' (Patnaik 2000: 235 cited by Mooij 2005: 25). This analysis is shared by some international observers who question the ability of developing countries to resist the forces of globalisation (see Hochraich 2002 for Asian countries). In many such cases, it expresses a macro-structural perspective that posits the dominance of the economic sphere over the political, and the hegemonic power of the North over the South. Not only do these perspectives underestimate the capacity of India's leadership to negotiate with international organisations, including with regard to hard conditionalities, they give little importance to domestic political interests favourable to reforms. Lastly, they ignore the strategic interests of elites within the Indian state in pursuing reforms, which reflect internal political calculations as well as external considerations, including aspirations for state power in the international arena (Racine 2003).

At the same time, it would be naive to imagine that the integration of markets on a global scale and the dominance of financial capitalism do not impose constraints on national policy-making. Yet, as Béatrice Hibou (2004) has argued in the context of the global wave of neo-liberal reform, states are not powerless to act in the economic sphere; they are *adapting* to external as well as internal constraints, even when this takes the form of privatisation, delegation of state power or other forms of indirect government. It is the narrow definition of notions of state sovereignty and legitimacy, she argues, that needs to be critically re-examined (ibid.: 46). This state theory has direct relevance for India's reform process, as I will argue throughout this book.

One debate in India questions whether ideology or 'outcomes' are driving the reform process, but this is less central to the discussion here than the changes in governance that have emerged and the fact that the reform agenda was endogenously produced, despite being calibrated on international norms.

Only detailed studies can help us understand how incentives generated by economic changes in the global economy translate into institutional and policy change in specific countries. John Echeverri-Gent (2004) argues that although globalisation creates powerful incentives, it does not dictate specific policy responses; these emerge as a result of political processes within the country, involving state (policy-making) actors as well as private sector actors, both of whom operate at various scales. On a related note, Jean-François Bayart (2004), writing about globalisation, reminds us that the universality of institutions and of political or economic ideologies does not level or erase the historical trajectories of the societies that appropriate them.[4]

3.3 A first phase of policy reform in the 1980s

There is now quite ample evidence to argue that the policy shift away from the Nehruvian model actually started in the 1980s, albeit in embryonic form, and that the liberalisation reforms of the early 1990s, although much more radical, are linked in significant ways to the earlier phase. In effect, there is continuity both with regard to the policy-makers in the central government, the agents of change, and to the political strategy driving action that consists in building alliances with the business community and improving the environment for private sector actors.

Until the early 2000s standard narratives about India's economic 'emergence' generally placed the starting point in 1991, when India started liberalising its trade policies and deregulating its domestic economy. In simplistic accounts, radical reforms had 'unleashed' market forces and resulted in strong growth. Although this often ideologically-driven version of India's recent economic performance has since been qualified to some extent, there is still considerable debate on the issue (see Ahluwalia 2004). One of the most serious challenges to this version came from economists who were able to show that the crucial turning point in the transition to high growth took place around 1980, a full decade before liberalisation. Annual growth during the 1980s averaged 5.7 per cent whereas in the in the earlier phase, 1950–80, it was only about 3.5 per cent, which works out to an average of only 1.7 per cent in per capita terms (Rodrik and Subramanian 2004). For Rodrik and Subramanian (2004), the crucial catalyst that explains this rupture was an attitudinal change on the part of India's national leadership towards the business community. When Indira Gandhi returned to power in 1980, she aligned herself with the private sector and tamed down her previous 'socialist' rhetoric: 'The national government's attitude towards business went from being outright hostile to supportive' (ibid.: 2).

But as these economists insist, this new orientation was 'pro-business' *not* 'pro-market.' They show that even in the absence of any concrete deregulation in the first years, not to mention anything resembling liberalisation, the attitudinal change was sufficient to modify the perceptions of the business community and to translate into increased investment and growth. Interestingly, it was in the medium and large-scale industrial sector where the productivity surge was the most evident in the 1980s, compared to infrastructure and agriculture. This is interpreted to mean that the policy reorientation was most beneficial to incumbents, i.e., well-established business houses, which is consistent with the political strategy that inspired it. As Atul Kohli (1989) has argued, after losing power to the Janata party in the 1977 elections, Indira Gandhi realised she needed to revise her political strategy, and so concentrated her energy on winning support from both the Hindu majority, by appealing more openly to Hindu chauvinism and industrial and commercial groups. The objective was to broaden her support base beyond the poor, though she was careful not to abandon her popular socialist leader image. Although he does not discount that other factors played some part in this shift towards more economic efficiency, including pressures from within the bureaucracy for policy change and conditionalities linked to an IMF loan taken in 1981, Kohli argues that Indira Gandhi's economic policies are best understood as an integral part of her overall *political strategy* to gain support from business groups (1989).

This policy reorientation went further with Rajiv Gandhi's government in 1985 and was reinforced with more substantive measures aimed at deregulating industrial investments and improving the environment for domestic business. Elected in late 1984 on a 'sympathy wave' following the assassination of Indira Gandhi, the Congress government enjoyed a comfortable majority in Parliament (415 out of 545 seats). Immediately after elections, it announced a series of deregulation measures favourable to the private sector including de-licensing of certain categories of industries, allowing companies in a number of industries to extend the scope of their operations to related activities or to expand their capacity. There were also steps taken to marginally lower trade barriers and import restrictions and reduce taxes. Economic modernisation and support for importing technology were emphasised. For Kohli 'there was a genuine attempt at a new beginning; an attempt was made to make a decisive shift from the state-controlled and imports substitution model to a liberal model of development' (1989: 311).

This initial set of policy reforms met with little resistance, probably because of the strong electoral legitimacy of the government and the good will towards Rajiv Gandhi, whose mother's assassination hoisted him onto the political scene, seemingly against his will. But subsequent attempts to undertake more fundamental reforms, like reducing massive subsidies in petroleum, foodgrains and fertiliser, provoked a 'political revolt' that ultimately forced the government to backtrack (Varshney 1999). Notwithstanding this backtracking, the 'timid' reforms of the 1980s, as they are often described, had a surprisingly strong impact on raising productivity, as well as GDP growth. According to Rodrik and Subramanian, this seemingly disproportionate impact was possible because India 'was very far from its long run or steady-state level of income *given the level of its domestic institutions*' (2004: 16–17, italics added). In other words, if we accept the theory that institutions are a major determinant of growth, then India's economic and political institutions should have produced (or at least *allowed*) a much higher income level than actually prevailed in the 1960s and 1970s.[5] According to their calculations: 'India's level of income was about a quarter of what it should be given the strength of its *economic institutions*. On the other hand, *if political institutions are the true long-run determinant of income*, India's income is about 15 percent of what it should be. India has thus been a significant under-achiever in the sense that it has not exploited the potential created by having done the really hard work of building institutions' (2004: 17, emphasis added).

This study, which was somewhat coolly received by at least one prominent member of the policy-making establishment,[6] turned a number of received ideas on their heads. For one, it showed that growth in the 1980s took place precisely in those manufacturing sectors that had been patiently built up over the previous decades through import substitution policy. So in other words, rather than completely discrediting the earlier policy regime, India could be seen to be harvesting the fruits of earlier efforts. The more 'friendly' environment that emerged as a result of these policy changes was attractive for new entrants and for new activities:

> It is perhaps not a coincidence that some of the IT powerhouses that would begin to fuel India's growth a decade or so later got established in the early 1980s, just as the economic environment was turning more business-friendly. For example, Wipro first ventured into IT in 1980, and Infosys was founded in 1981. These firms eventually were able to reap handsome benefits from India's prior public investments in higher educa-tion (the Indian Institutes of Technology – IITs – in particular) once the policy environment turned permissive.
>
> (Rodrik and Subarmanian 2004: 20)

These debates underscore the fact that for many people within and without India, and for different reasons, it is important to be able to identify the moment of rupture with the old economic policy regime. Like China's 1978 moment, a large section of India's elites would like a temporal landmark for turning the page on state-controlled development, and starting down the path of growth *and* more intense international engagement. Jean-Luc Racine has analysed this as a 'change of paradigm', fully assumed by India's leadership in the early 1990s, marking the end of a somewhat defensive stance and the beginning a new phase of assertiveness on the international scene (2003).

3.4 Policy-making in a multiscalar framework

In examining the reform process and the political strategies driving it, it is necessary to inquire about the actors, starting with the policy-making elites. Béatrice Hibou reminds us that to apprehend the state it is impossible to separate: (1) the state and power; (2) the state and ruling elites; in order to understand the state, it is necessary to understand the people in power, their games, their strategies and their historically grounded practices (2004: 21). Thus for instance the capture of wealth by state elites cannot be considered to go against the state, because they make up the state, they are the state; graft is a political practice (ibid.).

It is a fact that key architects of India's 1991 reform programme were also associated with the earlier attempt at liberalisation in the 1980s, in the Rajiv Gandhi era. These advisors were professional economists, many of whom had experience at the World Bank or other international agencies.[7] In his analysis of the economic policy-makers of the 1980s, Kohli argues: 'While clearly a competent group of managers, economists and bureaucrats, they were all marked by *a technocratic rather than a political image*' (1989: 312, emphasis added), and he goes on to note that since Rajiv and his crucial political aides 'had a managerial and technocratic image, there was a sense that the political leaders and their technical advisors were cut from the same cloth' (ibid.). This analysis, first published in 1989, foretells in many ways the evolution of the following decades, wherein economic advisors and experts of various kinds have come to occupy a critical place in both central and regional state structures; more precisely, they have been *invited* by policy-makers to occupy this critical place. So while it is true that technocrats may draft reforms, politicians have to manage them, and they are often willing to backtrack when reforms provoke an overly hostile reaction. Rob Jenkins reminds us of the 'pervasiveness of politics in the reform process'; politics shape reforms and are in turn shaped by them (2004: 261).

These remarks lend support to the economic analysis cited above that places the key rupture in the 1980s in the context of deep political change within India. As discussed, India throughout the 1960s and 1970s was moving gradually away from a one dominant party system towards greater competition at all levels. This was in part the result of social mobilisation occurring to a large degree in the context of identity politics, i.e., political mobilisation on the basis of essential characteristics like language, caste or religion, and the affirmation in electoral politics of subaltern groups, mainly Dalits and 'Other Backward Classes' (OBCs). In the late 1980s and early 1990s, the National Front, under Prime Minister V. P. Singh, introduced affirmative action for OBCs for jobs in the central government administration (27 per cent), ten years after the Mandal Commission recommended it. That decision was hotly contested by upper castes, which ultimately contributed in uniting the OBCs to fight a common cause (Jaffrelot 2003: 349). OBCs have been breaking away from mainstream parties, where they had been co-opted by the social elites who have dominated Indian politics since independence. Along with Dalits, they are forming interest groups and caste coalitions and are starting to vote for parties that correspond to their social profile and that will presumably represent their interests.

Arguably this type of mobilisation reinforces caste feelings, and its also contributes to stoking tension between upper and lower castes and classes.

Then again, it has been argued that caste and community allegiances have favoured democracy by becoming the focus for political mobilisation and by being vehicles for the pursuit of group interests (Austin 1999: 646). This mobilisation is having a decisive impact on *who participates in politics*, especially in northern India where upper castes have dominated since independence. Here, the representation of Dalits and lower castes in Parliament and State legislatures has dramatically increased in the last ten years, and subaltern-led parties have formed governments in several north Indian States in recent years – a development that has been termed 'a silent revolution' (Jaffrelot 2003).

Another equally important development during this period, also a manifestation of identity politics, was the rise of Hindu nationalism. Exploiting the 'inferiority complex' of the majority Hindu population and fuelling religious animosity between Hindus and Muslims in some regions, the nationalist Bharatiya Janata Party (BJP) mobilised Hindus across castes, classes and regions. The BJP rose spectacularly through the 1980s in northern India especially and became the second largest party in Parliament in 1991, behind the Congress.

As will be clear by now, I am arguing that India's political development is the key to understanding the reform process. This does not discount the importance of other contextual factors, two of which probably played a significant role in the decision to liberalise the economy: changing geopolitics and pressures from India's large diaspora.

India's reform process was no doubt influenced in substantial ways by the collapse of the USSR and by the tremendous impacts it had on global geopolitics. Unlike many developing countries, India quite effectively managed to maintain good relations with both superpowers, and benefited in some ways from their rivalry. The effective elimination of a counterbalance to American hegemony was a new parameter India's leadership was quick to integrate (Racine 2003). Moreover, China's spectacular economic performance in the 1980s had not gone unnoticed. According to Nayar, India's political leaders were motivated to pursue reforms 'beyond conditionalities' by their 'awe at the advance made by the economies of East and Southeast Asia' (Nayar 2005: 233). National security issues have no doubt been a central part of the larger quest for state power; India's weak economic position in terms of share of world output and trade was perceived by many in foreign policy circles to jeopardize its national security (ibid.: 236).

These important geopolitical considerations, which are beyond the scope of this book, nevertheless underscore the necessity of a multiscale approach for apprehending the changes in India's economic governance. This is all the more the case in an open society like India's with unrestricted access to ideas from the outside. Even if India's middle classes had only limited access to goods and services and international travel before liberalisation, because of high customs' duties and an inconvertible currency, India's open society allowed them to stay informed about changes taking place in the world. Although it may be stating the obvious, there can be little doubt that the global circulation of goods, people, and norms and practices, *did* create pressures in favour of liberalisation and contributed to shaping the process in significant ways. The circulation of people is particularly relevant in the case of India as it has a very large diaspora, and one that is characterised, at least in the US, by high educational levels and high incomes.[8] This is a direct result of the selective immigration policy of the US, reserving visas for professionally qualified elite. Devesh Kapur argues that the US-based diaspora in particular influenced economic ideas in India and consequently the trajectory of economic reforms, especially economists trained in top universities that went back to India. But he insists this was possible because of four interrelated factors: (1) specific characteristics of the diaspora ('elite migration': skilled individuals but also possessing social capital and access to influential networks); (2) the timing of liberalisation (first- and second-generation migrants were still attached to India); (3) the institutional configuration of the home country and its receptivity to new ideas; and (4) the willingness of migrants to return home, which are linked to the reasons for leaving in the first place (i.e., better economic prospects) (Kapur 2004).

Kapur insists that India's reforms were more 'home-grown' than in some other countries, notwithstanding foreign influence, because of India's institutions:

> India's institutional structure – a strong bureaucracy and a parliamentary system – means that a returning technocrat has to spend time in an advisory capacity before he can move to decisionmaking roles. This creates trust while also providing them a better sense of the political nuances that are critical if policies are to be adopted and implemented. The fact that would-be decisionmakers must pay at least some organizational dues to the system means that returning economists are required to replant themselves back in the 'home' turf.
>
> (2004: 375)

Of particular interest here, the diaspora came to exert increasing influence at all levels of society as more and more Indians settled abroad. As Indian society's engagement with the outside world has increased in recent decades, it has been in part mediated by its citizens abroad. India's leadership has explicitly tried to mobilise Indians and people of Indian origin with a view to enhancing economic ties, perhaps most explicitly in the US (Racine 2008; Therwath 2008).[9]

Jagdish Bhagwati, a renowned trade economist and vigorous supporter of economic reforms, recently published an opinion piece about the influence of the diaspora in which he cited a conversation with the Prime Minister Manmohan Singh, who as Finance Minister in 1991 was a major architect of the reform programme:

> He told me that, when he was spearheading the reforms as the finance minister, Prime Minister Narasimha Rao had lent his full support largely because many members of his own family, who were abroad, had told

him that India's policies made no sense and that they had diminished our standing in the world (...) our diaspora ceaselessly brought home to these elites [policymakers] the fact that these policies had little rationale; they lived often in countries where our policies would have been laughed out of court.[10]

Of course, this particular public intellectual has been explicit in his ideological commitment to free trade,[11] but it is nonetheless interesting to note the emphasis he gives to outsiders' perceptions as a motivating factor for India's policy-making elites. Incidentally, P. V. Narasimha Rao, the first South Indian to become a Prime Minister, was from Andhra Pradesh, a large State in South India (population 84 million in 2011). It is a fact that Andhra Pradesh has strongly contributed to elite migration to the US, among engineers in particular; Andhra Pradesh natives were the largest single group in Silicon Valley at the height of the new economy boom. In the 1980s private engineering and medical colleges had mushroomed across the State, and it became a middle class dream to send a son or daughter abroad. Based on a large survey conducted in the US in 2003, it is estimated that nearly one-quarter of all households in India have immediate or extended family members abroad (Kapur 2004: 379).

3.5 The politics of reforms

Although not engaging directly with the concept of state scales, the literature on the politics of economic reforms in India offers relevant insights for understanding which state actors, at which state scales, are driving the reform process and how they are managing it.[12] At issue is to understand how India's democratic and federal political institutions enabled political elites to usher in liberal market reforms that went against the immediate interests of both powerful organised groups and the country's large poor population (more than one-quarter live below the poverty line). It is generally assumed that top-down reform initiatives cannot on their own be sustained without a broader consensus among social actors at different scales. In this context, it is useful to recall that the issue of reforms has been singularly absent in electoral contests in India: not only have voters never been asked to support or reject the reform agenda, but election surveys carried out in the 1990s have regularly indicated that a large majority of Indian voters were not aware there was such a thing as a reform programme.[13] This raises important questions about the political processes underlying and accompanying reforms. Two major studies offer quite different interpretations.

For Ashutosh Varshney (1999), at the time economic reforms were adopted, India's political class was preoccupied with other more pressing issues for 'mass politics', linked mainly to lower caste mobilisation and to Hindu–Muslim tensions. He categorizes economic reforms as 'elite politics', the kind discussed in institutionalised settings, e.g., within the bureaucracy or in Parliament; in contrast, 'mass politics' takes place on the streets, and concerns issues that unleash passions and emotions (Varshney 1999: 223). In 1991, when the newly elected Congress government introduced reforms, the Hindu nationalist BJP had become the second largest party in the country and the Congress party's main rival. The socialist Janata party and the communists were opposed to reforms, but they were even more concerned about the growing popularity of the BJP, and so refused to join with it to vote against reforms in Parliament. He concludes: 'India's economic reforms kept progressing because the political context had made Hindu–Muslim relations and caste animosities the prime determinant of political coalitions' (ibid.: 248, italics removed). Varshney also argues that reforms that touch elite politics are the ones that have gone the furthest (e.g., devaluation, restructuration of capital markets, trade liberalisation, etc.), compared to those that affect the masses (e.g., reducing subsidies). If privatisation and labour legislation reforms have been lagging, it's because they could trickle down to mass politics. In this analysis, reforms are not a political issue, and the government has been careful to keep it out of the realm of mass politics, having learned from the experience of the 1980s.

In another study published the same year, Rob Jenkins (1999) put the focus on the working of India's political institutions, including the federal arrangements, to explain how reforms were implemented without directly consulting the electorate. With careful attention to detail, he mobilised an impressive corpus of evidence to show that political elites at national and regional levels, working through formal and informal institutions, used obfuscatory tactics and stealth, as well as considerable creativity and skill, to defuse opposition to specific reforms and build coalitions of support. Gradualism or the 'sequencing' of reforms allowed officials to manage the negative effects through negotiation, compensation, and building new alliances, it also gave politicians and officials opportunities to adapt, and see how they could exploit new possibilities thrown up by deregulation and privatisation, in the broad sense of the word.[14] Reforms set in motion a rearrangement of business–state relations at all levels. Large manufacturing firms, many of which enjoyed comfortable monopoly-like situations prior to reforms, felt threatened by import liberalisation, as did small scale industries, but these blocs were not monolithic, and negotiations and deals could be made with this or that faction; the gradual 'piece-meal' implementation of reforms allowed officials to maintain their control over the process, indeed to backtrack on occasion. Moreover, regional industrialists could perceive advantages to a shift in decision making from the central ministries to State governments, more easily accessible to them. In some States, such as Andhra Pradesh, regional-based business groups are closely linked to political parties; moreover, in this State economic and political elites tend to have similar ethnic and subregional backgrounds (Srinivasulu 2003; Baru 2000; Benbabaali 2009), which presumably facilitates cooperation.

Of particular interest for this study, Jenkins shows that State-level politicians and civil servants, far from passively implementing New Delhi's decrees, negotiated, often driving a hard bargain, according to the political imperatives prevailing in their State. Moreover, cooperating on a particular reform did not prevent them from claiming publicly that they had no choice but to follow the diktat from New Delhi, especially if it helped gain mileage in party politics. Jenkins illustrates with an example:

> The (BJP) chief minister from of Rajasthan stated in 1994 that the [S]tate's new mining policy, which was significantly more liberal towards the private sector, was a matter of necessity: 'the new economic policies being pursued by the centre had left the [S]tates to fend for themselves'. These and other liberalising moves were rejected as 'sheer hypocrisy' by the Rajasthan Congress president, Paras Ram Maderna: 'It is shocking that while the [S]tate BJP leadership charges the Centre with taking loans from world bodies, burdening the nation with debts, it is itself securing huge loans running into thousands of crores [tens of billions of rupees] from international agencies'.
>
> (1999: 144–5)

As this example suggests, when analysing the politics of reform at the State level, it is necessary to distinguish public posturing and rhetoric from actions on the ground. Incentives generated by partisan politics or concern about alienating adversely affected interest groups may lead State-level leaders to publicly oppose specific policies, but this does not stop them from selectively implementing measures viewed as compatible with their interests and objectives. The positioning of State governments *vis-à-vis* reforms and the way they present their positions publicly depend on their constituencies, and more broadly on the *regional political systems*, which emerge from territorialised mobilisation processes.

3.6 Regional political systems

In a comparative study of Tamil Nadu and Andhra Pradesh covering the 1990s and early 2000s, I demonstrated that although the two States had in fact enacted broadly similar policies for attracting investors, their packaging of these policies was entirely different (Kennedy 2004a). Tamil Nadu's policy-makers quietly went about modifying the business climate through the amendment of existing rules and regulations, mainly by government order as opposed to a more transparent legislative process. In contrast, the Andhra Pradesh government under Chief Minister Chandrababu Naidu opted to 'trumpet' its policy changes, asserting a radical rupture in the State's policies, indeed more radical than what actually occurred. To explain these different approaches, I examined specific features of each State's political system and engaged with two existing theories about how relatively poor or industrially underdeveloped States react to market reforms. A summary of that analysis will allow me to expose an explanatory framework that will be useful throughout the remainder of this book.

The explanation centred on the degree of fragmentation in the regional party system of each State, which was seen as a reflection of social dynamics. In both Tamil Nadu and Andhra Pradesh, a two-party system is the norm; two large parties contest power and traditionally alternate in forming the government. They 'accommodate' smaller groupings within their organisations, which are often based on caste or subregional identities. Tamil Nadu's political scene is dominated by the Dravida Munnetra Kazhagam or DMK and the ADMK,[15] both of which have their roots in lower caste mobilisation, starting with the anti-Brahmin movement of the first half of the twentieth century. These rival formations compete intensely for the support of middle and lower castes and Dalits, groups that have started forming their own caste-based political parties in recent years.[16] These organisations pledge their support to one or the other major party as opportunities arise, driving hard bargains in the process. Because of this fluid situation, neither established party has been willing to risk alienating the groups represented by these new organisations, which tend to oppose liberalisation,[17] thereby destabilising governing coalitions.

Political realities in Andhra Pradesh were quite different at the time: the TDP had emerged in the 1980s as a rival to the Congress party and these two main parties alternated with each other in a relatively stable balance. The State's two dominant castes, Reddys and Kammas, dominated the Congress Party and the TDP, respectively.[18] I argued that the relative stability of the two-party system allowed the TDP leadership to adopt an aggressive policy stance on economic reform without taking too much of a political risk. However, a more critical factor was the TDP's social base, which represents to a much greater degree upper and middle castes/classes than either the DMK or the ADMK. As K. Srinivasulu has argued, the TDP's pro-liberalisation reforms, based on promoting 'global growth sectors' such as IT and business services, were responsive to the demands and policy preferences of an 'urban entrepreneurial class', which constituted one influential section of the party's support base (Srinivasulu 2003). The question of social bases is a key element of State-level 'political regimes', as we saw earlier in the case of Kerala. These policies sought to rescale the State's economy in favour of tertiary activities. To some extent they have succeeded: in terms of State income, the contribution of the primary sector (agriculture, fishing) declined from 32 per cent in 1995–2000 (compared to 30 per cent for all-India average) to 29 per cent between 2000–5 and services increased from 44 per cent to 49 per cent in the same period. I will come back to the case of Andhra Pradesh in more detail in the next chapter.

The results of this comparative analysis provide evidence to counter a theoretical model that contends that poorer States are less likely than rich States to embark on economic reforms because they do not expect to be in a position to gain, for instance, in terms of attracting new investments, and because they fear that central government redistribution based on cross-regional subsidisation will be phased out (Jenkins 1999: 9). Yet Andhra Pradesh, whose socioeconomic indicators were below the national average in the early

1990s, embarked on bold reforms. I argued that an approach based on local and regional social dynamics offered a more powerful explanatory framework for understanding policy choices than a priori assumptions based on categories like 'rich' and 'poor' States. This approach will be mobilised in Chapter 4 to contrast State governments' responses to the economic reform agenda and in Chapter 5 to the national Special Economic Zone policy.

3.7 Conclusion

This chapter examined the process of economic reforms, the context, the contents and the actors. Whereas numerous internal and external constraints contributed to India's decision to adopt reforms, it was argued that endogenous factors explain the depth and duration of reforms. This position does not deny that the decision was responsive to incentives generated by changes in the global economy or that India's policy-making elites were influenced by global actors and ideas. What I emphasise, however, is that India's political elites are driving the reform process, and that it is inextricably linked to a larger process of political change reflecting the country's political development over the last decades. Increased political competition at all spatial scales reflects the intense mobilisation that is occurring, including a marked trend in favour of identity-based movements, illustrated by a new wave of subaltern political mobilisation in the Hindi belt and the rise of Hindu nationalism.

A first round of reforms in the 1980s, more pro-business than pro-market, produced rapid gains in growth, linked to productivity increases in the manufacturing sector. These economic outcomes were largely a result of the earlier import substitution policies, which had enabled the establishment of a solid industrial base. The new policy environment and an emphasis on technology and modernisation created conducive conditions for the emergence of home-grown IT companies, like Wipro and Infosys, which made their initial investments in the early 1980s.

It is important to make the point that there is continuity between the old and new policy regimes, and that even radical reforms, like those adopted in 1991, were mediated through existing institutions and within a particular economic governance regime. We saw that there was continuity among bureaucratic actors elaborating economic policies in New Delhi in the 1980s and 1990s, and it can be assumed that networks between political elites and established economic actors were still in place, at both national and regional levels. Informal institutions, such as networks of influence, played a crucial role as well as the skills that allowed politicians to negotiate and build coalitions of support for reforms (Jenkins 1999).

Largely based on an analysis of the literature, the discussion of regional political regimes and recent social mobilisation patterns lays the foundation for the next chapter which will address the manner in which subnational States have responded to the new policy environment.

Notes

1 India's weighted average duty rate dropped from more than 75 per cent in 1990 to 29 per cent in 2002 (Mukherji 2007: 133).
2 Another consequence of the crisis with deleterious financial implications was the abrupt stoppage of remittances from expatriate labour in Kuwait and elsewhere in the Gulf (Nayar 2005).
3 Rahul Mukherji makes a similar argument asserting that India's pro-trade executive was able to successfully exploit a synergistic issue-linkage with the IMF and domestic interest groups at the time of the financial crisis (2007).
4 The original quote: 'l'universalisation des institutions et des idéologies politiques ou économiques (…) n'arase pas les trajectoires historiques des sociétés qui se les approprient' (Bayart 2004: 29–30).
5 See also Rodrik *et al.* (2002).
6 See Ahluwalia (2004). See also the following note on this key policy actor.
7 Montek Singh Ahluwalia, for instance, a key architect of India's economic reform programme, was posted at the World Bank (1968–79). Since 2004 he has held the top post (Deputy Chairman) in the Planning Commission. Manmohan Singh, currently the Prime Minister of India, was the Finance Minister in 1991. A trade economist trained at Cambridge and Oxford, he worked for several years at the UN in New York.
8 Indians in the US are almost twenty times more likely to be college educated than Indians in India (Kapur 2004: 367).
9 During his first visit to the US after becoming Prime Minister in 2004, Manmohan Singh specifically addressed business leaders and urged them to play a role in connecting the two economies (Therwath 2008).
10 J. Bhagwati, 'Diaspora impact on a changing India', *Business Standard*, 8 January 2010.
11 He is the author, *inter alia*, of *In Defense of Globalisation* (Bhagwati 2004).
12 See Jos Mooij's review of the literature in the introduction (Mooij 2005). See also Jenkins (1999) and Varshney (1999).
13 According to a CSDS survey carried out in 1996, only 19 per cent of the electorate had knowledge of economic reforms (Yadav and Singh 1996, cited by Varshney 1999: 224).
14 For a discussion of the broad concept of privatisation, see Hibou (2004).
15 The Anna Dravida Munnetra Kazhagam (ADMK) was formed when the DMK split in 1972. The official name was later changed to AIADMK, All India ADMK, but it is still usually referred to simply as ADMK.
16 For a more in-depth study of party system change in Tamil Nadu, see Wyatt (2009).
17 The political rhetoric of organised lower caste/class groups usually equates liberalisation with a pro-rich policy agenda, but because they are pragmatic when it comes to making political alliances, they may not necessarily hold a dominant party accountable for its actual policies. This is why public posturing can be as important as actual policies.
18 For instance, they are consistently overrepresented in the State legislative assembly. Although the estimated weight in the population is 8 per cent for Reddys and 5 per cent for Kammas, their representation in the Assembly following the 2004 election was respectively 32 per cent and 11 per cent. See Vaugier-Chatterjee (2009: 289).

4 Reforms and the rescaling of state spaces

Using empirical case material, this chapter analyses how different States are modifying their policy frameworks and their relation to space and territory in response to the changes brought about by economic reforms. By examining two distinct policy areas, *promotional policies* for attracting new investments and *fiscal restructuring*, the aim is to explain what has changed in the last two decades in India's multilevel governance structure.

Using the conceptual framework introduced in Chapter 1 and further developed in the preceding chapter, I analyse the variable responses of State governments to reforms as well as their differentiated capacity to exercise control over the scope and pace of structural reforms. The framework combines a political economy approach with attention to institutions, the political agency of state actors and spatial restructuring.

4.1 Subnational states in the rescaling literature

In the specialised literature on rescaling, there is relatively little attention to subnational territorial states per se. Rather the central focus is on rescaling of the nation-state and the emergence of urban local governments, municipalities and metropolitan regions, as strategic sites of economic governance.[1] This is particularly the case in studies on Europe where state restructuring in relation to the European Union, a supranational scale, tends to put the spotlight on the nation-state. A simple explanation for this research gap is that unitary states do not generally have subnational regional entities with any degree of political autonomy and so the issue does not arise. But a more substantive reason, which will be the focus here, is that subnational governments are often assumed to lack agency, especially with regard to globalisation processes, because of limited political mandates or financial weakness, or both.

Indeed, at the core of much contemporary literature on globalisation is the issue of agency of nation-states and subnational states, including metropolitan regions and municipalities. Subnational states are often represented as powerless, situated at the receiving end of strategies that they can not control. As Darel Paul points out, subnational states are commonly viewed simply as 'local filters for global processes' (2002: 467), 'an arena in which national policy and national agency are played out' (2002: 471); there is a tendency to interpret entrepreneurial strategies deployed at locales scales as 'a reflection of uncontrollable (at the local scale) competitive processes and beggar-thy-neighbor dynamics which, rather than express local agency, in fact eliminate it' (Paul 2002: 471, citing Eisenschitz and Gough 1993: 138). Even when it is conceded that 'subnational state economic development policies are "central to the con- temporary economy", this centrality is *assigned* to subnational states rather than seized by them and by other local actors' (Paul 2002: 471, emphasis added).

As pointed out in Chapter 1, international political economy theory often posits regionalisation and/or new localisms as concomitant processes of globalis- ation and does not give much importance *a priori* to subnational processes or to their contribution to political and economic restructuring. This view is countered to some extent however by another theoretical proposition according to which scalar arrangements are being rearticulated *both upward and downward* 'to establish rehierarchized social, economic, and political geographies' (Brenner *et al.* 2003: 16). To critically discuss these propositions, the analysis will focus primarily on subnational scales.

Paul argues that subnational states have emerged in last thirty years as major 'sites of regulation' of the global political economy:

> This regulation is realized in part through subnational state provision of the physical infrastructure necessary for globalized production and con- sumption, e.g. highways, water and air ports, fibre optic networks. It is also realized through the use of investment incentives such as locally situated means of production (especially land and the local built envir- onment), favourable access to local labour supplies, lucrative tax holidays, concessionary government loans.
>
> (Paul 2002: 468)

He asserts 'the new world order depends upon locally scaled practices organised through subnational states in ways quite distinct from the narrow functional role played by the local in the past' (ibid.: 470) and that 'authority exercised at subnational scales through subnational states has implications far beyond the local or even national scales' (2005: 7). On the basis of research on States and provinces in the US and Canada, Paul demonstrates that subnational states currently exercise considerably more autonomy with regard to economic development policies, for instance, through their powers over taxation, infrastructure development, land use, labour relations, and job training (Paul 2005). Moreover, 'As the leading voices for a locale to "go global", subnational state officials exercise considerable agency in attracting foreign investment, networking transnationally, promoting exports and (re)building the city in a global mode' (Paul 2002: 471).

This chapter will engage with these theoretical propositions by examining case material from several Indian States. I proceed on the basis of several hypotheses:

- Because they are more intensively engaged in global activities than in the past, *India's subnational states are also more likely to be solicited by state and non-state actors to participate in economic governance.* This could result in formal or informal devolution of authority from the national state (e.g., administrative reforms); incentives from national or supranational actors to improve the investment climate and balance the budget; conditional lending by international development agencies to subnational states. It could also take the form of appeals by transnational corporations directly to subnational states to negotiate terms of investment.
- *Regional political elites are taking pro-active measures to participate in economic governance, to seize perceived opportunities for shaping economic outcomes within the territorial borders they control.* However, the effective implementation of such a strategy is highly contingent on existing patterns of economic governance in a given context. In particular, the relationship between political and economic elites appears to be a critical factor.
- *Processes occurring in India at subnational scales shape, to an increasing extent, overall changes in economic governance.* This suggests a new interpretation of subnational dynamics, which are not only a 'side effect' but equally *constitutive* of new scalar constructions that affect overall governance and, it can be assumed, economic outcomes.

4.2 Competitive regions: promotional policies for industrial development

Prior to the economic reforms of the 1990s, as previously discussed, the central state pursued a planned approach to industrial development, in which the production of some goods and services were reserved exclusively for public sector enterprises, whereas others were produced both by public and private firms. Private firms were required to submit proposals for new industrial units or plans for expansion of existing units to central government agencies for approval, including the proposed geographical location of the investment. In this institutional arrangement, State governments could not directly influence national industrial policy, although they could use their skills and resources to try to bargain for a better deal. This could be done through formal administrative channels, 'invited space', or by exerting pressure on national policy-makers through informal channels, such as political parties, 'claimed space'.[2] Within the limits of their political jurisdictions and budgetary capabilities, they could pursue economic development policies, as the example of Kerala illustrated.

I propose to examine here what has changed after liberalisation, starting from the following propositions:

- The dismantling of licence-permit raj has changed the rules of the game and modified, in the process, the policy scope of State governments, especially with regard to industrial development policies. Regional industrial policies and related policy initiatives are currently rearticulating inherited scalar arrangements and in the process new geographies are emerging in the form of new state spaces and also, new economic spaces.

- Scales are not produced only by state actors, but also by private actors. A non-rigid political economy approach[3] can offer insights into which groups benefit, and to the ruling party's traditional support bases; the assumption being that the interests of these groups *inform* the policy direction without necessarily dictating it. This approach combines attention to local institutions and practices, the result of a singular historical development rooted in specific forms of collective action.

Although primarily concerned with industrial development, I will not limit my analysis to industrial policy *stricto sensu*. Rather, I will explore a broader field of public action in order to take into account policies that influence, more or less directly, industrial development. This is in part imposed by the nature of industry itself as a kind of meta-sector, which tends to structure the economy through its various linkages to employment, allied services, energy and environment (Huchet 2010: 26–8). Essentially, it is a methodological choice dictated by field observation; as Jean-François Huchet has argued with regard to China, a more extensive definition of industrial policy leaves scope for considering other policy changes with direct repercussions for industrial development (ibid.). It is a well-established premise in theories of economic geography that infrastructure is a key factor for attracting investment and hence a key determinant of growth. Infrastructure development has become a central policy thrust of State governments – a key component of promotional policies designed to make their territories more attractive to private investors.

In the first years following liberalisation, most States took measures of some kind to improve their 'investment climate', to employ a term commonly used in business reports and comparative studies by consulting agencies and other investment intermediaries. This usually involved some combination of the following measures: (1) simplification of investment procedures; (2) public investments in select infrastructure; (3) incentives packages in the form of direct or indirect financial assistance; and (4) policy innovations to meet specific goals or as an ad hoc response, for example, enhancing the mandates to industrial development corporations to allow them to build up land banks through the acquisition of private land or conversion of publicly held land. For the most part, these promotional policies, as I call them, were based on existing models of international 'best practices' or were 'inspired' by other States;[4] they were not necessarily designed for the specific characteristics of the regional economy. They are briefly examined in the following paragraphs.

Streamlining investment procedures

Simplifying investment procedures and rules was a relatively straightforward way of improving the business environment and one that was certain to draw approval from the private sector. It mainly involved streamlining procedures for new investment proposals, which required 'clearances' from a large number of government departments (power, water, labour, environment, building codes, urban planning, etc.). Investors could get discouraged along the way by delays, but also uncooperative officials, demands for bribes, etc. To simplify the application process, many States introduced a 'single-window clearance' (SWC) mechanism, the idea being to accompany investors through bureaucratic channels and accelerate the approval process. Although easy to announce, these SWC instruments have not always functioned as smoothly as promised.[5] As we will see in other examples below, there can be various obstacles to implementation, which correspond to a lack of administrative capacity, a social or ideological divide between the political leadership and the bureaucracy, and built-in incentives to maintain the existing system. One way to make the SWC more effective was to put time limits on how long a file could be left pending in a given department, a measure put in place in Haryana in the 2000s. Other strategies, deployed in Tamil Nadu, consisted in delegating responsibilities to lower levels of administration and inviting private investors to start construction *even before receiving clearances*:

> The [S]tate government has given the single window clearance system additional powers by empowering the chief executives of the various industrial complexes, growth centers and industrial estates in the public and private sectors to grant all clearances which an industry would require without the need to go around seeking clearances from various government departments. Additionally, via a new law, *The Industrial Township Area Development Authority Act of 1997*, the government has granted powers of single window clearance to an authority in case of every industrial township and industrial park. Furthermore, in order to speed up the process of setting-up private industry, the government has permitted the private industry to go ahead with construction of its factory without waiting for the plan approval from the local body [subject to certifications by a registered architect and commitment to carry corrective actions if rules were violated].
>
> (Bajpai and Sachs 1999: 7–8)

Infrastructure for growth

Infrastructure networks such as roads, electricity, water supply and drainage, fall within the mandates of State governments, as well as social infrastructure, e.g., education and health care. Investment needs in these areas are colossal and although infrastructure development is high on the list of priorities of State governments, their financial capacity is limited. In the two decades since market reforms were introduced, new norms and practices have emerged with regard to financing infrastructure. The central government's early decision to liberalise private investment in infrastructure provision (roads, transport systems, ports) had immediate repercussions on the scope of action of regional political leaders as it created opportunities for them to enter into partnerships with private sector actors (e.g., delegation, joint ventures, etc.), including foreign investors, and to imagine new regulatory arrangements to accompany these partnerships. This expanded the policy repertoire of regional governments and arguably gave them wider scope for influencing economic outcomes, as well as access to resources for patronage politics and funding campaigns (Jenkins 1999).

Incentives packages

Regarding incentives for industrial investments, these usually included project finance (e.g., access to subsidised capital, interest subsidies), guaranteed supply of key inputs such as power and water and/or concessional rates for these inputs, as well as fiscal incentives or tax holidays, usually in the form of sales tax exemption or deferment (either for a fixed number of years or for a specified amount, expressed in terms of the fixed capital investment amount). For so-called 'thrust' industries, those that State governments were particularly keen to promote, such as IT, it was not unusual to offer additional incentives (longer tax breaks, more capital subsidy, etc). In one of the first studies of the kind, released in 1999, Bajpai and Sachs compared fifteen of India's largest States on the basis of criteria such as investment incentives, power sector reforms, industrial and infrastructural reforms and tax reform (Bajpai and Sachs 1999). It is interesting to note that at the time of the study twelve out of fifteen States had some kind of project finance such as capital subsidies or interest subsidies on loans, and the same number offered fiscal incentives packages to investors (out of which eleven proposed sales tax concessions), ten States had simplified their rules and twelve had put in place arrangements to speed up decision making. This suggests a convergence in practices, although implementation on the ground certainly varied across these States. In the case of Tamil Nadu, the size of investments could also serve as a criterion for determining the degree of subsidies and benefits, as the following example illustrates.

'Super mega projects' in Tamil Nadu

In 1995, the ADMK government under the chief ministership of Jayalalitha defined a new category of investments, 'super mega projects', which had an initial investment of at least Rs 1,500 crores in the first 5–7 years (222 million euros in 2012 figures).[6] In exchange, firms would receive a sales tax deferral/waiver for 14 years, or 21 years if the quantum of sales tax deferral/waiver did not reach 100 per cent of the investment in fixed assets by the fourteenth year.[7] Additional perquisites included sales tax exemption on capital equipment and inputs procured within the State of Tamil Nadu, full exemption from tax on land transactions (stamp duty) and exemption of tax on electricity, in addition to a guarantee of uninterrupted power. Moreover, such 'super mega projects' were eligible for generous capital subsidies, among the highest in the country at the time: an investment above Rs 200 crores drew a subsidy of Rs 1 crore.[8]

In fact, the 'super mega project' category was initially conceived to benefit a specific investor, Mahindra-Ford,[9] who had agreed to locate a large automobile plant near Chennai after a countrywide search. This is apparent from the fact that the new incentives for 'super mega projects' were issued by government Order just one day before the Memorandum of Understanding was signed with the car manufacturer (Subramanian 1996).[10] Tamil Nadu had lobbied hard to win the contract, competing with Maharashtra and Haryana among other States, already specialised in the car sector and strategically located near the largest end markets. Today Chennai, the capital of Tamil Nadu, is considered one of the main automobile clusters in the country (Huchet and Ruet 2006: 183).

This example underscores a very important fact: State governments have at their disposal a range of instruments, which allow them to respond to opportunities as and when they arise, and more importantly *to make opportunities happen*. Setting up investment promotion agencies with a wide-reaching mandate and sending delegations to foreign countries to drum up business are some of the ways that State governments have tried to influence economic outcomes. In some States, such as Gujarat, these practices pre-date liberalisation,[11] but most States started proactive economic development initiatives only in the 1990s or later. Tamil Nadu, probably one of the first, set up its Guidance Bureau in 1992 as the single window for investment proposals. This can be contrasted with Madhya Pradesh, a large State in central India, which set up its investment facilitation corporation, TRIFAC, in 2004. Such variations continue to characterise India's economic governance, and suggest that caution is needed in generalising findings from one State to another.

Policy innovations

Evidence compiled from empirical studies suggests that regional political elites do enjoy a fairly large degree of discretionary decision-making powers, which allow them to invent customised responses to investment proposals, without prior permission from New Delhi. It has been observed that State governments do not usually make public their negotiations with private investors, employing the same stealthy practices described in the last chapter.[12] Rather than seeking legislative sanction for the special deals they broker, they tend to issue decrees or government orders. A crucial area where State-level political elites have shown great willingness to intervene is with regard to providing land for industrial projects as well as other infrastructure. This may well have been the deciding factor in Mahindra-Ford's decision to choose Tamil Nadu over other States in 1995. According to unofficial reports, the government agreed to develop the production site for Mahindra-Ford at a nominal cost, as part of the deal. The land, which belonged to the Chennai Metropolitan Development Authority, a public planning agency, was transformed into a customised industrial park called Maraimalai Nagar. As I analysed earlier:

> This points to a strategy that does not appear in official documents, i.e. that industrial estates may be developed *ad hoc* to accommodate a particular firm. This was apparently the case for two other large investment projects: Hyundai Motors at Irungattukottai [1996] and Saint Gobain Glass at Sriperumbudur [1998]. The two latter sites are designated as industrial estates of the State Industries Promotion Corporation of Tamil Nadu (SIPCOT), with space to accommodate additional firms.
>
> (Kennedy 2007b: 326)

Indeed, the development of industrial estates, equipped with good-quality infrastructure (roads, power, telecommunications, water) and located in strategic sites near major roads, railways, seaports or airports, is considered an effective way of attracting investment.[13] It provides minimal assurances to private investors about the quality and quantity of infrastructure available. This policy instrument was used by State governments well before liberalisation, but my research shows that it is now being deployed quite differently; regional policy-makers have adapted it to new conditions and to their changing perceptions of state territorial space. Again, Tamil Nadu will be used to illustrate.

4.3 Changing perceptions of subnational territory

In 1975, Tamil Nadu had thirty-six industrial estates, the second largest number in the country at the time after Gujarat (sixty-eight estates) (Sinha 2005: 145). The Tamil Nadu government used this industrial estate policy to achieve two main goals: (1) offer support to investors in small-scale industries; and (2) attract investment to relatively underdeveloped areas of the State, with the purpose of promoting more balanced regional development.[14] These industrial parks or estates were usually developed by specialised public agencies, such as the Small Industries Promotion Corporation (SIPCO). In 1972 another fully government-owned agency, SIPCOT (State Industries Promotion Corporation of Tamil Nadu), was created and given a mandate to develop industrial parks. Until the mid-1990s, *all* of SIPCOT's estates were located in designated backward districts or subdistricts (*talukas*), usually at a consider- able distance from major urban agglomerations.[15] However, starting in 1995, SIPCOT began to build new industrial estates in close proximity to Chennai,

Table 4.1 SIPCOT industrial estates in Tamil Nadu, 1973–98

Name/place	Starting year	Characteristics of location	Surface area (in acres)[a]
Ranipet – phase 1	1973	Backward district	730
Hosur – phase 1	1974	Backward district (40km from Bengaluru)	1,236
Manamadurai	1980	Backward district	492
Pudukkottai	1983	Backward district	421
Cuddalore – phase 1	1984	Backward district	519
Tuticorin	1984	Backward district	1,155
Gummidipoondi – ph. 1	1984	Backward district (45km from Chennai)	801
Ranipet – phase 2	1989	Backward district	133
Hosur – phase 2	1989	Backward district (40km from Bengaluru)	457
Gummidipoondi – ph. 2	1991	Backward district (45km from Chennai)	645
Cuddalore – phase 2	1992	Backward district	220
Gummidipoondi – EPIP (Export promotion industrial park)	1995	Backward district (45km from Chennai)	224
Irungattukottai	1996	35km from Chennai	1,447
Sriperumbudur	1998	44km from Chennai	1,833

Source: Data collected by author at the SIPCOT office, Chennai, and updated with information from the website: www.sipcot.com
Note a: 1 acre = 0.405 hectare.

the State's largest city and arguably its most attractive investment destination. Moreover, the estates developed in the second half of the 1990s, such as Irungattukottai and Sriperumbudur, were much larger than most earlier ones as Table 4.1 shows.

This trend continued throughout the 2000s; very large estates were constructed within the metropolitan region of Chennai, e.g., Siruseri IT Park (1,000 acres, 30km from Chennai) and Oragadam Industrial Park (around 3,000 acres, 50km from the capital). Like for the Ford example above, the opening of these parks often coincided with the launching of a large-scale investment project e.g., Saint Gobain at SIPCOT Industrial Park in Sriperumbudur, Hyundai Motors and ancillaries at SIPCOT Industrial Park in Irungattukottai. As a result, these parks took on sectoral specialisations, turning them into potential clusters.

This example of SIPCOT locations provides a forceful illustration of how the scalar logics underlying industrial estate development shifted from promotion of regional dispersal, with reference to the State's *internal economic geographies*, to promotion of 'competitive spaces' conceived on a global scale. In both cases, the political jurisdiction is the State's territorial boundaries, but the scalar frame of reference of political action changes. This has important theoretical implications; it effectively redefines state space and introduces a disconnect with the territorial dimension of state space. It also has important practical repercussions; State governments in India wield wide-ranging power over land and many of them are evidently in the process of rethinking their mandate with regard to land-based public goods, most notably commons and other types of government-owned land. Land rights and property development for industry have become crucial issues in India; indeed core debates about development, for instance about how to promote economic growth *with* social justice, have crystallised in recent years around the issue of land and the mediating power of the state over land transactions. This issue will be addressed in more detail in Chapter 5.

As the previous discussion makes clear, liberalisation had the indirect effect of expanding the policy prerogatives of State governments giving them a greater stake in economic governance. Adapting to the opportunities and constraints generated by institutional change at the national scale, regional political elites gradually started putting in place strategies for making their investment climate more attractive. Yet, as similar policies were implemented across the country offering identical incentives packages, it became increasingly evident that States were in competition with each other, at least for some types of industrial activities. Not surprisingly this encouraged a 'beggar-thy-neighbour' approach whereby States offered more and more concessions, such as tax holidays, which fed a negative downward spiral. In 1999, under pressure from the central government, the chief ministers came together and agreed to put an end to harmful tax wars between their States. Floor rates for sales tax were put in place, and the practice of offering sales tax exemption/deferral as an incentive for industrial investment was abolished for future projects (Purohit 2008: 204). Among the major arguments put forward in favour of these reforms was the loss of revenue for States, estimated to be about 25 per cent of their sales tax base (ibid.).

This example indicates that the central government is reacting to current practices, here growing inter-State competition, and taking on a regulatory role in the sense of ensuring compliance with overarching rules. In general, the central state continues to maintain a firm hold on financial aspects of macro-economic policy-making, and to occupy a dominant position *vis-à-vis* the States with regard to finances. A brief examination of public finance reforms in the next section will serve to balance the impression that subnational states have gained policy scope across the board; it will illustrate that although there has been a scaling down of some arenas of policy-making, e.g., industrial development, there has been a scaling up with regard to public finance management.

4.4 Reform of States' public finances and central directives

Public finance reform, including restructuring State-level finances, is a policy area in which the central government has taken the lead, but which requires the cooperation of the States to succeed. As mentioned in Chapter 2, federal financial relations are a very sensitive area and a source of federal tension, due to several interrelated factors. These can be summarised as follows:

- State governments are dependent on the Union for financing their budgets. The main reason for this is tax powers are centralised and spending responsibilities are decentralised: States have primary responsibility for social spending and social infrastructure development including education, health; this disconnect created a perpetual 'vertical fiscal gap' (Chelliah 2005: 3400).
- The absence of a direct link between spending and revenue generating capacity at the State-level meant there was no built-in incentive for States to practice fiscal rigour and this contributed to the generation of unsustainable deficits.
- The Constitution made provisions for the vertical fiscal gap to be filled by sharing tax revenues, most of which are collected by the Centre for reasons of efficiency. As for *horizontal gaps*, reflecting the differing capacities of States to raise fiscal revenues and provide public services, they were to be addressed through grants-in-aid to States. However, in practice, the Finance Commissions did not keep these two types of gaps clearly separate (Chelliah 2005).
- Plan assistance allocated to the States from the Planning Commission, of which 30 per cent were grants and 70 per cent were loans, did *not* take into consideration the capacity of the State to repay, nor its existing level of debt.

These features of India's fiscal federalism, which were not at all new, started being perceived as a serious problem in the 1990s for two different reasons. First, the central state was committed to pursuing fiscal restructuring and was confronted with the fact that its finances were inextricably linked with those of the States. Second, fiscal performance at both central and State levels had objectively gotten worse and there was growing pressure on both the central government and State governments to undertake fiscal reforms. In fact, the situation had started deteriorating from the 1980s; the combined fiscal deficit was over 9 per cent of GDP by 1990–1. The situation worsened considerably in the late 1990s following the decision to raise the salaries of all public sector employees (the Fifth central pay commission awards) (World Bank 2005). Not surprisingly, poorer States found it more difficult to manage than States with more buoyant tax revenues. Fiscal deficits as a ratio of GDP are considered high in seven of the sixteen major States (Odisha, West Bengal, Punjab, Rajasthan, Gujarat, Kerala and Uttar Pradesh). Except for Gujarat, all of these States have high interest payments on their debt, in proportion to their revenue.

Cascading effects and structural reforms

Economic reforms had, from the outset, numerous direct and indirect consequences on State-level finances. One direct consequence of fiscal consolidation measures, implemented as part of the initial stabilisation package, was a decline of central transfers to States as a percentage of GDP (from 4.9 per cent in 1990 to 3.8 per cent in 1999). A second example, of an indirect effect, is equally critical: financial sector deregulation made financing States' debt more expensive by allowing higher interest rates; interest payments as a percentage of total revenue expenditure increased from 8 per cent in 1980 to 22 per cent in 2003 (Chakraborty *et al.* 2009: 40).[16] This had the effect of reducing States' primary expenditure (net of interest payments). Still, high growth in the post reform period has also had a favourable impact overall on regional finances. For instance, from 1993 to 2003, revenue receipts increased on the average by 66.5 per cent in absolute value terms; per capita receipts also increased in all States, but these were higher in 'richer' States, i.e., those whose revenue is above the national average (Robin 2009: 6) (see Table 4.2 in Appendix showing State per capita income). In this same period, almost all States increased their per capita expenditures on capital investments, which can be seen as contributing to medium and long-term development outcomes (Robin 2009: 10).

Restructuring public finance is often included in the nebulous category of 'second-generation reforms'.[17] Although there is some debate about its definition, there is generally a consensus about the fact that they require greater implication on the part of State governments in part because they involve areas under the constitutional purview of States. They usually include, for instance, restructuring public utilities (for electricity: this means unbundling production, distribution and regulation function, and removing political interference), modifying labour laws (notably hiring and firing clauses) and restructuring public finance.

Starting in the late 1990s, the central state began to put in place new types of arrangements for federal financial relations. It began to negotiate financial assistance with States, for instance, through MOUs, and to introduce incentives to improve the fiscal performance of States. The Fiscal Reforms Facility, started in 2000–1, linked a portion of central grants to the fiscal performance of States, and external funding agencies also tied a portion of fund transfers to the achievement of fiscal adjustment targets (World Bank 2005).

A few years later, Parliament adopted a law on Fiscal Responsibility and Budget Management (FRBM), with effect from 2004, which compelled the central government to reduce its fiscal deficit gradually so that by 2009 it would not exceed 3 per cent of GDP. In principle, this concerned only the central government, but in reality, State governments had little choice but to follow suit, especially as the 12th Finance Commission (formed in 2002) made fiscal responsibility legislation a precondition for availing debt relief (Chakraborty *et al.* 2009). Between 2002 and 2007, all but two of India's twenty-eight States (West Bengal and Sikkim) had enacted some form of fiscal responsibility legislation.

These qualitative changes in federal relations marked a significant break in existing practices, which although top-down, nonetheless strove to distribute resources in a neutral manner. For instance, central planners did not question the contents of States' budgets, the estimated revenue receipts and expenditure, so as not to impinge on their autonomy.[18] This practice, reflecting a *norm* in federal relations that had been in place for several decades, started changing; the Finance Commissions operating in the 2000s intervened to modify the projections of revenues receipts and expenditures submitted by the States to them. For example, the 12th Finance Commission drastically reduced (by four times!) the aggregate gap between receipts and expenditure by increasing the revenue projections and cutting expenditure by 23 per cent (which worked out to 2 per cent of GDP) (Chelliah 2005: 3401, citing Twelfth Finance Commission Report 2004:119). Although the Centre has always been in a dominant position *vis-à-vis* the States in financial matters, these practices suggest a process of scaling up of fiscal management and control.

This example indicates the determination of the central state to put State-level financial reform on the agenda and thereby reorder scalar arrangements of state space in the field of federal financial relations. It illustrates the continued relevance in certain policy areas of the national frame of reference whereby state space is concomitant with national territorial scale. Moreover, it raises crucial questions about the capacity of India's States, within the existing institutional framework, to manage their finances and to define the scope and pace of structural reform at the State level. This question is all the more relevant given that under the reordered scalar arrangements, State governments can no longer depend on New Delhi in the same way as before for capital investments and budgetary support. The larger issue then is the relative financial autonomy of States and the discretionary resources at their disposal for prioritising policies and funding actions. We saw earlier indications of increased policy scope for States; the question here is whether fiscal restructuring has reduced their 'fiscal space'. Fiscal space has been defined as 'room in a government's budget that allows it to provide resources for a desired purpose without jeopardizing the sustainability of its financial position or the stability of the economy' (Heller 2005). To avoid conceptual confusion with other meanings of space used here, we will use the term 'fiscal scope' rather than 'fiscal space'.

4.5 Fiscal scope and subnational state capacity

Various tools can be used to measure the discretionary resources that State governments have at their disposal. Not surprisingly, the size and growth rate of the regional economy, measured by gross state domestic product or GSDP, and revenue receipts are key factors determining subnational state capacity, although these have to be considered in relation to other measures such as fiscal deficit, public debt and interest payments.

In seeking to compare fiscal scope across Indian States, scholars have devised specific measures to take account of Indian realities. These reflect for instance that States can increase their access to resources depending on their relationship with the central government. As discussed in Chapter 2, there is a degree of discretion in the size of the deficit that the central government allows a State government to run, which means that States with more leverage can obtain more resources (Nooruddin and Chhibber 2008). This can have an important impact on spending, for instance in an election year, thereby contributing to the political survival of the ruling party. In measuring fiscal scope then, central loans can be used as a proxy for the deficits allowed by the Centre. Another important aspect to take into account in measuring fiscal scope is the relative size of 'committed expenditures', e.g., on civil administration, mainly salaries and benefits and debt servicing. For all practical purposes a State government is not in a position to suppress these, and hence they are perceived by officials as a given.[19] Expressed as a share of total revenues, it indicates both the size of the State's economy and its fiscal performance; when population is also taken into account, States can be compared on a per capita basis.

Depending on the methods used to measure fiscal scope, the results can vary widely. One study of India's sixteen largest States found that between 1993 to 2003, fiscal scope decreased for *all* States by 17 per cent on average (Robin 2009).[20] However, measured in per capita terms, the findings were less clear-cut. One method indicated that fiscal scope increased for some States and decreased for others and that committed expenditures increased on average more rapidly than total revenue receipts. In West Bengal, an 'extreme' case, committed expenditure increased by 3.17, whereas revenue receipts only grew by 1.6, indicating that the economy did not expand commensurate with expenditures (Robin 2009: 16). In terms of fiscal scope, it ranked lowest among States. Let us recall from the discussion in Chapter 2 that West Bengal is a State that has had a confrontational relationship with the central government. Led by a communist party from 1977 until 2011, it has followed largely autonomous policies, at least rhetorically.[21] West Bengal has a large public sector and large committed expenditure in the form of salaries. For many years, it refused to sign the FRBM Act,[22] on the grounds that it would reduce welfare measures and curb the ability of the State to pursue its education and health policies.[23]

Notwithstanding, the above-mentioned study found that West Bengal ranks well with regard to tax efforts, tapping its taxable resources, but these are simply not sufficient to increase its revenues. This suggests that it cannot count on its tax powers and must find ways to build 'earning assets'.[24] In this context, it should be noted that West Bengal has suffered a long period of de-industrialisation. Recent efforts by the government to attract private investment have not been very successful one reason being that several projects have come up against strong popular opposition (e.g., Singur and Nandigram). As commentators have pointed out, the electoral defeat of the communist-led coalition in 2011 was in part the consequence of the government's handling of those popular protests.

This example underscores one of the contradictions currently underway whereby States enjoy more policy scope, but may not have the fiscal strength to take advantage of it; their constitutional tax powers are too restricted and their tax bases often too narrow to allow them to balance their budgets (Purohit 2008). As a result, a majority of States remain largely dependent on central transfers. Yet, here again, there are important differences among States. A State with strong industrial growth has a greater capacity to raise revenues through taxing these industries (property tax, professional tax) than a State with an agricultural base.[25] Yet one very interesting finding was that the States with the most restricted fiscal scope are not necessarily the poorest States, even though it was confirmed that 'poor' States such as UP, Bihar and Odisha do not have much fiscal space. Likewise, the richest States, those with the largest revenue receipts, such as Punjab and Himachal Pradesh, did not necessarily have the soundest financial bases (Robin 2009: 22).

4.6 Analytical narratives of State-level reforms

Unlike promotional policies, which States have implemented voluntarily, structural reforms are more difficult to put in place, politically speaking; the losers are more easily identified and the gains, if gains there are, will only be reaped in the uncertain future. Although the Centre may exert pressure on States to implement reforms, as was seen with the FRBM, States can and do resist that pressure. So what motivates certain States to undertake structural reforms?

This section will explore this question through analytical narratives of the context and sequencing of policies in Odisha and Andhra Pradesh.[26] By situating their respective policies in relation to their institutions and political economies, the aim is to identify and discuss factors that contribute to explaining variations in policy and fiscal scope across States with regard to structural reforms.

Fiscal consolidation under duress in Odisha

Odisha has several distinguishing features;[27] it is a 'poor' State in terms of per capita income (below national average, see Table 4.2 in the Appendix) as well as in the high incidence of poverty in the overall population (47 per cent compared to 26 per cent for India as a whole). Three-quarters of the population relies on agriculture for its livelihood. Odisha's society is characterised by an unusually high proportion of social groups that have suffered historically from discrimination: Scheduled Tribes and Scheduled Castes contribute respectively 22 per cent and 16 per cent to the total population. These groups are over-represented among the State's poor population as they make up 64 per cent of the total.

At the same time, Odisha has occasionally been at the forefront among States in implementing structural reforms e.g., in the power sector and also in fiscal consolidation, making it a poster child for the World Bank and other international lenders, notably the UK's Department for International Development. How can this situation be interpreted?

By the late 1990s, Odisha's public finances were in a critical condition. Whereas its public debt as percentage of GSDP was around 30 per cent in 1980, by 2002 it was 65 per cent (Chelliah, 2005: 3402, cited by Robin 2009). Its interest payments in 2002 were 30 per cent of its income, up from 14 per cent in 1991; it was in a debt trap and its long-term growth prospects looked quite compromised. The government was at the point where it was having difficulty paying its employees. In 1999 it signed a protocol with the central government to reduce its expenses and raise resources. In 2005 it followed New Delhi's lead in adopting its own fiscal responsibility law and restructured its debt, which reduced its interest payments as a percentage of current expenditure (Robin 2010). In addition, it took steps to increase revenue by introducing VAT in its territory and increasing royalties on the mining and metalworking industries. It also took drastic measures to reduce expenditure by freezing salaries and recruitment in the civil service[28] and privatised a number of the State's public sector units and cooperative societies.

At about the same time, in the early 2000s, the State government radically redefined its industrial policy shifting the focus from reliance on public investment to enabling private investors; the main strategy consisted in attracting investment from national and international investors in the mining industries to exploit the State's remarkable mineral wealth. Odisha concentrates a large proportion of the country's mineral deposits: 95 per cent of chromite ore, 92 per cent of nickel, more than half of the bauxite deposits, 33 per cent of iron ore, and 24 per cent of coal (Government of Orissa 2009). It put in place promotional policies along the lines indicated above: simplification of investment procedures, fiscal incentives and an effort to improve infrastructures. In 2007, a new industrial promotion agency, 'Team Orissa' was created to guide and assist investors and act as a single-window for clearances. Like in other States, the government has shown responsiveness to demands made by industrial investors, for example, for making land available. It has also shown its political will to repress popular protests of industrial projects.[29] Several high-profile mining projects, including a huge steel project by the South Korean firm POSCO, are strongly opposed by local groups on both social and environmental grounds.

Odisha's economic performance did improve along with the rest of the country, especially in the 2000s. GSDP grew at 8.5 per cent on average during the Tenth Plan period (2002–7), compared to 5.5 percent during the previous plan (1997–2002). However, its per capita income remains well below the national average (INR 16,149 versus INR 24,295 in 2007–8, see Table 4.2 in the Appendix). Between 2002 and 2007 growth was driven mainly by the mining sector, which grew by almost 20 per cent. Private investments, especially in extractive industries increased rapidly in the 2000s. The State no doubt benefited from the abolition of the freight equalisation policy, mentioned in Chapter 2, which had prevented it from exploiting its comparative advantage in mineral deposits.

Although fiscal restructuring measures allowed Odisha to recover from its severe crisis, it has also set the State on a path that appears relatively irreversible. Ideologically speaking, its policies are now closely calibrated on 'international best practices', as defined by the World Bank. This is no accident as the World Bank was very closely involved with Odisha's structural reforms from the very beginning (Robin 2010).

How can Odisha's decision to implement structural reforms be explained in political economy terms? Generally speaking there is a low level of political mobilisation among the State's middle and lower caste and class groups.[30] Politics in Odisha are dominated by a numerically small elite, mainly from upper caste groups. This is the case for elected officials but also the State bureaucracy, mainly composed of Brahmins and Karnas (Kumar 2004: 115).

In theory, the Khandayats, an intermediary caste that makes up the largest OBC group, could wield important political clout because of its demographic strength, but the group is not homogeneous nor well integrated (ibid.). In fact, the distribution of landed resources is relatively even between Khandayats and high caste groups, and there have not been social conflicts around this issue as in some other regions, which can act as a catalyst for OBC mobilisation (Robin 2010). In contrast to OBCs in the neighbouring State of Bihar, Yadavs in particular, the Khandayats have not mounted a political challenge to traditionally dominant groups, rather '[t]hey have aligned with one or the other upper caste in order to obtain a share of political power' (Kumar 2004: 129). Politics in Odisha are characterised by intra-elite competition, leading some observers to conclude that 'It is unlikely, here, that changes of party-regime are of any great significance for policy or its implementation' (Harriss 1999: 3372).

Moreover, there is an unusually strong personal element in regional politics. Naveen Patnaik, who has been the Chief Minister since 2000, followed in his father's footsteps taking over leadership of the Janata Party after his death in 1997. In 2009 the regional party led by Naveen Patnaik, the Biju Janata Dal, won a third consecutive term in office, a rare occurrence in State legislative assemblies.

Regarding the tribal groups, which constitute 22 per cent of the total population, their extreme diversity has probably hindered any attempt to mobilise as a united group. Although there is a high level of participation in elections, more in-depth studies underscore the distance that separates marginalised social groups from the political elites (de Haan and Dubey 2005, Robin 2010). Widespread passivity on the part of lower castes and tribal groups has allowed the government to pursue its 'investor friendly' policy on the grounds that it will bring development to the State. The social costs of this policy however are high and unevenly distributed. Large-scale mining projects almost always involve displacing people and the destruction of cultural and natural environments.[31] Odisha's current development policies do not directly address the strong geographical disparities in the State (the poverty rate is three times higher in the southern region than in the coastal region), nor the State's stark social inequalities (Robin 2010).

Andhra Pradesh – an example of chosen reforms?

The context in which Andhra Pradesh decided to adopt reforms, under Chandrababu Naidu's watch as Chief Minister (1995–2004), was very different.

Admittedly, the State's financial situation was not on very solid foundations when Naidu took over as Chief Minister in 1995; his predecessor, N. T. Rama Rao, was known for his popular policies, e.g., subsidies for rice, free electricity for farmers (for irrigation pumps), which had created serious budget deficits. However, despite there being objective pressure to put in place a fiscal consolidation policy, this was not the rationale put forth. Naidu took a different tack and claimed that a radical reform programme to liberalise the regional economy was an opportunity for the State.[32] By situating the reform programme within a regionalist discourse, Naidu could claim that it would give the State more autonomy *vis-à-vis* New Delhi and allow the State to forge its own development path. In this context, it is useful to recall that the TDP was formed in the early 1980s in opposition to the national Congress party with the objective of protecting regional interests and restoring regional pride (see Chapter 3). Also mentioned in the preceding chapter, the TDP is responsive to the interests of dominant caste groups, which are a key component of its social base.[33] To garner support from other groups, whose numerical strength it needs to win elections, it accommodates lower castes within the party, as is evident from the caste affiliations of its elected members,[34] and also targets schemes to benefit specific groups, e.g., women.

In analysing policy documents, such as 'Andhra Pradesh: Vision 2020' (Government of Andhra Pradesh 1999) and political discourse from this period,[35] the implicit message is that only the State government has the legitimacy to decide the State's fate. By pursuing well-defined, high-profile policies, it was fulfilling its mission to look after the State's interests and promote its welfare. Naidu spoke publicly about the necessity of decentralising India's federal system and asserted that unless powers were devolved as close as possible to the theatre of action, speed and efficiency (of reforms) would not be achieved.[36] He referred to the new paradigm emerging as a result of global networks and the 'information age', in which federal governments will have a diminished role, and predicted that just as geography is condemned to becoming history, so is centralisation. Calls for devolution of financial resources and policy autonomy are not new, especially coming from regional parties, but what is of interest here is their explicit link to liberalisation and globalisation processes.

The message projected by Naidu's government is that Andhra Pradesh is an autonomous unit, acting of its own volition and within the scope of its rights and responsibilities. In the 350-page *Vision 2020* document, there is hardly any mention of the central government except to say that the State will need to exert influence on the Centre to incite it to implement a number of reforms.[37] In practice, the Andhra Pradesh government did appear to act independently *vis-à-vis* New Delhi in many respects and engaged directly with actors operating at supranational or transnational scales including private investors (e.g., Microsoft, which decided to locate in Hyderabad its first R&D centre outside the US), international aid agencies (e.g., World Bank, DFID) and political leaders (e.g., at the World Economic Forum). A striking example is the large loan that the State government negotiated with the World Bank in 1998, the first of its kind to a subnational entity.

Apparently non-threatening to the BJP-led ruling coalition in New Delhi, political allies of the TDP, this stance was primarily targeted at a regional audience and aimed to enhance the State government's political legitimacy 'at home'. The government justified its support of economic reforms on the contention that they 'liberated' the Andhra people from Delhi's yoke and allowed them to follow their own development path.

The policy documents contain references to other nation-states, citing development experiences from East Asia or Latin America, for example. The obvious suggestion is that Andhra Pradesh is an actor in the international arena, competing on a level footing with other countries. In fact, the title of *Vision 2020* was directly inspired by Malaysia's *Vision 2002* document.[38] To finance that ambitious plan, the State government declared it was prepared to act on its own, by generating revenue through tighter fiscal and budgetary management, attracting private investment, and garnering loans and foreign aid. It did indeed take out a large loan from the World Bank, but what is important here, and marks a contrast with Odisha, the political leadership did not wait for those loans to start the reform programme. This suggests more 'ownership', a more deliberately chosen strategy. This does not imply, however, that Andhra Pradesh's reform programme was somehow more democratic than in Odisha. On the contrary, Chandrababu Naidu's approach was top-down, even authoritarian, and policies were severely criticised within the State for neglecting agriculture and for being generally ill-adapted to the reality of the regional economy (Reddy 1999).

Analyses of Andhra Pradesh's reforms under Chandrababu Naidu indicated that they were less radical than they claimed to be – more 'hype' than reality (Mooij 2007) – and that alongside politically difficult structural reforms such as cutting subsidies and privatising cooperatives and public sector enterprises, the government was careful to cultivate key constituencies through targeted social programmes (Kennedy 2004a). What makes this example interesting is what it says about the degree of discretionary power that State governments can wield. In comparison to Odisha, the Andhra Pradesh government appears to have had more control over the reform process, its initial launching and its sequencing on the ground. This more ample policy scope can perhaps be partly explained by a less constraining financial situation, but social and political factors most certainly weighed in the balance.

Unlike Odisha and many other States, Andhra Pradesh can boast of having an endogenous capitalist class, large-scale industrialists who are natives to the State (Baru 2000). Of particular importance here, political elites and economic elites are largely from the same caste backgrounds, which coincide to some extent with a common subregional background as well, i.e., coastal Andhra. These elites belong to dominant, landowning castes for the most part (e.g., Kamma, Reddy, Kapu, Velama, Raju), many of whom were settled in the fertile deltas of the Godavari and Krishna rivers. Irrigation projects and the green revolution were instrumental in helping these groups achieve upward social mobility throughout the twentieth century.[39] As a result, these groups migrated to the cities to avail higher education and started investing in non-agricultural activities; a few industrious individuals built empires, especially from the 1970s and 1980s, in media (Eenadu group), fertiliser and chemicals (Nagarjuna group), pharmaceuticals (Dr Reddy's Labs), and computer software services (Satyam) to name just a few. The social and cultural proximity between political and economic actors is no doubt a crucial consideration in understanding how consensus is reached in Andhra Pradesh's political economy; it helps explain how Naidu was able to build a coalition of support for the structural reform agenda and defend it in regional, national and international fora.[40] Interviews conducted with officials in business and industrial organisations in the early 2000s indicated broad satisfaction with the government's policies; they felt the government was responsive to their demands.[41] Relations between business groups and government were to some extent institutionalised through regular consultations, demonstrated by the fact the industries department of the State government invited regional trade organisations to consultative meetings to get inputs on proposed policy measures. All of these factors combined help explain the State's approach to reforms.

National-scale political factors are also important. When *Vision 2020* was launched in 1998, Naidu was already fairly well known on the national political scene; he had emerged as a key negotiator after the general elections in 1996, helping to bring together the thirteen-party coalition that became the United Front government. But it was when that government fell and new elections in 1998 brought a hung Parliament that Naidu very skilfully (and unscrupulously) seized an opportunity to enhance his State's policy *and* fiscal scope. He extended his party's support to the BJP so that it could form a coalition government. Although the TDP's twenty-nine MPs made it the largest partner of the coalition, and hence in a position to claim plum ministerial portfolios, Naidu decided not to participate in the government but rather to extend support *from outside*. In that way, he could keep his independence, negotiating his support on a case-by-case basis and, at the same time, benefit from privileged access to the inner circles of power. This underscores the importance of multiscalar processes in the art and practice of government at the State level: a State government's manoeuvring room, whether expressed as fiscal scope or policy scope, depends in part on its place within the larger political game.

On its own turf in Andhra Pradesh, TDP's policies can be analysed as a strategy to re-territorialise state space at the regional scale, on one hand, and benefit dominant economic interests implanted in the State, on the other.[42] Beyond the sensationalist rhetoric, promising to usher in a 'golden age' for the State (*Swarna Andhra*), a radical reform agenda of this type expresses a willingness to realise a new model of governance *at the regional scale*, including an economic environment appealing to business. As we will see in the following chapters, the Andhra Pradesh government is actively engaged in promoting its territory to private investors and facilitating projects already in the pipeline. Even though the ruling party has since changed—Congress won the Assembly elections in 2004 and again in 2009—this aspect of the policy regime has not been altered significantly.[43]

4.7 Conclusion

This chapter documented how economic reforms, by deregulating private industrial investments and dismantling the centralised management of the economy resulted in an expanded policy scope for regional governments. Within the first decade following the adoption of reforms in 1991, most State governments had put in place a broadly similar set of promotional policies intended to attract new investment. This included simplified procedures, tax holidays, infrastructural investments designed to accompany private initiatives (e.g., industrial estates), and discretionary policies for allocating land or providing other critical inputs. State-level industrial policies, sometimes specifically adapted to regional conditions like Odisha's policies for the mining sector, and sometimes the expression of a proactive stance like IT in the case of Tamil Nadu or Andhra Pradesh, aim to influence economic geographies and to restructure the regional economy. In the process, the subnational state's rapport with its territory is being redefined. Structural reforms at the regional scale also reorder state spaces by redefining the role of state in society, its rapport with private sector actors (e.g., privatisation of public sector units), or by fiscal restructuring of the state's revenues and expenditure.[44]

This research broadly corroborates Darel Paul's assertion that subnational states exercise more autonomy and more agency than in the past and are increasingly important for shaping economic governance; they contribute to 'the regularization of global capital circulation and accumulation', for instance, through infrastructure provision, energy supply, regulatory agencies, etc. (2002: 470).[45] While careful not to overstate the capacity of the local scale to influence conditions beyond its scale, it was argued here that subnational scales in India represent significant intermediary architectures between global capitalism and local political economies. Subnational States do exert extensive influence over economic governance within their territorial boundaries. They exercise autonomy, for instance, in their negotiations of cost-sharing with private sectors partners, e.g., with respect to land or equity agreements in joint ventures, and the degree to which they enforce social and environmental regulations. At the same time, it was seen that they are limited in their ability to influence the broad rules of the game at the national scale. Unlike the national state they do not have at their disposal tools, such as monetary policies, for regulating key economic conditions and their fiscal scope is restricted by their relatively weak fiscal powers. In that sense, State-level autonomy is contingent. The research underscored one of the contradictions currently observed whereby States enjoy more policy scope but may not have the fiscal scope to make use of it effectively.

The examples analysed in this chapter emphasized that the scalar changes observed are not primarily the result of a reassignment of powers and responsibilities between state actors such as occurs in devolution of powers; nor is it a zero-sum game where powers are removed from the central state and attributed to regional States. There has been a growing overlap with regard to economic development, with both levels simultaneously elaborating policies. Notwithstanding, State governments have a wider scope of action with regard to economic development policies and they contribute, more then in the pre-reform period, to aggregately defining economic governance.

Institutions governing fiscal federalism, the sharing of fiscal resources, have not undergone fundamental change and State governments remain dependent on fiscal transfers. Yet, State governments can no longer count on the Centre in the same way as before, e.g., for capital investments and budgetary support. Moreover it was seen that the central state has become more interventionist in the last decade in its efforts to impose fiscal rigour on States, impinging in some cases on their autonomy. This expresses the volition of the central state to continue to exert influence over national territory, over public finances and over fiscal conditions in general, for instance in orchestrating the decision to discontinue sales tax incentives. It indicates the contested nature of state spaces and the constant political tensions surrounding the scalar arrangements of the state.

In the final part (Section 4.6), analytical narratives were used to explore why and in what contexts States adopt structural reform policies. As the cases of Odisha and Andhra Pradesh showed, there is considerable variation in the way States position themselves *vis-à-vis* economic reform. In Odisha, drastic decisions were taken in a context of crisis. Does it mean the State was *compelled* to turn towards the central government, and then towards the World Bank and accept fiscal restructuring? Probably not, but its choices were certainly very limited. Evidently its leadership calculated that such a move would not provoke adverse political consequences, given the social alignments in the State. In the case of Andhra Pradesh, the State government decided to undertake reforms at a time when it was not financially sound and when its regional economy was performing below the national average. Yet it was able to assert a degree of control over the reform process. Socio-political factors, operating at various scales, were mobilised to explain variations in state capacity. The conclusion suggested by these brief narratives is that political capacity cannot be assumed to be identical across States. It is a function of institutions and political economy, as well as the skill of political leadership.

States can be compared and contrasted also with regard to territorialisation processes, which reflect the degree to which particular scales – here State boundaries – represent a relevant scale for collective action. The analysis of structural reforms in Odisha, adopted in a context of severe fiscal constraints, indicated a policy process influenced by experts from outside the State. In that sense the policy framework that was adopted appeared like a form of delegation, following generic prescriptions, and less the result of an endogenous social process. It was recalled that a small elite group dominates politics in the State and that social mobilisation among subaltern groups was limited. In

Andhra Pradesh the decision to reform was packaged as part of a political strategy on the part of the Telugu Desam Party and articulated with the party's regionalist rhetoric, which makes explicit reference to State territory (land of the Telugus) and identity. Moreover, the presence of regionally based economic elites, their density, and their links to political establishment are crucial factors in explaining the State's capacity to put in place an economic development strategy. This example is more characteristic of a territorialisation process, to the extent that the dominant class interests expressed in this agenda are territorially rooted and mobilised.

4.8 Appendix

Table 4.2 Per capita income of States 1999–2008 at constant prices

States/UT	1999–2000	2002–3	2003–4	2004–5	2005–6	2006–7	2007–8
1. Andhra Pradesh	15,507	17,486	18,961	19,871	21,334	22,835	25,044
2. Arunachal Pradesh	13,990	15,832	17,340	19,339	18,081	20,087	20,570
3. Assam	12,282	13,072	13,675	13,946	14,419	15,152	15,857
4. Bihar	5786	6658	6117	6772	6719	8167	8,703
5. Jharkhand	11,549	10,563	11,173	12,869	12,950	14,252	15,303
6. Goa	42,296	40,602	42,206	45,394	52,201	56,021	60,232
7. Gujarat	18,864	19,509	22,387	23,346	25,487	27,027	NA
8. Haryana	23,229	26,726	28,861	30,822	32,975	37,314	39,796
9. Himachal Pradesh	20,806	23,234	24,377	26,278	27,443	28,639	30,586
10. Jammu & Kashmir	13,816	14,341	14,848	15,414	16,086	16,817	17,590
11. Karnataka	17,502	18,115	18,236	19,847	21,913	22,952	25,226
12. Kerala	19,461	21,942	23,156	25,118	27,220	30,044	32,961
13. Madhya Pradesh	12,384	10,880	11,870	12,032	12,567	12,881	13,299
14. Chhattisgarh	11,629	11,716	13,661	14,070	14,694	15,660	16,740
15. Maharashtra	23,011	23,447	24,859	16,603	28,683	30,982	33,302
16. Manipur	13,260	12,319	13,389	14,334	14,559	15,047	15,270
17. Meghalaya	14,355	15,882	16,658	17,595	18,501	19,292	20,094
18. Mizoram	16,443	18,429	18,555	18,904	18,616	19,220	19,750
19. Nagaland	13,819	17,122	17,958	18,147	18,318	NA	NA
20. Odisha	10,567	10,575	11,951	13,329	13,957	15,528	16,149
21. Punjab	25,631	25,995	27,075	27,905	28,487	30,041	31,439
22. Rajastan	13,619	12,054	15,579	14,908	15,541	16,460	17,334
23. Sikkim	14,890	17,065	18,159	19,332	20,777	22,167	23,761
24. Tamil Nadu	19,432	19,662	20,707	22,975	25,558	28,320	29,445
25. Tripura	14,119	17,752	18,554	19,825	21,524	22,987	NA
26. Uttar Pradesh	9749	9806	10,120	10,421	10,758	11,334	11,939
27. Uttaranchal	13,516	16,530	17,542	19,524	20,355	22,178	NA
28. West Bengal	15,888	17,567	18,374	19,367	20,212	21,753	23,229
29. A&N Island	24,005	25,487	27,229	27,267	28,637	31,009	NA
30. Chandigarh	44,502	55,991	59,406	62,352	66,134	70,361	75,480
31. Delhi	38,913	40,929	41,930	45,157	48,885	54,821	60,189
32. Pondicherry	30,865	39,159	40,338	34,863	36,397	38,488	40,931
All India	*15,881*	*17,101*	*18,301*	*19,331*	*20,868*	*22,580*	*24,295*

Source: French Institute of Pondicherry, compiled by Eric Denis, 2011

Notes

1 A notable exception is Paul (2002, 2005).
2 I am using quite liberally Cornwall's concepts, developed in the framework of her research on community participation in governance networks. This framework is useful for distinguishing between different types of action, associated with varying degrees of agency. See Cornwall (2002).
3 As opposed to a more deterministic class-based explanation of the state, which tends to assume the state is captured and does not have autonomy.
4 In the early 1990s, government officials in Tamil Nadu studied promotional agencies in Maharashtra and Gujarat before setting up their Industrial Guidance and Export Promotion Bureau in 1992 (Sinha 2005: 157).
5 This conclusion was drawn from interviews with officials in the Industries Department, in Andhra Pradesh and Haryana respectively.
6 This discussion is based on Kennedy (2007b).
7 These clarifications were provided during an interview with a senior official in the Industries Ministry, Government of Tamil Nadu, Chennai, 29 June 2000.
8 One crore is the equivalent of ten million.
9 Mahindra subsequently sold its equity and Ford is the sole owner today.
10 Incidentally Subramanian (1996) estimated the loss to the State exchequer from the sales tax exemptions would be Rs 300 crore (42 million euros in 2012 figures).
11 Sinha notes that Gujarat set up an investment promotion office in 1977 (2005: 297, note 19).
12 Here the crucial role of the press can be acknowledged.
13 In Bajpai and Sach's study thirteen of fifteen States were recorded as providing quality infrastructure in select areas in the form of large industrial parks (1999: Appendix III, p. 14).
14 State governments were able to strengthen their own efforts on these lines by relying on central government schemes with similar aims, for instance 'backward areas' development, which made available special incentives packages for designated districts (credit facilities, tax holidays, capital subsidy and import facilities). Like other such entitlement programmes (here places rather than human beneficiaries), they tend to generate pressure to replicate and by 1984 the central government had recognised 247 districts as 'backward', almost two-thirds of the total (Rosen 1988: 76).
15 This was, *inter alia*, in keeping with central government regulations that strictly prohibited locating industries within 50km of urban areas.
16 Robin calculated that from 1993 to 2003, interest payments expressed as a ratio of revenue receipts increased in almost all States; in some cases this ratio was extremely high (more than 52 per cent for West Bengal in 2003–4) (Robin 2009: 8).
17 According to Rob Jenkins, the second generation of reform, mainly in the 2000s, required the creation and development of institutions, e.g., sectoral regulatory bodies such as the Telecom Regulatory Authority. See Jenkins (2004).
18 Perhaps inevitably, given the incentives for States to overestimate the revenues, this hands-off approach resulted in perpetual revenue deficits. Yet as Chelliah (2005) argues, the original fault lies in the design of federal fiscal relations, rather than with the States.
19 Nooruddin and Chhibber designed this method on the basis of interviews with civil servants (2008: 1077).
20 These measures take account of the size of the deficit the Centre allows the State to run (government loans are taken as a proxy), which enhance discretionary resources; the size of committed expenditures, effectively reduces discretionary resources, but which must be seen in relation to the State's overall capacity to mobilise revenue.

21 Barbara Harriss-White's (2007) study of commodity markets in West Bengal seriously questioned the ruling parties' commitment to social justice on the basis of its regulation of rural markets.

22 The State government finally passed the law in July 2010, less than a year before being voted out of office.

23 'Replying to a debate in the Assembly on the West Bengal Taxation Laws (Amendment) Bill, 2008, (Finance Minister Asim Dasgupta) said the FRMBA was a constraint on welfare measures like recruitment of doctors and teachers.' Cf. 'Bengal will not implement fiscal management act: minister', *Business Standard*, 13 August 2008.

24 Dipankar Dasgupta, *The Telegraph*, 14 May 2011, 'Two lakh crore and counting'.

25 It may be recalled that most States do not tax agricultural incomes, for electoral reasons, although it is within their purview.

26 Dani Rodrik popularised the use of analytical narratives in his edited book, *In Search of Prosperity* (2003), as a tool to explore gaps in the literature on growth, in particular to explain variations in performance by exploring 'deep determinants' like geography, market integration and institutions.

27 This analysis of Odisha and Andhra Pradesh draws on Kennedy *et al.* (2013), unless otherwise indicated.

28 According to the World Bank (2008), approximately 80,000 government jobs were abolished between 1998 and 2005.

29 Twelve people were killed in police firing in Kalinga Nagar on 2 January 2006 (Banerjee forthcoming)

30 As John Harriss reminds us, 'there is no neat mapping between "class" and "caste", but there are strong correlations, for example between land ownership and caste position' (1999).

31 Although rehabilitation packages exist, most studies indicate that displaced people suffer a deterioration of their standard of living compared to that before displacement (Meher 2008, quoted by Mishra 2010: 50).

32 These ideas are laid out in detail in Naidu's book *Plain Speaking*, see Naidu and Ninan (2000).

33 In the 1999 assembly election, the TDP–BJP alliance secured 65 per cent of the upper caste vote, 64 per cent of 'peasant OBCs', and 47 per cent of 'lower OBCs' and 33 per cent of the Dalit vote (against 64 per cent for Congress) (CSDS with Suri 1999: Table 9).

34 In 2004, 33 per cent of TDP's MLAs were from OBCs (other backward classes), a sharp increase from 1999 (12 per cent) and 20 per cent were from Scheduled Castes and Scheduled Tribes. See Vaugier-Chatterjee (2009: 295).

35 This section draws on my unpublished paper 'Mobilizing regional identity in pursuit of Swarna Andhra. Strategies to foster growth and engage with globalization in Andhra Pradesh', presented at the Symposium 'Regions and Regional Consciousness in India', Arizona State University, 7–9 March 2004.

36 World Economic Forum held in Delhi in December 1999 (press release).

37 For example, 'Regulatory change (...) will not be possible without the Centre's participation and co-operation. Therefore, to create a favourable regulatory climate, the State will not only have to undertake significant initiatives at the State level *but also influence the Centre to act*' (GoAP 1999: 41, emphasis added).

38 These are clear indications of travelling concepts, circulated by international transfer agents such as McKinsey consultants. See Stone (2004).

39 See also Benbabaali (2009) for a study of Kamma cultural dominance in Hyderabad.

40 Naidu attended the World Economic Forum, for instance, and pleaded alongside Catalonia's Jordi Pujol in favour of greater subnational autonomy.

41 Author interviews conducted at FAPCCI (Federation of Andhra Pradesh Chambers of Commerce and Industry), and at the CII (Confederation of Indian Industry) in Hyderabad, March 2002.

42 As mentioned above, the TDP–BJP alliance secured 65 per cent of the upper caste vote in the 1999 assembly elections (CSDS, with Suri 1999).

43 This corroborates the analysis of political scientists who have observed, starting in the late 1980s, that '[W]hile the parties in power changed, the stability of the polity continued. The success of a party seemed to lie in building a strong and charismatic personality on the one hand and carrying out populist policies on the other, capable of appealing to a broad spectrum of disadvantaged groups' (G. Ram Reddy 1989: 287, cited in Harriss 1999: 3373).

44 The latter are examples of non-territorial rescaling of state spaces.

45 See also Painter and Goodwin who refer to subnational state as 'sites of regulation' of the global political economy (1995: 342). It should be noted that these scholars use a looser definition of regulation than the one generally assigned in French regulation theory wherein the overarching accumulation regime and the régulation mode that accompany it are anchored in, and emerge from, dominant institutional forms apprehended at the national scale. It is a conceptual framework that reflects the more integrated economic space of advanced industrial economies.

5 State spatial strategies via Special Economic Zones

It can be recalled that following independence, the goals of the Indian state were similar to those of all modern national states, i.e., to normalise national space and to organise social and economic activities on the national scale. In theoretical terms, modern national states are driven to 'rationalize, unify and homogenize social relations within their territorial boundaries' (Lefebvre, cited by Brenner 2004: 42). Such national and nationalist efforts continue in India, most obviously in rhetoric, but also in terms of state action. However, *in the realm of economic development*, other types of spatial strategies have emerged in parallel, some of which compete with those that continue to be framed against national territory.

In this chapter, I will argue that the 2005 Special Economic Zone (SEZ) Act represents a forceful illustration of a rescaling strategy from several different points of view. It aims to redefine India's engagement with global capitalism, and put it on a fast track. This has implications both for Indian firms aspiring to trade in global markets and for transnational firms seeking to use India as an export platform. At the same time, and this will be the main focus here, I will argue that the SEZ policy is rescaling geographies of statehood by redefining state spaces within India's federal set-up and putting into motion processes of reterritorialisation at subnational spatial scales.

Because the construction of scales is a contested process and because territory is constantly 'worked' by social forces, organisational scales for political, economic and social relations are not static. As Brenner reminds us, 'territorialisation, on any spatial scale, must be viewed as a historically specific, incomplete, and conflictual *process* rather than as a pregiven, natural, or permanent condition' (2004: 43). Here the focus is on a prominent policy initiative of the central state but whose implementation relies fundamentally on its encounters with subnational state spaces and strategies. This process has implications for territorialisation at different spatial scales, for economic governance and for organising collective action.

5.1 India's revamped SEZ policy

An SEZ is a delineated space cut out of the institutional fabric of national territory and governed by a specific regulatory framework. The 2005 SEZ law offers attractive incentives to private developers to set up economic zones and fit them out for export-oriented production of goods and services. It is assumed that such platforms equipped with the best infrastructure possible will attract private firms, which are also eligible under the SEZ Act to benefit from duty-free import of inputs, tax holidays on profits, as well as other advantages compared to *outside the zone* in the real economy. In principle, these zones do not have vocation to interact with the domestic economy or the 'domestic trade area' as it is called in SEZ policy documents.

There were several precursors to the SEZ Act of 2005. Indeed, as the government likes to boast, India was the first Asian country to promote export zones as early as 1965 when it established an export processing zone (EPZ) in Kandla, on the western coast of Gujarat. This was followed in 1974 by the establishment of a zone in the (then) suburbs of Bombay at Santa Cruz (SEEPZ), which exports electronics, software and jewellery. There were eight major 'first generation' export zones. Except for one private zone (in Surat, Gujarat), these EPZs were set up by the central government with infrastructure funded by the State governments (Menon and Mitra 2009: 14). These EPZs never represented a dominant sector of the economy; their performance was not remarkable with the exception of SEEPZ in Bombay, which accounted for half of the total value of exports from EPZs in 2004–5 (Grasset and Landy 2007: 612). In that same year, the share of all the zones combined in total exports was only 5 per cent, 1 per cent of factory employment and about one-third of 1 per cent of manufacturing investment (Aggarwal 2006: 4534).[1]

The current avatar of the export zone scheme started taking shape in 2000, and was directly inspired by the Chinese example. It was announced by the Commerce Minister following a trip to China, in the framework of a new Export and Import Policy, called EXIM 2000. Under this policy, which borrowed the Chinese term 'Special Economic Zone', new zones, with a minimum size of 1,000 hectares, could be set up by the public or private sector; existing EPZs were converted into SEZs and became eligible for additional advantages.

This policy was replaced a few years later by a law, the SEZ Act 2005, accompanied by a set of extensive rules released in February 2006. The passage through Parliament was intended to give legitimacy to the policy, underscore the commitment of the central government, and reassure investors about continuity in the event of a change of government. In effect, a new Congress-led coalition government had taken power in 2004, and it threw its full support behind the SEZ approach as a key instrument for achieving national economic goals, which included deeper engagement with global markets.

The SEZ Act's official objectives are: (1) generation of additional economic activity; (2) promotion of exports of goods and services; (3) promotion of investment from domestic and foreign sources; (4) creation of employment opportunities; and (5) development of infrastructure facilities.[2] Put in these terms, the aims of the policy appear irreproachable. But other proponents of the policy express the rationale somewhat differently, emphasising all that is wrong with *existing economic governance in India*, making SEZ look less like a motor for achieving a goal than a refuge for investors, who will be spared Indian realities:

> The promotion of SEZs is an attempt to deal with infrastructural deficiencies, procedural complexities, bureaucratic hassles and barriers raised by monetary, trade, fiscal, taxation, tariff and labour policies. These structural bottlenecks affect the investment climate adversely by increasing production and transaction costs.
>
> (Aggarwal 2006: 4533)

Another commonly stated rationale for pursuing SEZ is that India's requirements in infrastructure are so great that the government could not possibly take them up on its own. By framing a comprehensive package of fiscal incentives (tax holidays, de-taxed inputs), the aim is that private investors, both domestic and international, will come forward and develop the much-needed infrastructure, introducing state-of-the-art technology in the process. Individual firms will then lease space within these zones from the promoters, either turnkey premises or a plot to build their own plants. These firms or 'units' are eligible too for tax holidays (100 per cent exemption on export income for the first five years, 50 per cent for the next five, and 50 per cent on reinvested export profits for five more years) as well as tax exemptions on all inputs from the domestic trade area or from imports.

Beyond state-of-the-art production platforms, the SEZ law seeks to create 'self-contained zones' that include *non-processing areas*, for residential and commercial purposes, in addition to the *processing area*, used for producing goods and services. In other words, an SEZ is intended to be a private township, wherein the SEZ developer would take over the role of the local municipal government:

> In fact, the SEZ developer would have to fill in all the processes and services that would be needed for the SEZ units to operate at peak efficiency. These services include civic amenities, infrastructure such as roads, sewage disposal, green/open spaces, housing, supply of power and water, and education. Self-sufficiency and planned infrastructure have the added advantage that non-processing areas can be kept free of unplanned habitation like slums, which might later turn into a political *fait accompli*.
>
> (Menon and Mitra 2009: 16)

Thus the mandate of the SEZ promoter is extended beyond infrastructure provision to city-building. Yet the SEZ law leaves many issues unaddressed, for instance how private services for basic needs (water, electricity, schools, health clinics) would be run and what their cost would be. Presumably all social categories would live in the zone (workers, supervisors, managers). Would they all have access to the same services? This is a highly unrealistic

Table 5.1 Land requirements for various categories of SEZ

Sector	Minimum land requirement (hectares)	Minimum Land requirement in special states and union territories (ha)	Minimum built-up processing area requirement
Multi-product	1,000	200	50% of total area
Sector specific	100	50	50%
IT/ITES	10		100%
Gems and jewellery	10		50%
Biotech	10		40%

Source: adapted from Mody (2010) (based on SEZ Rules 2006, Ministry of Commerce and Industry, Government of India)

assumption given India's socially segregated society. As sceptics have pointed out, what would stop unplanned habitation, i.e., slums, from coming up just outside the zone, thereby producing the very result the law claimed to prevent? Lastly, a fundamental question: would residents have elected representatives in zone management? In fact, in as many as fifteen States, the SEZ laws or policies propose to consider these zones as 'industrial townships', a category that falls outside the realm of local self-government; it is likely that a small nominated committee would act as a substitute for the local authority (Sivaramakrishnan 2009: 90). Given that most large zones created by the 2005 Act are still under construction, these governance issues are largely theoretical but figure prominently in the SEZ debates.

Another defining feature of the current SEZ scheme, which explains the developments one can observe on the ground, is the definition of various categories of SEZs with differing minimum area requirements. The two main categories are multi-product and sector specific, the latter containing several subcategories such as IT/ITES, gems and jewellery, biotech and handicrafts (see Table 5.1). This marks a major difference with the early Chinese zones, few in number but which cover very large areas, encompassing rural and urban areas.[3] As of now, most of India's SEZs are very small in size.

5.2 Economic performance and spatial effects of SEZs

Before moving to my analysis of SEZs as a state spatial strategy, it is useful to relate some key aspects of the SEZ experience in India. This provides important context for understanding how various state scales, as well as social actors, are responding to the policy. A first remark: the SEZ policy framework has generated an enthusiastic response from private investors, and from some State governments, judging from the number of proposals received, especially in the first few years (2006–9). By November 2011, 582 projects had received 'formal approval' from the central government. Of these, 380 were 'notified', meaning that the promoter, having shown proof of land ownership and having obtained all the required clearances from State and local authorities,

Table 5.2 Growth rate of exports from SEZs, 2006–11

Years	Growth rate (year to year)
2006–07	52%
2007–08	93%
2008–09	50%
2009–10	121%
2010–11	43%

Source: GoI n.d (6)

was given permission to start construction of the zone. However, take-off has been quite slow: only 173 zones were fully operational in April 2013, of which 19 are pre-2005 zones. The global financial crisis has had a dampening effect on SEZ development, fewer and fewer proposals are submitted for approval, and there have been requests for de-notification.

The government claims to be satisfied with the level of exports coming from SEZs, which have grown rapidly as indicated in Table 5.2.

In terms of sectoral distribution, zones specialised in IT and IT-enabled services (business process outsourcing, or BPO) have received by far the largest number of applications. In late 2011, 80 of 143 operational SEZs were in this category. Among sector-specific notified SEZs, the other sectors most strongly represented after IT are: pharmaceuticals/chemicals, biotech and engineering. As Table 5.1 indicates, the SEZ Act authorises very small zones in the IT and biotech sectors (10 hectares), basically the equivalent of a business park. For critics, this indicates one of the perverse effects of the SEZ policy. It allows property developers to benefit from major tax breaks for developing office buildings for IT-related activities, which are, in any case, in high demand. Indeed, IT services are among the fastest growing sectors in the Indian economy and are already export oriented. Moreover, infrastructure requirements for the IT industry are not particularly challenging and do not require specialisation.

This pattern is related to another feature of India's SEZs, i.e., the fact they have primarily been promoted by Indian firms. The share of foreign direct investment (FDI) in total investment is only 11 per cent (Aggarwal 2012: 144). Here too, the policy has not produced the expected results. It should be noted, however, that international financial capital is nonetheless contributing to SEZ development indirectly, for instance via private equity funds channelled to real estate firms for property development. Foreign investment in real estate was deregulated in 2005 and private equity investments in Indian real estate rose sharply in 2006 and 2007, before falling off after 2008. India's real estate market is a prime destination for financial capital because of the high returns it generates.

A common assumption about export zones is that countries with a comparative advantage in labour costs, such as India, will attract investments in labour-intensive manufacturing. This has not been confirmed in the case of

India, neither for SEZs nor for the economy as a whole. Instead, economic restructuring in the 1990s and 2000s resulted in strong growth in tertiary sector activities (Nagaraj 2008). Productivity gains have been impressive but employment has not progressed as expected and has even declined in relative terms in the organised sector of the economy. Manufacturing is taking place in some SEZs, notably the multi-product zones of which there were 17 in operation in late 2011 (out of a total of 143 notified zones), and is planned in some sector-specific zones. It is noteworthy that only five notified SEZs are in leather and footwear and 12 in textiles, despite India's traditional specialisation in these sectors, and their labour-intensive character. With regard to the policy's stated objective of creating large-scale employment in manufacturing, the empirical evidence suggests a rather mediocre performance. According to official figures, approximately 579,708 jobs had been created by June 2011 under the 2005 Act.[4] This figure should be appreciated in relation to the size of India's labour force, estimated at 420 million.

A final unexpected outcome of the SEZ policy has been the popular protests. In almost every part of the country where SEZ projects have been proposed, there has been some form of protest, and in many cases prolonged mobilisation. Mainly large-scale zones have run into problems with land acquisition in the face of resistance from local farmers and stakeholders. What has aroused much anger, and led to large-scale anti-SEZ mobilisation, is the perception that State governments are lending support to SEZ developers against the larger interests of the State and its citizens. For instance, many State governments have invoked the power of public domain in the name of 'public purpose', to justify forcibly requisitioning land from private landowners, that they then cede to SEZ developers. A dramatic example is Nandigram, West Bengal, in which small landowners and tenant farmers resisted giving up their land for a proposed chemical hub, promoted by the Salim Group from Indonesia and supported by the State government. In March 2007 after a protracted struggle between local protesters, mobilised largely by the opposition Trinamul Congress party, the State government sent in the police, which fired on the crowd killing fourteen people. This was followed by several months of protracted struggles, before the West Bengal government cancelled the project and announced it would find another location for the chemical hub. This dramatic episode epitomised the manner in which SEZ policy translates in local space, in specific places, where it encounters subnational state spatial strategies as well as resistance from social forces. I will discuss anti-SEZ mobilisation in Section 5.7.

Spatial effects

To a large extent spatial effects generated by the SEZ policy reflect pre-existing industrial geographies: investments have concentrated in industrially developed regions, and more specifically near the country's largest urban agglomerations. These areas are relatively better equipped with infrastructure (energy, ports/airports, telecommunications) and in many cases the proximity to large cities ensures adequate labour supply and other supporting services, including quality housing and education. As previously mentioned, a large proportion of total projects are in IT and IT-related services, which employ qualified engineers and technicians for the former, and English-speaking graduates for the latter. Large cities are more likely to respond to these labour needs and provide the lifestyles young professionals are seeking.

Map 5.1 in the Appendix 5.9 locates the formally approved SEZ projects specialised in IT as of 2010, and shows the concentration in the largest cities. The National Capital Region (NCR) with 63 IT zones had the highest concentration; most of these zones are located in the periphery of Delhi: 28 in Gurgaon (Haryana) and 26 in NOIDA (Uttar Pradesh). NCR is followed by Hyderabad (48), Bengaluru (ex Bangalore) (26), Chennai (24), Kolkata (14), Pune (13) and Mumbai (12).

All types of zones combined, SEZs are geographically concentrated in a small number of States (see Table 5.4 in Appendix 5.9). In April 2013, out of 386 notified zones, 301 were located in just six States, approximately 78 per cent of the total. These States – Andhra Pradesh, Gujarat, Haryana, Karnataka, Maharashtra and Tamil Nadu – are among the most industrially developed in India. The country's largest metropolitan areas (Delhi, Mumbai, Bengaluru, Hyderabad, Chennai), with the exception of Kolkata, are located within these States or in close proximity (Haryana surrounds the National Capital Region of Delhi on three sides). In terms of total exports from SEZs, six States account for 92 per cent of the total: Andhra Pradesh, Gujarat, Kerala, Karnataka, Maharashtra and Tamil Nadu (GoI n.d.: 11).

In much finer detail, Map 5.2 (in Appendix 5.9) represents the district-wise distribution of the 582 formally approved SEZ. It shows that only 130 districts out of a total of 615 have one or more zones. Almost half of these (58) have only one zone; 16 districts have between 8 and 40 zones and together regroup 330 SEZs, approximately 57 per cent of the total. The dark grey patches in metropolitan regions is clearly apparent as is the broader trend of SEZ development in the faster-growing regions of the country, the South and the West as well as coastal areas. It is striking to see the almost total absence of SEZ projects in the densely populated Gangetic Plain of northern India, situated on a diagonal between Delhi and Kolkata (States of Uttar Pradesh, Bihar and Jharkhand).

5.3 Rescaling economic regulation

The previous section briefly sketched the economic performance of the SEZ policy and its spatial impacts. The emphasis in this section will be on governance aspects of SEZ implementation, and on the implications for state rescaling.

The SEZ policy is extremely complex in that it interacts with many other policies and regulations, such as tax, trade and employment to name a few. Its implementation requires the involvement of many government departments as well as all levels of government, including the local level for land-use regulations (zoning) and building rules. In some key respects, I will argue, SEZ governance resembles a throwback to the centralised economic management of the licence-raj days, albeit without the control over location. The central state is again in the role of rule maker *vis-à-vis* State and local governments, and has interposed itself as an 'intermediary architecture' between capital investors and the physical implantation of capital in space. The SEZ policy can be expressed as a strategy to rescale the national economy through the creation of exceptional spaces conceived to ensure seamless interaction with the global economy and with international investors. Such 'zoning technologies', which have been widely used throughout the world,[5] have been analysed as examples of 'neoliberal exceptions' aimed at producing new economic possibilities but also 'spaces, and techniques for governing the population' (Ong 2006: 7).

SEZs are conceived as a key component of the central government's strategy to stimulate growth, and especially boost exports, but it is applied within limited geographical areas. In this respect it does not attempt to solve all the problems that continue to characterise India's investment climate and that would require a reformed economic policy regime for the national territorial economy as a whole. Rob Jenkins questions whether the SEZ policy should be seen as bold – ushering in radical change in India's engagement with globalisation and neo-liberalism – or instead as excessively timid, indicating the reluctance of policy-makers to face opposition by implementing deeper reforms. He concludes:

> SEZs represent an attractive way, politically speaking, of introducing reforms from which liberalizers have otherwise shied away. The SEZ policy is a convenient means of overcoming the huge obstacles (bureaucratic and legal, but ultimately political) to urban redevelopment. Barriers range from the diversity of agencies and authorities with overlapping jurisdictions (each with its own set of entrenched political defenders), to outmoded legislation such as the Urban Land Ceiling Act and the Rent Control Act, which have proven difficult to revise.
>
> (Jenkins 2011: 53)

It is a fact that State governments have been reluctant to implement reforms in sensitive policy areas, like industrial relations and labour laws, but the central state has not performed better on that count, preferring to rely on States to negotiate 'awkward political dilemmas' (Jenkins 2004: 334). It is convenient for central policy-makers to reproach States. One of the architects of the 2005 Act is on record as saying:

> The strongest pro-SEZ argument is that the DTA [Domestic Trade Area], *one that is driven by the States – all of which have differing economic persuasions* – has long been unable to meet any of these expectations [generate economic activity, develop infrastructure, increase investment,

raise net export earnings, boost employment, induct R&D]. That apart, the Centre has no choice either. Witness India's vast heterogeneity, and the bitter diversity of opinion on liberalization. New Delhi can do no better than to adopt a policy package which, even if it falls well short of the ideal is yet the best that would be attainable while steering clear of unsettling dissension or harm.

(Menon and Mitra 2009: 8, italics added)

Despite such rhetoric blaming the States for the country's economic short-comings, the policy can be interpreted as the proof of the central state's unwillingness in the current era of national coalition governments to compel State governments to take up the unfinished reform agenda.[6] So while expressing political weakness on one level, the SEZ policy also expresses the central state's volition to define bold national-scale initiatives for promoting economic development, here specifically, export growth.

SEZ governance structure

The governance structure reflects the commanding role of the central government in the formal implementation process. Bureaucrats have been the driving force behind the policy, from its inception until today; a special SEZ Division at the Ministry of Commerce in New Delhi serves as headquarters. The Board of Approvals, presented as the single window approval mechanism, is the key implementing institution. It is composed of nineteen *ex officio* members, mostly from central government ministries and departments (commerce, finance, taxes, industrial production, science and technology, urban development, etc.). One nominee from the concerned State government is included on the Board of Approvals as well as the 'Development Commissioner' of the concerned region. At this formal level, the governance structure bears an uncanny resemblance to the central approval committee of the licence-permit raj era. A key difference is the territorial organisation, which involves the deputation of central government functionaries, who occupy a crucial position in the SEZ implementation architecture. These Development Commissioners are high-ranking civil servants – not below the rank of Deputy Secretary to the Government of India – who answer directly to the Minister of Commerce. National territory is divided into seven large SEZ Zones, each of which is headed by a Development Commissioner who looks after all the SEZs in that geographical area; this constitutes the ad hoc territorial command and control structure of the SEZ policy framework. It is a 'nested' structure in the sense that the Development Commissioner also chairs the governance structure at the level of the individual SEZ, the Unit Approval Committee. Its primary duty is to approve the proposals for setting up of units (firms) in a given SEZ. It includes representatives from the central government (Ministry of Commerce, the Customs Department, the Income Tax Department) as well as the State government and the promoter.

State governments are co-opted into this centralised governance structure, and are expected to give their full cooperation to SEZ implementation. For instance, a developer can submit the proposal for the establishment of an SEZ either to the concerned State government or directly to the central Board of Approvals. However, the Board of Approvals will not make a decision on a proposal unless the State government has given its recommendation. If channelled through the State government, the latter is required to forward the proposal to the Board of Approvals with its recommendation, 'for' or 'against', within forty-five days from the date of receipt.[7] It is important because by giving a favourable recommendation, the State government is in effect committing to providing essential services to the proposed SEZ, i.e., bringing networked infrastructure to the gates of the zone. In this context, it is not surprising that some States question whether they stand to reap a net gain from this policy, an issue I will return to below.

Notwithstanding the predominant role of the central government bureaucracy, an Empowered Group of Ministers (EGoM), an institutional arrangement for promoting inter-ministerial coordination,[8] was formed for the SEZ policy to provide political oversight to the Board of Approvals. It included, in addition to the Commerce Minister, the External Affairs Minister and the Finance Minister. As Balveer Arora has remarked, an EGoM for the SEZ policy is particularly important 'because it involves a complex interplay of Central powers and responsibilities with States' interests and jurisdictions (such as land acquisition and relief and rehabilitation of displaced persons)' (Arora 2007: 7). The SEZ EGoM has weighed in occasionally, especially in response to popular protests, thereby fulfilling its duty to ensure the political sustainability of the policy. For instance in 2007, following sustained agitation around land issues in Nandigram that resulted in police firing, it ordered State governments not to use state machinery to acquire land for SEZ developers, i.e., through the land acquisition legislation. This directive, concerning a State subject, has not been systematically applied, as I shall discuss next. The SEZ EGoM weighed in again when it decided to reduce the maximum size of multi-product SEZs from 10,000 to 5,000 hectares,[9] considering that large zones would inevitably provoke land conflicts. This ceiling rule was amended in May 2009, to give the central Board of Approvals the discretion to disregard the 5,000 hectare ceiling in certain cases.[10] I will return below to the issue of land and the implication of State governments.

Another significant amendment concerns the minimum processing area for multi-product SEZs: it was raised twice from 25 per cent to 35 per cent and then to 50 per cent following criticism that real estate firms, as opposed to more specialised industrial builders, were drawn to zone development solely for the opportunities it availed for residential and commercial property development, and that there was little interest or expertise in providing state-of-the-art industrial infrastructure, the policy's ostensible *raison d'être*. Given the strong demand for housing and strong consumer demand, such a market response was not surprising, but in the face of widespread unrest about land, it has become increasingly difficult for the government to justify the industrial township model.

Interestingly, the central government has *not* presented a united front with regard to the SEZ policy, with the Ministry of Finance openly opposing the tax benefits and underscoring the tremendous loss to the exchequer in foregone revenues.[11] The Ministry of Finance even appealed to the EGoM to consider repealing the Act, on the grounds that it was not WTO compliant, and that other countries might retaliate, to which the Commerce Ministry countered that it was an act of Parliament.[12] This is a useful reminder that the state is not a monolithic entity and that strategies pursued by various departments may compete with each other.

5.4 Implementing the SEZ policy in a multiscalar state

To understand the manner in which the SEZ policy is playing out in space and how it is restructuring state spaces in India, it is critical to examine its encounter with subnational state strategies. State-level studies have shown that States have reacted very differently to the policy.[13] A number of States enacted their own SEZ policies after the first central SEZ policy was announced in 2000, and six have also passed SEZ laws.[14] At present, most States are content to function with an SEZ policy, which has the advantage of being easily revised: a new government can announce its own new SEZ policy. In principle, State government policy and legislation must be compliant with the central Act and rules, but research indicate that there are radically divergent approaches among India's States, including practices that do not conform to the policy.

The SEZ Act leaves certain core issues to the discretion of State governments, for instance with regard to labour issues.[15] The assumption is that in the absence of explicit rules to the contrary, existing labour legislation will apply. It is noteworthy that Maharashtra's draft SEZ bill, which dates from 2002, was stalled because of clauses restricting trade union activity and the application of labour laws (Mody 2010: 9). Only Gujarat's Act, ratified in 2004, clearly addresses the issue of how labour-related laws will apply in an SEZ; the Act is 'designed to provide flexibility with respect to which provisions within existing labour laws would be applicable with SEZs. [It] allows the government to amend any of sixteen pieces of labour-related legislation "as and when considered necessary"' (Mody 2010: 10).[16]

Other States apparently prefer a less explicit approach to this sensitive issue. In some cases, States have declared units within SEZs as public utilities, which allows derogations from regular labour laws including the right to strike.[17] These measures have important implications for workers' rights in SEZs. In other cases, States have decided to delegate the power of the Labour Commissioner, the top-ranking officer in the State in charge of labour relations, to the Development Commissioner, thereby further concentrating power in the hands of the central government officer.[18] The rationale for this delegation of powers is that the Development Commissioner is in touch with the management of the firms located in the zone and through frequent inter-action develops a good 'understanding' with them.[19] Thus, in the event of a labour dispute, the Development Commissioner could exercise influence over the company's management to find a rapid resolution to the problem before it degenerated. What is implied but not explicitly stated is that Labour Com-missioners, because they are more professionally qualified to deal with these issues, would be more likely to allow labour representatives to register claims within the legal framework.[20]

The Commerce Department is favourable to this delegation of powers of the Labour Commissioner. This arrangement was put in place with the State government of Uttar Pradesh where the vast majority of SEZs are located on the eastern periphery of Delhi, in NOIDA and Greater NOIDA. These SEZs pre-date the 2005 Act for the most part, and were already administered by the Commerce Department. Although a Development Commissioner insisted during an interview that State labour laws apply within SEZs, as per the Act, he also stated that the managers of NOIDA refused to provide office space to trade unions, with a view to restricting their influence in the zone.[21]

This analysis underscores the Commerce Department's strong preference for placing as much responsibility as possible with the Development Com-missioners, in order to streamline the implementation of the policy across national territory, and the *differing economic persuasions* of the Indian States. The territorial organisation of the SEZ governance structure effectively attempts to supersede subnational territorial jurisdictions.

The SEZ Division in the Department of Commerce conducted a review of the SEZ policy in view of recommending changes. Frustration with State governments, accused of not fully complying with the SEZ Act, transpires clearly from this document:

> The six year experience has shown that while the SEZ Act contains pro-visions that give it an overriding effect over inconsistent provisions in other legislations, this has not translated at the ground level into fulfill-ment of State Government obligations and an effective single window mechanism at the State level. Developers often complain that many State Governments do not follow the SEZ Act in letter and spirit, thereby denying them crucial benefits at the ground level.
>
> (GoI n.d.: 25)

The Commerce Department tries to influence State government practices *vis-à-vis* SEZs, to convince them to embrace the letter and the spirit of the law.[22] However, this often involves putting the SEZ spirit above the interests of the State governments, which explains why the latter are reluctant to cooperate. This can be illustrated with an example: The State of Haryana levies devel-opment charges on SEZ promoters for meeting some of the costs of bringing infrastructure to the zone, such as roads, electricity, water and sewerage (i.e., external development charges) and for developing basic infrastructure within the zone (i.e., internal development charges). The Development Commissioner in charge of Haryana stated in an interview in July 2009 that he had written to the State government 'on behalf of developers' to request it to stop levying these development charges on grounds that they go against the SEZ Act. Six months later, the same official indicated that no decision had been taken but that a high-level meeting had been held with the Haryana government to formally request that development charges be discontinued. He considered that State governments should facilitate private investments since they had given their recommendation for the SEZ to the Board of Approvals, and that this was tantamount to a commitment.[23] An official at the Department of Industries in Haryana indicated that the State government would not agree to completely eliminate these charges, 'otherwise the costs will have to be borne by somebody else', although it was considering reducing them.[24] The officer explained that in Gurgaon, which is immediately contiguous to Delhi on the southern extremity and where *all* the notified SEZs in the State are located, real estate prices are extremely high. In order to develop peripheral roads for new SEZs, the State government is required to pay market prices for land (which at the time of the interview in 2010 were Rs 10 million per acre, approximately €2,500/m^2). In this light, the 'uncooperative' attitude of the Haryana government can be understood in relation to its relatively high capacity to attract investments, in particular to its territory near Delhi. The State can reasonably question what it has to gain from an SEZ policy that has produced thirty very small IT export zones in the heart of Gurgaon, the city with the highest number of SEZs in the country. Gurgaon is booming and does not need tax exemptions to render it attractive (the city's population grew by more than 73 per cent between 2001 and 2011!).

The example of development charges levied by Haryana suggests the burden that SEZs place on State government finances, and underscores the contradiction with the stated rationale for making SEZs into townships i.e., to ensure that private investors bore all development costs: 'The underlying intent for sequestering that proportion of land [non-processing area] is to allow SEZs to function independently, to provide accountability and better infrastructure. All these get achieved *without straining already existing municipal, or other, services*' (Menon and Mitra 2009: 16, italics added).

In its review of the policy, the Commerce Department insists that State governments must do more to extend their services to SEZs:

> External connectivity and provision of utility services are of vital importance for an SEZ. Connectivity issues range from connectivity with the major rail / road arteries, extension of the Mass Rapid Transit System (MRTS) to the SEZ, rail connectivity to dry ports, establishment of cargo airports etc. State Government must take adequate steps to provide connectivity and public utility services such as water, drainage connections etc. for the SEZs.
> (GoI n.d.: 26)

But Haryana, for one, has taken decisions to limit its responsibility *vis-à-vis* developers. In January 2011 it announced that no additional SEZs would be allowed in Gurgaon until a new water supply system was in place, or unless the developer could show that it would arrange it own supplies (not from groundwater sources).[25] This illustrates how in certain policy contexts State governments *do* assert their right to withhold cooperation, especially when there is a direct conflict with their territorial interests.

This discussion has centred on the complex articulation between state spaces in relation to a specific form of economic rescaling, complete with an ad hoc governance framework. I propose to view the SEZ policy framework as emblematic of the manner in which the central state is positioning itself as an intermediary architecture between the global economy and the various scales that make up the national economy. The examples analysed here suggest a constant pull between the central state and the regional States, which are indicative of their overlapping territorial jurisdictions as well as their distinct political strategies with regard to territorial economic development. The central government ministries try to obtain 'compliance' and 'cooperation' from State governments through various means. The latter respond in a differing fashion, according to their 'economic persuasions', in ways which express agency but integrate at the same time constraints. Variations among States can be observed with regard to formal arrangements (Acts or policies, explicit delegation of the powers of the Labour Commission) as well as implementation on the ground, as I will show in the following sections.

5.5 Land – a State 'subject'?

The SEZ Act has been controversial since it was first announced and there have been numerous ongoing campaigns around the country, some opposing specific projects while others call for a repeal of the Act. Protests have centred on land issues above all else, and for that reason I will examine this issue in some detail. In some cases, local stakeholders (owners, tenants, users with collective rights) refuse the principle of parting with their land or renouncing their land rights. In others, landowners are willing to sell but want higher compensation rates than those offered by government agencies trying to expropriate them. What has most fuelled protests is State government intervention in land deals, which has taken the form of State-level parastatal agencies forcibly acquiring land from private parties in order to transfer it to SEZ developers or these agencies 'assisting' promoters to buy from the 'market'.

Although land is a crucial input for industrial development everywhere in the world, the manner in which this use is perceived by particular social groups depends very much on alternative, often competing, uses. Agriculture is still the major provider of livelihoods in India, and many social groups attach tremendous symbolic importance to land, in addition to its utility as a resource or a fixed asset. Although agriculture accounts for only one-quarter of national income, approximately 65 per cent of Indians depend on it for earning a living, with significant variations across States. So why do State governments risk social unrest and potential political fall-out by assisting SEZ promoters to take possession of agricultural land?

As discussed in Chapter 4, State governments are openly competing with each other for investments, and providing inexpensive land to investors is a crucial factor in many deals, especially large-scale projects. Yet price is only one aspect of the issue. Perhaps more important for an investor are clear-cut, legally binding, property titles on land. In fact, obtaining unencumbered land titles in India is very difficult, a situation that directly affects the functioning of land markets. Explaining why requires a brief detour through India's system of land tenure and property records.[26]

Although much land was brought under private ownership during the colonial period, India does not have a uniform private property regime across its vast territory. Various categories of land coexist including collectively held lands, e.g., 'tribal lands'. Reserved and protected forests and lands classified as barren remain under the stewardship of the state. Legal institutions governing land originate primarily from the colonial period and reflect the colonial emphasis on tax collection. For instance, the Registration Act of 1908 establishes proof of land transactions, but does not establish the legality of the transactions: ownership rights remain presumptive only. The Registrar's Office, where land transactions are registered, does not authenticate land titles based on cadastral maps, for instance, and so does not offer a guarantee that there are no outstanding claims on the land. This explains why buying land on the market involves potentially high transaction costs.

Given the primacy of well-functioning property rights in any model of capitalist economic development, it is not surprising the Indian government has an agenda for reforming the current system of titling and property records. In 2008 it merged two existing centrally sponsored schemes to form the 'National Land Resource Modernization Programme', with the stated objective of moving towards *conclusive titling* (as opposed to presumptive). Under this programme, land records and registration are digitalised and ground surveys are conducted to update maps and records. Going a step further in 2010, a 'Land Titling' bill was introduced in Parliament, but not voted upon, with the following goal: 'to provide for the establishment, administration and management of a system of conclusive property titles with title guarantee and indemnification against losses due to inaccuracies in property titles, through registration of immovable properties' (2010: 1).[27] The proposed legislation clearly aims to reassure investors, as it claims to provide 'an environment conducive to facilitating easier access to capital and, therefore, enhanced agricultural productivity per unit of land, efficient property transactions and security of tenure and property rights' (2010: 45).[28]

In proposing these reforms, the Indian government is clearly concerned about conformity with international standards, and it has commissioned studies from international agencies and experts.[29] These efforts are yet another illustration of how the central state is currently seeking to adapt its institutional framework to facilitate capitalist development and adhere to the norms of the global economy. The perceived urgency to reform a system that has been in place for decades can be seen as a reflection of the central state's commitment to economic reforms. On one level, it could be argued that these reforms are long overdue, and that security of tenure is in the public interest. Indeed, inaccurate property records and ambiguous land rights are partly to blame for large-scale land grabbing. But the issue is not so simple. As I just mentioned, there are coexisting systems of use and ownership rights, and imposing a rigid system premised on the principle of private property will inevitably lead to a loss of rights for certain categories of people, often including those who are already the most economically vulnerable. As Eric Denis points out, there are radical implications of moving from a deeds registration system to a title registration system, because '(d)eeds differ according to the customs of the place, personal status, reinforced by the regional specificity of the legal framework and the inclusion of local customary laws. There may be a title deed, *patta*, *kabuliyat*, gift deed, habitation deed or simply a *khazana* or tax receipt depending on the place. In most cases, the deeds will be in local languages and will encompass multi layers of right of use and ownership' (2010).

Moreover, a new system may exacerbate the problem in many places by 'officialising' inaccurate records, or records that have been falsified in anticipation of this current 'opportunity' by people with access to information.[30] What these proposed reforms do not adequately recognise is the social dimension of the problem, that insecurity is a reflection of the broader social and legal environment, characterised by institutionalised inequality among social groups, and that allows powerful players, both state officials and private investors, to act with impunity. Moreover, it is unrealistic to expect that decades, or even centuries, of land records can be sorted out in one go or that the computerisation of lands records and transactions will automatically end corruption.[31]

It is explicitly stated that the parliamentary bill is intended to serve as a 'model law' for all the States (and Union territories with legislature) in order to ensure uniformity across the national territory. The law would put in place a new institutional set-up in each State, including specific recommendations for a titling authority, led by high-ranking civil servants, a district-level 'Land Titling Tribunal', electronic records, etc. Some States have already implemented reforms in these areas, usually assisted by the central government, for instance the CARD system in Andhra Pradesh in the 1990s (Caseley 2004) and the Bhoomi system in Karnataka in the early 2000s (Lobo and Balakrishnan 2002).

In light of this discussion, which has highlighted some of the obstacles to litigation-free land titles, it is perhaps easier to understand why States choose to play the role of intermediary and why they are actively building up 'land banks', i.e., stocks of available land to have on hand for investment projects. When the government acquires land from private parties using official machinery, notably the Land Acquisition Act 1894, the title then becomes legally secure and the investor has the non-negligible advantage of purchasing land with no encumbrances.

Another aspect that comes into the picture when purchasing property is the issue of land use: land designated for agriculture cannot be converted to non-agricultural uses (industrial, commercial, etc.) without permission from the State or local government. Traditionally, land conversion has been an onerous task, requiring time, money and usually support from a powerful patron. However, when a government agency acquires the land, it can arrange for this conversion at the same time, for the benefit of the buyer. Moreover, the classification of land, as agricultural or non-agricultural, has a direct bearing on its sale price, with the former priced considerably lower than the latter. That is why property dealers, if they can successfully convert land use, stand to make large profits in a turnaround sale. Conversely, farmers tend to lose out, whether they are selling to private parties or to the government. In general, the worst possible scenario for a landowner is to be forced to sell land to the government because compensation is inevitably lower than market value. This is because compensation is fixed by law on the basis of recent land transactions and these are systematically under-reported to avoid paying the high transaction tax (stamp duty). Finally, the focus on land ownership tends to neglect the interests of the many other stakeholders who depend on land for livelihood or security.

5.6 State-level strategies for developing SEZs

As with industrial development generally, State governments have adopted different strategies with regard to land issues in their approach to SEZ development. In some cases, like the ones examined here, these strategies underscore the assertion of relatively autonomous subnational regulatory frameworks operating within a national policy framework. In effect, the centralised framework is permeated by subnational strategies; the result is a variegated pattern of SEZ regulation across national territory.

Perhaps more than any other State, Andhra Pradesh has actively promoted SEZ development. In 2013, it had the largest number of formally approved SEZ projects (109 out of 588) and also notified SEZs in the country (76 out of 386), almost one-fifth of the total (see Table 5.4 in the Appendix, Section 5.9). Likewise, it has more operational SEZs than any other State (37). Beyond just 'facilitating', the State has taken the lead in promoting its own SEZs, alone or in partnership with private sector investors.[32] Concerning the 56 notified SEZs in the State in 2009, the pattern was as follows: 12 were developed solely by the State's industrial infrastructure corporation (APIIC); one was a joint venture between APIIC and a consortium for 'Fab City', specialising in semi-conductors; two IT-related SEZs were promoted by urban development authorities; 21 were 'assisted' by APIIC; and the remaining 20 were promoted by private companies.[33] 'Assisted by APIIC', according to an official interviewed in 2009, meant the State government gave the land for the project, and this was calculated as equity participation (the State owned between 11 per cent and 26 per cent equity stake at that time), but these were not joint ventures per se.[34] This official clarified that the SEZs promoted by APIIC were not considered 'public' because APIIC is a semi-autonomous corporation and can generate profits.

Parastatal organisations, like APIIC, and its equivalent in other States, operate in a grey zone between the public and private spheres, and allow State governments much greater room to manoeuvre in their dealings with the private sector. In many cases, arrangements are negotiated and special purpose vehicles are elaborated in an entirely opaque manner. However, sometimes these dealings come into the public light, usually in the form of a scandal involving politicians. In 2011, one such high-profile financial scandal erupted with regard to an SEZ 'assisted by APIIC', Emaar Hills Township, and the Convention Center just next to it, both located on prime property at Gachi Bowli near HITEC City in Hyderabad's western suburbs. The Central Bureau of Investigation focused its enquiry on the conditions surrounding the decision to reduce APIIC's equity stake from 49 per cent to 26 per cent and to raise the share of Emaar Properties, a Dubai-based real estate company, from 51 per cent to 74 per cent. The assumption was that two successive chief ministers benefited from some kind of pay-off from the real estate company.[35] This example lends credence to the criticism that many SEZs, instead of producing goods and services for export, are simply an instrument for allowing private parties (and their willing partners in State government) to profit from property speculation. Equally important, it shows how the SEZ policy has opened up a whole range of opportunities for regional political elites who choose to exploit them through 'partnerships' of various kinds.

At the same time that it can act like a quasi-private corporation, the APIIC is also empowered to exercise classical state functions, most notably the right of eminent domain, which allows the state to requisition property from landowners in the name of 'public purpose'. This ambiguity of state action exercised through industrial development corporations, has been observed in many States. Tamil Nadu was one of the first States to commission its agencies to build up a land bank so as to be in a position to propose locations to private investors as opportunities arose. In 1997 it amended its land acquisition legislation (Acquisition of Land for Industrial Purposes Act of 1997) to speed up the process of acquiring land for large projects (Bajpai and Sachs 1999: 8). This restricted legal recourse to the compensation amount, and allowed the process to move forward without waiting for the litigation to run its course.

Andhra Pradesh's approach to SEZs can perhaps best be understood in the context of the 'regime' change that took place in the State in the 1990s, which has been characterised as a broad consensus among the major political parties in favour of liberalisation of the regional economy and an economic development model based on a larger role for private capital (Srinivasulu 2004). However, this 'model' should not be confused with a pure market economy model, as the above discussion makes clear: the State government is very actively involved

in the economy, acting as an entrepreneur or through public–private partnerships designed to ensure favourable terms for investors and, in some cases at
least, lucrative kick-backs for officials.

The case of Haryana, examined in the next section, illustrates State-level
implementation of the SEZ policy in greater detail. More importantly, it
demonstrates how a subnational state puts in place a custom-made regulatory
regime adapted to its economic development strategies and political imperatives.

A case study of Haryana's SEZ strategy[36]

In Haryana, the State government has followed a very different line of action
from that of Andhra Pradesh. It has not promoted its own SEZs, nor come
forward to assist private SEZ developers in acquiring land, with the exception
of the Reliance-Haryana SEZ, to which I will return in a moment. This
position may be linked to the State's already attractive geographical location
and strong economy, so it has no perceived *need* to promote SEZs. It may
also be linked to the fact that one of the State's industrial specialisations,
the automotive industry, is largely turned towards the domestic market, so
export zones are not a priority. This does not mean, however, that the State is
not aggressively pursuing industrial development and assisting investors with
land. Like Andhra Pradesh, the Haryana government, through its industrial
infrastructure development corporation, the HSIIDC, has been building up a
land bank, and developing large-scale industrial townships, in particular,
along the national highway connecting Delhi and Mumbai. Like other States
(see Chapter 4) Haryana changed its strategy towards industrial development
and started acquiring larger areas of land from the mid-1990s. Whereas
HSIIDC had acquired approximately 1,500 acres between 1973 and 1994, it
acquired 1,000 acres in 1995 alone (at Bawal for an industrial growth centre)
and in 1996 it began acquisition of 1,800 acres for an Industrial Model
Township in Manesar, just 35km south of Delhi.[37]

With regard to SEZs, Haryana welcomed the national Act in 2005 and was
one of the first States to follow up with its own legislation the same year.
There has been a good political relationship between the State and central
governments, both led by the Congress party since 2005. Perhaps in order to
demonstrate its enthusiasm for the national SEZ policy, the State government
announced plans in 2005 to develop an SEZ project 'New Gurgaon', well
situated in the bustling satellite city of Gurgaon, contiguous to Delhi. The land
had been acquired during the previous administration from private landowners, through expropriation for 'public purpose'. The following paragraphs
describe in some detail this project and analyse the interplay of economic and
political strategies deployed across various scales.

In December 2005 the State government signed an MOU with Reliance
Industries, India's largest private corporation, for jointly setting up a large-
scale SEZ in Haryana. At this point in time, the State had not yet decided, or
at least not publicly, to bring into this partnership the attractive plot of land it

had acquired in central Gurgaon. This controversial decision was announced six months later when the joint venture was formed: the partners announced their plans to develop India's largest multi-purpose SEZ on 10,000 hectares of land, called Reliance-Haryana SEZ (RHSEZ), comprising manufacturing, services and agri-business, complete with cargo airport and power plant. The press relayed the gargantuan projections of investments (Rs 100,000 crore or €14.6 billion) and employment (500,000 jobs). Straddling the Gurgaon and Jhajjar districts of Haryana, the project was strategically placed in relation to Delhi, the country's fastest growing urban agglomeration, with access to the national highway and the international airport.[38] Mukesh Ambani, the CEO of Reliance, was quoted as saying: 'The challenge for us is to think in terms of "Team India", where we can compete globally with countries such as China, Malaysia, Singapore, and Dubai (...) We will attract capital to our SEZ in a way that is most competitive. We will create an infrastructure showpiece that can catapult India into the mainstream of global investment.'[39]

The government's decision to drop the 'New Gurgaon' SEZ project and enter into a high-profile joint venture with Reliance provoked immediate protest. On one hand, the landowners in Gurgaon whose properties had been acquired were furious that after using the 'public purpose' clause, the government sold the land to Reliance, a Fortune 500 company run by India's wealthiest individual, for practically the same undervalued price for which it had been acquired.[40] On the other hand, farmers in Jhajjar District were surprised to see their lands comprised in the project and worried that a joint venture might mean forced acquisition by the State government. Opposition parties in the State were quick to seize the opportunity to throw their support behind these two sets of stakeholders, whose mobilisation is analysed in Section 5.7 next.

At about the same time, no doubt in response to this negative publicity, the State government put in place a series of policies designed to significantly enhance compensation and improve the overall rehabilitation package for 'land acquisition oustees'. This policy response, when analysed in relation to the overall political economy of the State, illustrates an explicit territorialisation strategy prompted by the national SEZ policy and by the liberalisation agenda more generally. Taken together, they form the basis of the State's custom-made regulatory regime, operating within the boundaries of its jurisdiction, which seeks to condition the interface between the State government and private investors.

In May 2006, Haryana's Department of Industries finalised a policy dealing with 'acquisition of land for private deployment and in public–private partnership for setting up of SEZs, Technology Cities, Industrial Parks and Industrial Model Townships, etc.'. As this long title suggests, it integrates the SEZ concept as part of the policy landscape but is not restricted to it. It outlines the conditions under which the government intends to assist private investors, according to the size of the project, its specific location within the State's territorial boundaries (e.g., the National Capital Region, designated 'backward areas', etc.), and whether or not the government is a partner in the venture. In the case where the State's equity share is 26 per cent or more, it will acquire the entire plot of land for the project. The policy also outlines the responsibilities of private investors who are assisted by the government, and here we observe the terms and conditions that were applied to Reliance. Significantly, they include a number of aspects that usually fall squarely within the purview of state action, such as taking charge of rehabilitation measures for affected people, providing essential services for relocated villages, running training institutes, offering employment to at least one member of each family whose land is acquired for the project, and a quota of 25 per cent of employment reserved for Haryana residents.[41] This final 'condition', which appears more a pious (and popular) wish than an enforceable provision, refers to the fact that Haryana's factories employ primarily labour from other States. Although factory managers have a preference for hiring migrants because they are less integrated in local society and hence easier to handle, this pattern also reflects Haryana's relatively high standard of living: many Haryana natives find factory wages simply too low.

Taking a step further its efforts to ensure better compensation, comparable to market rates,[42] in April 2007 the State government issued a schedule of minimum floor rates for different areas of the State to be paid by the government in the case of expropriation under the Land Acquisition Act 1894. The National Capital Region in particular continues to be the object of intense real estate speculation and to keep pace with the market, the government revised the initial floor rates in November 2010, doubling them in Gurgaon from Rs 2 million per acre to Rs 4 million per acre. Rates in neighbouring Faridabad were increased from Rs 1.6 million per acre to Rs 3 million per acre during the same period. In other regions of Haryana, outside the National Capital Region, rates were revised from Rs 800,000 per acre to Rs 1.2 million per acre (GoH 2010). This policy of issuing differential floor rates, which recognises and formalises the differentiation of the State's territory, expresses a territorialisation strategy in relation to an economic development objective. It is responsive to landowners, but at the same time underscores the State government's intention to continue to build up a land bank in strategic places in the State to facilitate capital investments. This subnational strategy contributes to the construction of new scales, which are adapted to capitalist restructuring very much in keeping with the transformations observed in Europe by Brenner (1998).

Another key policy concerns the rehabilitation and resettlement of land-owners ('land acquisition oustees'). It provides for additional compensation to be paid every year for 33 years in the form of 'annuity', on the basis of a fixed amount per acre, to be increased annually (GoH 2007; GoH 2010). Initially fixed at Rs 15,000 per acre, to be increased by Rs 500 per year, it was enhanced in 2010 to Rs 21,000 per acre per year, with annual increases of Rs 750. Significantly, land acquired for an SEZ is considered a special case, and the annuity is *double* the amount (Rs 30,0000 per acre, increased to Rs 42,000 per acre in 2010), to be paid by the private promoter. In addition, depending on the amounts of land given up, landowners can claim rights to plots of land held by public agencies either for residential purposes (e.g., if 75 per cent of an owner's total holdings are acquired) or to commercial plots.

This policy, which is the first of its kind in India, has captured the attention of politicians and policy-makers in Delhi who were quick to advocate the 'Haryana model' for the whole country.[43] Because it addresses the demands of one key set of stakeholders, landowners, this Rehabilitation and Resettlement model was seen as a first step to making the SEZ policy more politically sustainable on the ground in the medium to long term. This was clearly the calculation of the Haryana government, which was also concerned with calming agitation around the RHSEZ in the short run. As we will see now, a section of Haryana's farmers were able to organise collective action against the government's SEZ policy.

5.7 Anti-SEZ mobilisation and policy responsiveness

Practically every State with an SEZ project has witnessed some amount of protest, although the magnitude of the movements, the types of actors involved, and the outcomes have varied tremendously.[44] Social movements reflect to some degree the relative conduciveness of the local political environment to allow or enable collective action. As argued in Chapter 4, each State has distinct social institutions which have evolved historically and which condition the scope for collective action. Likewise, a State's response to social mobilisation varies, as it depends on the particular configurations of its political economy.

Goa offers no doubt the most spectacular case of mobilisation since it resulted in the cancellation of *all* the SEZ projects in the State. According to Solano Da Silva (forthcoming), the anti-SEZ activism, which developed into a broad-based movement in the course of 2007, mobilised on two main issues: identity loss and land appropriation by non-Goans. It can be recalled that Goa is the smallest State in India in terms of both population (fewer than 1.5 million in 2011) and landmass and it has a distinct cultural identity linked to the long Portuguese presence. The massive employment projections put forward by the SEZ promoters, around 300,000, were used by activists to argue that the State would be invaded by non-Goans. Likewise, the amount of territory – and the fact that the State had agreed to supply or acquire land for transformation into SEZs – were presented as a threat to the Goan lifestyle and environment. Moreover, the opposition BJP succeeded in making SEZs an electoral issue in a by-election, which further drew attention to the case and forced the government to take a public stand. Finally, in a matter of six months, the movement built up momentum and maintained pressure on the State government until it finally announced it would cancel all SEZ projects in the State. The anti-SEZ movement very effectively tapped into the specific features of Goan society to broaden the base for mobilisation and ultimately prevail on the State government to incline to its demands.

The situation in Haryana is radically different in several respects. The protests have centred around one project, albeit a very large one, the RHSEZ, and have largely focused on the amount of compensation, rather than on the SEZ principle or industrialisation generally.[45] Two separate groups have been mobilising to oppose RHSEZ, each with their own sets of demands and grievances. In Gurgaon, individuals whose lands were acquired by the government have filed a lawsuit and formed an organisation to contest the grounds on which their lands were acquired, as well as the change in purpose. They are claiming enhanced compensation, and an equity share in the project. In Jhajjar District, one group of farmers is trying to convince others not to sell to Reliance; in doing so, they have used various arguments: the purchase price offered, duplicity on the part of Reliance in particular regarding the promises of employment, long-term security, etc.[46] These idioms—mistrust of government and private industrialists, security of landed property—resonate with people's perceptions and have been effective to some extent.

In Jhajjar, the local ad hoc association, which calls itself the *Kisan Mazdoor Sangharsh Samiti* (KMSS), or the Council for Farmers' and Workers' Struggles, brought together members from the approximately twenty-four villages affected by the project. Despite its name, the association is primarily a network of Jat landowners, most if not all of whom belong to the locally dominant Guliya clan. Their organisational structure appears to rely to a large extent on the traditional caste panchayat system. In addition, they have used their pre-existing ties to farmers' unions to try to sensitise farmers elsewhere in the State and country about SEZ and thereby build up pressure on the government. For instance, in April 2008 they organised with the Haryana unit of the *Bharatiya Krishak Samaj* (Indian Farmers' Forum), a week-long *kisan padyatra* (farmers' march). The focus of the protest was directed towards the 'anti-farmer' policies of the central and State governments, and 'land-grabbing' on the part of the State government for SEZ projects. The KMSS's president criticised the Haryana government for 'acting as a broker (*dalal*) in the interests of corporate houses'.[47] The capacity to link up with farmers' unions, which have traditionally played a strong role in Haryana politics, has most certainly strengthened the movement. It provides a contrast to many other anti-SEZ movements, which are restricted to the affected localities. Even though they insist that their association is apolitical, the leaders of KMSS have links to the opposition INLD party,[48] which gives the movement additional organisational strength as well as financial backing.

It is significant that although quite effective at networking with farmers groups, including from outside the State, the KMSS has been less successful in incorporating other local groups, such as tenants and agricultural labourers, who also stand to lose from the establishment of the RHSEZ. Because of this, the movement's base remains quite narrow, in contrast to the broad-based mobilisation in Goa, for instance, and has probably limited its effectiveness. One explanation may be the social divide in Haryana, compounded by deep-seated caste animosity. Caste consciousness is considered very strong and there have been cases of caste-related conflicts, including in Jhajjar district.[49] Dominant landowning groups in Haryana, Jats in particular, who constitute about a quarter of the electorate, tend to monopolise social and political power at all levels. Here the overlap of caste and class is particularly evident. Jat politicians have explicitly favoured their community, which has aggravated non-Jat groups and reinforced divisions. An election survey held in 2004 reported that the perception of Jat favouritism was shared by a majority of voters (80 per cent of Dalits), even 27 per cent of Jats in the survey agreed to this statement (Joshi, Rai 2009). In this context, it is evident that state strategies have, over time, contributed to shaping the stakes of ongoing socio-political struggles by defending the interests of particular (landed) interests.

As this discussion suggests, historically rooted factors are strong determinants of collective action, but it is important to underscore that in addition to these inherited social institutions, current policies also shape the conditions for collective action. For instance, the measures aimed at enhancing compensation rates and providing annuity are clearly aimed at appeasing dominant landowning groups and accommodating their interests. In doing so, the political establishment reiterates their position as key social partners in the State's economic development strategies, thereby reinforcing their privileged position within the territorial political system. So although the anti-SEZ mobilisation has not led to a change in the State government's SEZ policy or its strategy of amassing a land bank for industrialisation and urban infrastructure projects, it has nonetheless generated a policy response favourable to landed interests. Other social groups likely to lose out have not received equal attention. The revised Rehabilitation and Resettlement policy of 2010 includes a scheme for landless workers and rural artisans focused on technical training and preferential treatment for employment in new units, but the modalities are not spelled out in any detail, in particular how potential beneficiaries would be identified (GoH 2010: 7581). Moreover, the policy delegates key aspects of rehabilitation to the private sector, '(w)herever land is acquired for the Private Developers, they would be required to make arrangements for creation and up-gradation of the skill-sets of the affected persons and preference in employment of the affected persons/their dependants in the projects set-up over such land' (ibid.: 7582). Given the generally 'business-friendly' approach of the State government to industries, it seems unlikely that the implementation of such provisions would be enforced.

Policy response to policy 'losers'

In his analysis of the SEZ Act, Rob Jenkins argues that political elites in New Delhi expected opposition to the policy but were confident that dissent would be fragmented, both geographically and with regard to the basis for the opposition (ideological, technical, etc.), and could thus be managed (2011: 54). In particular they were counting on assistance from State governments, since ultimately the latter would be in charge of implementation and policy fine-tuning:

> Most [S]tate governments, they reasoned, would want to attract SEZ promoters–because they wanted to create jobs and build their economies,

and for less public-spirited reasons as well. Political managers in Delhi were confident of the ability of [S]tate-level politicians to arrange accommodations between contending groups and to compensate policy 'losers'.

(Ibid.)

In Haryana, political pragmatism has meant attending to the interests of landowning groups, which are demographically and economically powerful. In many respects, Haryana's recent policies take into account the evolution of Haryana's economy and society away from an agrarian base. Many landowners, especially around the National Capital Region and Chandigarh, have diversified their economic activities outside of agriculture and depend increasingly on the urban economy for their livelihood. Landed castes in Haryana are pulled in opposite directions by a classic modernisation dilemma: on one hand they identify with farmers (and the farm lobby); on the other hand they no longer earn their living exclusively from agriculture. Already many families rent out their land to tenant farmers and the younger generations are not engaged in farming. Like Punjab, Haryana's agricultural sector is capital intensive, as a result of land consolidation in the 1950s (Gill 2001) and the green revolution in the 1960s, and no longer resembles a peasant economy.[50] Although the 'farm' lobby remains strong, it no longer represents only farming interests, and there is a support base for an economic development policy based on industrialisation and urbanisation, especially real estate development. This is especially the case in the territory falling within the NCR, where all the key elements of a classic 'growth machine' can be found.[51] In metropolitan Delhi, the growth machine brings together property developers, landowners eager to see land values continue to appreciate, and politicians with interests in urban expansion.[52] In turn, the State government is investing heavily in this area in the form of large infrastructure projects, e.g., the Kundli–Manesar–Palwal Expressway. The State government's partnership in the RHSEZ megaproject, with a global corporate group, can be interpreted as the culmination of a strategy geared on adjusting to geo-economic opportunities. In addition to prestige, the State government hoped to generate income from its partnership.[53.]

This case study illustrates a dual process of rescaling occurring in Haryana. On one hand, the regional economy is rescaled and its geographical centre of gravity has shifted to Delhi and the NCR, one of India's most dynamic economic regions, and this has in turn prompted the State to reconfigure its territorial policies. For instance, subnational industrial policies have targeted specific places for regulation as part of a larger strategy aimed at enhancing territorial assets. On the other hand, Haryana politics have become rescaled over the last quarter-century and regional political stakes are increasingly articulated around the NCR, reflecting the importance of this area for the entire regional economy. As Table 5.3 makes clear, the NCR weighs heavily in terms of number of factories and industrial employment. In basic electoral terms too, 35 out of 90 seats in the Haryana legislature are in the NCR, allowing voters in this area to shape political outcomes for the entire State.[54]

Table 5.3 Industrial growth in Haryana and in Haryana's territory comprised in the National Capital Region (NCR)

		2002	*2007*	*Notes*
Number of registered industrial units (under Factory Act):	in Haryana as a whole	8,974	9,954	Increased by 980 units in five years, of which 661 are in the NCR (67% of total)
	in NCR	3,713 (41% of total)	4,374 (44% of total)	
Number of employees in industrial units:	in Haryana as a whole	540,338	681,416	Increased share of industrial employment reflects large size of units in NCR
	in NCR	293,939 (54% of total)	411,343 (60% of total)	

Source: Data collected by the author from the Labour Commissioner, Government of Haryana, December 2008

5.8 Conclusion

The aim of the chapter was not to evaluate the economic rationale or performance of India's SEZ policy but rather to analyse the politics of this controversial policy with particular attention to multi-level governance and state spatial strategies.

It was argued that the current SEZ policy illustrates a rescaling strategy *par excellence* in that it reconfigures the scalar organisation of economic activity – promoting the creation of enclaves dedicated to the production of goods and services for export – and at the same time creates new 'coordinates' of state territorial organisation (Brenner 1998). In substance, the policy allows for the parcelling of national territory and configures a special regulatory framework for governing these spaces. Figuratively, such exceptional spaces are extracted from national territorial fabric and are not intended to interact with the real economy. By proposing an attractive investment package and a largely deregulated environment for operations, the aim is to facilitate global flows of capital via transnational firms and via the Indian private sector, and to facilitate the latter's capacity to penetrate international markets for goods and services.

In the rhetoric surrounding the SEZ policy,[55] the imagined zones appear like clean slates, dedicated spaces for the production of goods and services totally unaffected by their surrounding environment in the broad sense: physical, social, political. In this sense, the policy gives expression to a modernist fantasy of an economy built on a *tabula rasa* (Bach 2011). The analysis in this chapter has shown how far that representation is from reality. Existing institutional and regulatory layers at every spatial scale shape the modalities for implementing the policy; likewise, existing patterns of socio-political relations and legacies of political mobilisation influence the reception of SEZs and condition, in turn, the policy response of central and State governments to protest movements and to pressure from organised interest groups.

In this sense the SEZ policy provides a window onto territorialisation processes occurring across the country, which are always contested, incomplete processes. The notion of a territorialisation *continuum* (Dubresson and Jaglin 2005) suggests a range of possibilities, giving expression to ongoing processes that arise from political strategies and power struggles among social actors at various scales. At the national scale, the policy clearly aims to create a unique framework for zones across the country, all governed by the same rules under a centralised command structure. In doing so, it effectively proposes to remove some economic activities from the 'domestic economy' *and* to remove regulatory oversight from State-level officials. It expresses a strategy to rescale geographies of statehood by redefining state spaces within the federal framework. It delegates implementation to State governments, who are expected to apply the law unquestioningly. In the SEZ fantasy of the central state, subnational states are submissive, embracing the 'letter and spirit' of the SEZ law in a disinterested manner. In reality, this attempt to delegate is contested, on one hand, by State governments asserting their prerogative to exercise authority over their political territories and, on the other hand, by social groups who mobilise to oppose SEZs and in doing so make claims to appropriate and control local space.

The implementation process, involving different levels of government as well as various departments at each level, has proved to be very complex. The analysis has shown how the passage of the policy through the ad hoc SEZ governance structure, mediated by federal institutions, sets in motion processes of state spatial rescaling, reconfiguring the scalar organisation of economic regulation. A *national* policy, the rules of which apply to the whole country, it nonetheless concerns only specific spatially delineated zones. Subnational states, with territorial jurisdiction over these spaces, find themselves directly confronted with the implementation of the policy, starting with the issue of land and extending to the terms of agreement with investors (e.g., development charges) and labour conditions inside the zones. Although subordinate to the central state in the formal SEZ governance structure, State governments can claim state space and shape the implementation process and thereby the conditions for capital accumulation. The example of State-level agencies intervening to supply land to private investors – complete with unencumbered titles and zoned for non-agricultural purposes – was a compelling illustration of this.

States have elaborated very different strategies with regard to the SEZ policy, and these strategies encounter those emanating from the central state, converging or diverging, with direct repercussions for what happens on the ground. At the same time, state strategies meet those of private actors, landowners, firms, residents and stakeholders of various kinds. Although the modalities deployed were very different, the cases of Andhra Pradesh and Haryana both illustrated autonomous processes of appropriation of the policy and assertion of subnational territorial control.

More than any other State in the country, Andhra Pradesh has forcefully promoted SEZs in its territory. This strategy is consistent with its aggressive style of territorial marketing noted in earlier chapters. Its political leadership opted to directly develop SEZs via semiautonomous public agencies and to 'assist' private firms in many others projects by providing equity stake in the form of land, thereby playing an entrepreneurial role. Involvement in public–private partnerships allows the subnational state to operate in a grey zone, with considerable room to negotiate deals in an opaque manner. In this respect, the Andhra Pradesh government has used the SEZ policy as a 'privatisation practice', to borrow Hibou's term (2004), that allows it to redraw the lines between public and private spheres.

In the case of Haryana, the State government was largely hands-off with regard to the many small IT SEZs in Gurgaon, but it became a joint venture partner with Reliance to build a mega-SEZ in metropolitan Delhi.[56] In part because of protests prompted by that decision, it drafted specific rules for land acquisition for SEZ projects, issued a schedule of compensation rates in the event of expropriation, and devised an original rehabilitation and resettlement policy, thereby significantly shaping the conditions for SEZ development and industrial investment more broadly in the State. These custom-made regulations are illustrations of locally scaled practices that produce the conditions under which capital is fixed.

5.9 Appendix

Table 5.4 State-wise distribution of SEZ projects, April 2013

State	Formal approvals	In-principle approvals	Notified SEZs
Andhra Pradesh	109	6	76
Chandigarh	2	0	2
Chhattisgarh	2	1	1
Delhi	3	0	0
Dadra & Nagar Haveli	2	0	1
Goa	7	0	3
Gujarat	47	7	32
Haryana	46	3	35
Himachal Pradesh	0	0	0
Jharkhand	1	0	1
Karnataka	62	1	41
Kerala	29	0	20
Madhya Pradesh	19	2	6
Maharashtra	103	16	64
Nagaland	2	0	1
Odisha	10	1	5
Pondicherry	1	1	0
Punjab	8	0	2
Rajasthan	10	1	10
Tamil Nadu	69	6	53
Uttar Pradesh	34	1	21
Uttarakhand	2	0	1
West Bengal	20	3	11
Grand total	*588*	*49*	*386*

Source: www.sezindia.nic.in (consulted 27 April 2013)

N
△

Chandigarh
Mohali Dehradun
National
Capital
Region*
Jaipur
Gwalior
Aransol
Jabalpur Bolpur
Gandhinagar Bhopal
Ahmedabad Chindwara Bilhai Bhardhaman Kolkata
Indore
Vadodara
Daman Pardi Khordha Bhubaneshwar
Mumbai
Pune
Hyderabad Vishakhâpatnam
Kurnool Kakinada
Goa
Thirupati
Bangalore
Mangalore Mandya Chennai
Kazaragod Khrisnagiri
Kannur Mysore Salem Pondicherry
Khozikode Coimbatore Thiruchirapalli
Ernakulam Madurai
Alappuzha
Thiruvananthapuram Thirunelveli

63
48
35
19
8
1

0   300 km

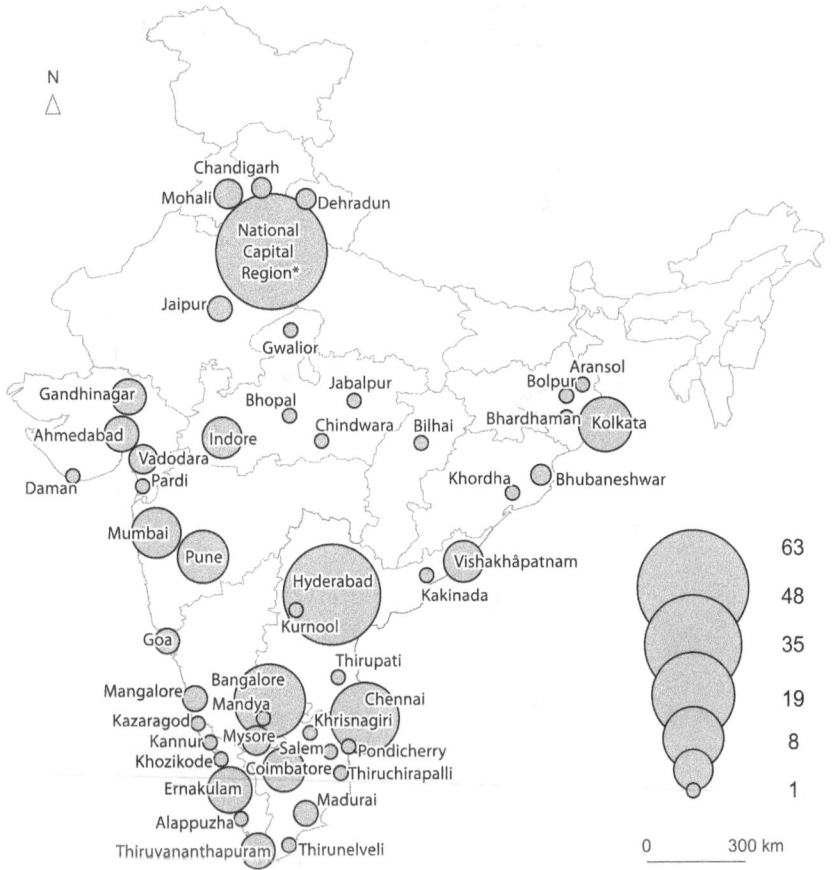

*The National Capital Region includes the districts of Gurgaon, Faridabad   ————— *Borders of States and Territories*
and Sonipat in Haryana, and Noida and Greater Noida in Uttar Pradesh

Map 5.1 Location of SEZ projects in the IT sector, 2006–10
Source: Ministry of Commerce and Industry, SEZ Board of Approval, www.sezindia.
nic.in, 2006–10. Map Design: Divya Leducq, 2013.

Distribution of the 582 Approved SEZ Projects in India by District.
November 2011.

Distribution of 582 SEZ by district (616 districts)

Districts having no SEZ (486 districts)
Districts having 1 SEZ (58 districts)
Districts having betwen 2 and 7 SEZ (54 districts)
Districts having 8 and 40 SEZ (18 districts)
- Geometrical Interval classification method (ArcGis10.0)

Source: Ministry of Commerce & Industry,
Government of India, November 2011.
http://sezindia.nic.in/index.asp

CEIAS - EHESS/CNRS, ©Catherine Finetin, CNRS 2013.

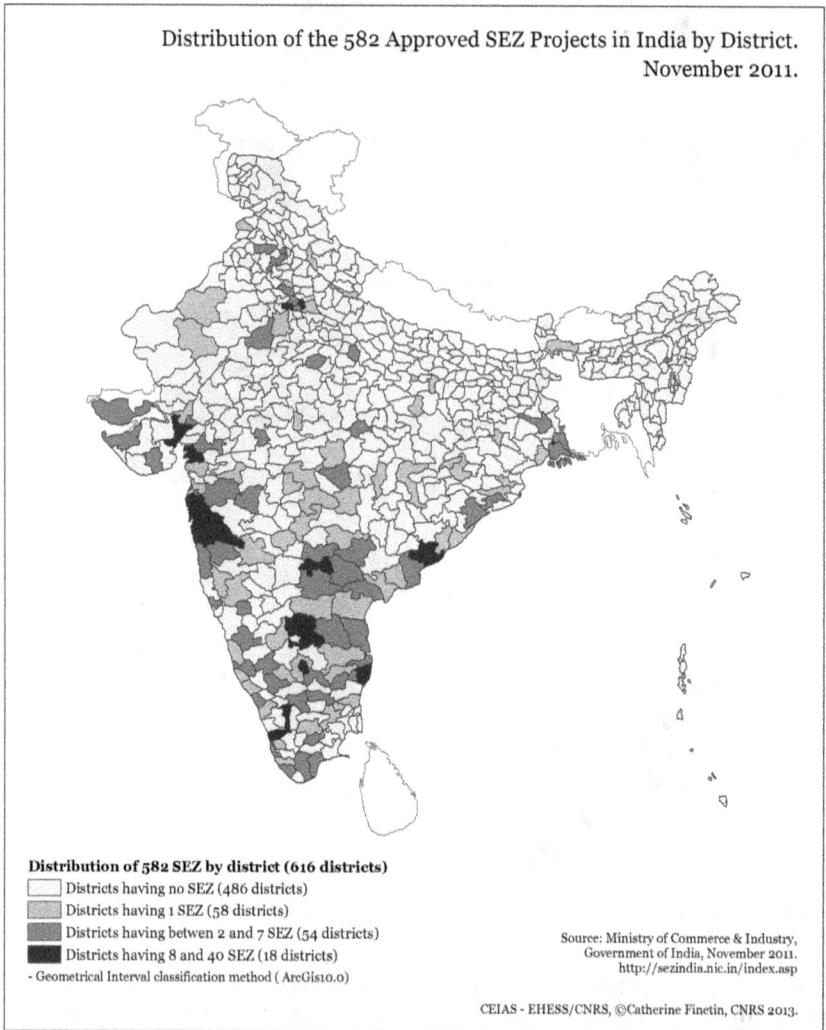

Map 5.2 District-wise distribution of SEZs, November 2011

Notes

1 Despite their weak performance in exports, some economists have argued that early EPZs made a long-term contribution to Indian industry by facilitating the insertion of domestic firms in global value chains. See for instance Aggarwal (2012: 172).

2 See the government website: www.sezindia.nic.in/about-introduction.asp, last consulted 30 October 2013.

3 In recent years, special zones have proliferated in and around Chinese cities, the expression of local economic development strategies and interregional competition. See Cunyi *et al.* (2012).

4 Total employment in all SEZs, including those converted from EPZs, was 714,412 (source: GoI n.d.: 5).

5 One-quarter of the world's manufacturing takes place within some 5,000 zones, which provide employment for over 41 million people according to the International Labour Organization, cited by Jonathan Bach (2011).

6 We saw in Chapter 4, with reference to financial sector reforms, that the central state has the capacity to take the lead on reforms when it chooses to do so, and design incentives for convincing State governments to follow.

7 See the official SEZ website: www.sezindia.nic.in/about-introduction.asp, last consulted 30 October 2013.

8 See Arora (2007).

9 Four companies were directly concerned by this amendment: Reliance Industries (Jhajjar, Haryana, 10,000 hectares), Gujarat Positra Port Infrastructure Ltd (Panvel, Maharashtra, 10,000 hectares), DLF Ltd (Gurgaon, Haryana, 8,097 hectares) and Omaxe Ltd (Alwar, Rajasthan, 6,070 hectares) (Mody 2010: 7).

10 As Anjali Mody (2010) points out, this allowed the merger of three SEZs of the Adani Group into a single SEZ in Gujarat. The minutes of 30th Board of Approvals meeting dated 22 December 2008, referred to this decision: http://sezindia. nic.in/writereaddata/BOA/Minutesof30thBOA22122008.pdf.

11 See *Business Standard*, 'Clarification sought on profits from SEZ units', Thursday, 21 February 2008.

12 See CNBC-TV18, 'FinMin says SEZ direct tax benefits not WTO compliant', Sunday, 24 February 2008, www.moneycontrol.com/news/business/finmin-says-sez-direct-tax-benefits-not-wto-compliant-327580.html.

13 The findings in this section derive largely from a collective research project covering eleven Indian States. Based at the Centre de Sciences Humaines and the Centre for Policy Research in Delhi, it was funded by the Ford Foundation (2008–10). An edited volume is forthcoming with Oxford University Press, New Delhi: see Jenkins *et al.* (forthcoming). The material on Haryana is from my chapter: see Kennedy (forthcoming).

14 West Bengal and Madhya Pradesh in 2003, Gujarat in 2004, and in the months following the passage of the central Act in mid-2005 Tamil Nadu and Haryana passed State-level SEZ legislation, joined by Punjab in 2009.

15 Section 49 of the SEZ Act explicitly states that the central government may not make any changes in 'matters relating to trade unions, industrial and labour disputes, welfare of labour including conditions of work, provident funds, employers' liability, workmen's compensation, invalidity and old age pensions and maternity benefits applicable in any Special Economic Zones' (GoI 2005: section 49(1)).

16 Gujarat prides itself on its 'business-friendly' investment climate and these 'labour unfriendly' clauses bear witness to the social compromises prevailing in that State more generally. Comparatively speaking, Gujarat ranks low in terms of industrial disputes and person-days lost due to strikes, which can serve as a proxy measure for the relative strength of organised labour there.

17 According to a guide for investors published in 2008 by the Export Promotion Council for EOUs and SEZs (EPCES), six States had declared SEZs to be public utilities: Andhra Pradesh, Madhya Pradesh, Maharashtra, West Bengal, Karnataka and Uttar Pradesh. See EPCES (2008).

18 This was done in Andhra Pradesh, West Bengal, Karnataka and Uttar Pradesh. See EPCES (2008).

19 Interview with Mr Suresh Chandra Panda, Development Commissioner for the northern zone (consisting of eight States and the Union Territory of Chandigarh), 3 July 2009, Delhi.

20 An official of the Andhra Pradesh government related that the Labour Ministry in New Delhi initially rejected the clause in that State's SEZ bill delegating these powers on the grounds that it would concentrate too much authority in the hands of the Development Commissioner ('both prosecutor and judge'). Interview with the Principal Secretary, Ministry of Industries and Commerce, Government of Andhra Pradesh, 15 October 2008, Hyderabad.

21 Interview with the Development Commissioner in charge of the northern zone, 3 July 2009, Delhi.

22 This transpired from interviews with several key officials in the Ministry of Commerce, conducted in 2008 and 2009.

23 Interview with the Development Commissioner in charge of the northern zone, 15 January 2010, Delhi.

24 Phone interview with the Secretary, Department of Industries, Government of Haryana, 15 January 2010.

25 See *Business Standard*, 'Gurgaon SEZ developers run into water hurdle', 20 January 2011.

26 Material for this section (5.5) is based largely on Kennedy and Vijayabaskar (2011).

27 See www.prsindia.org/uploads/media/draft/Draft%20Final%20Model%20Land%20 Titling%20Act-04.5.10.pdf. A revised version of the bill was proposed in 2011, and it is interesting to note that the clause 'with title guarantee and indemnification against losses due to inaccuracies in property titles' was removed. It states only: 'to provide for the establishment, administration and management of a system of conclusive property titles through registration of immovable properties' (2011: 1), available at www.prsindia.org/.

28 This statement also disappeared from the 2011 version.

29 Such as Hernando de Soto for urban land titles. USAID sponsored a study on reforming the land title registration system in Delhi, prepared by the Urban Institute in Washington, DC. The final report, dated 2007, offers concrete recommendations. See www.usaid.gov/in/our_work/pdfs/land_title_reg_system.pdf.

30 For a critical assessment of Karnataka's Bhoomi programme, see Benjamin *et al.* (2007).

31 Two separate studies of programmes aimed at computerising land records and transactions concluded that they did not eliminate corruption. For Andhra Pradesh, see Caseley (2004); for Karnataka, see Lobo and Balakrishnan (2002).

32 Out of ninety-six planned zones in 2009, almost 60 per cent were to be developed by public agencies alone or in partnership with private promoters. Information collected at the APIIC office by the author in October 2008 and April 2009.

33 Information collected at the APIIC office by the author on 1 April 2009.

34 Same as previous note.

35 See 'Naidu, YSR cut state's stake in Emaar', *Times of India*, 16 November 2011.

36 This case material is based on fieldwork conducted in Haryana during 2008–10. It is presented in greater detail in Jenkins *et al.* (forthcoming).

37 Interview with the Industries Secretary, Government of Haryana, Chandigarh, 19 November 2008.

38 See 'Reliance Ventures, HSIIDC to set up 25,000-acre SEZ in Haryana', *Business Line*, 20 June 2006.

39 See 'Reliance Ventures, HSIIDC to set up 25,000-acre SEZ in Haryana', *Business Line*, 20 June 2006.

40 According to a press report, the Government of Haryana received Rs 360 crore, to cover interest and administrative costs, against the Rs 300 crore it paid out as compensation. See 'Reliance Ventures, HSIIDC to set up 25,000-acre SEZ in Haryana', *Business Line*, 20 June 2006. Many observers and people interviewed speculated that Reliance actually paid much more money, unofficially.

41 I was not able to confirm whether the committee that was supposed to monitor the compliance of these Terms & Conditions, was ever formed, nor to what extent these Terms & Conditions have been implemented.

42 Author interview with the Commissioner & Secretary Industries Department, Government of Haryana, Chandigarh, 19 November 2008.

43 See 'Farmers to be protected in land deals: Sonia', *Economic Times*, 1 October 2008.

44 Analysis is this section is largely based on the eleven-State study mentioned in note 14; that study explicitly addressed subnational social movements and anti-SEZ mobilisation, and sought to analyse them in their respective State contexts. See Jenkins *et al.* (forthcoming).

45 Notwithstanding, one movement leader from Jhajjar spoke about the threat of SEZs to food security.

46 Author interview with Captain Satvir Singh Guliya, New Delhi, 25 March 2009. Unless otherwise indicated, the information on KMSS in this section is based on this interview.

47 See the press release issued at the press conference in IWPC in Delhi on 24 April 2008, http://asianfarmers.org/?p=454.

48 The president of the KMSS, Chaudhary Mahavir Guliya, is closely associated with the INLD. Interview with author, Jhajjar, 7 March 2009.

49 According to the sociologist Surinder S. Jodhka, 'Nowhere in north-western India is the discourse of caste as prevalent as it is in Haryana' (Jodhka 1999: 2218). See also Jodhka and Dhar (2003) for an analysis of a particularly violent case of caste violence in Jhajjar district in 2002, in which five Dalit men were killed by a mob for allegedly slaughtering a cow.

50 I am grateful to Surinder S. Jodhka, Professor of Sociology, Jawaharlal Nehru University, for insights into Haryana's economy and society. Personal communication, Delhi, 20 January 2010.

51 See Molotch (1976).

52 Politicians can make easy gains by acting as intermediaries between local landowners and property developers and industrialists.

53 'The Haryana Chief Minister, Mr Bhupinder Singh Hooda, said that the revenue of the State would rise by Rs 10,000 crore per year on account of the project.' See 'Reliance Ventures, HSIIDC to set up 25,000-acre SEZ in Haryana', *Business Line*, 20 June 2006.

54 See 'NCR holds key to Haryana winner', *Times of India*, 22 October 2009.

55 See for instance Menon and Mitra (2009).

56 In June 2013, the SEZ Board of Approvals announced its decision to denotify the RHSEZ. See 'Government allows RIL to surrender SEZ in India', *Economy Times*, 24 June 2013. Earlier, press reports related that the government of Haryana had requested Reliance to return the land it had bought after failing to realise the SEZ project, even after six years. See 'Reliance "agreeing" to give back SEZ land to govt: CM', *Times of India*, 3 March 2013.

6   State spaces and changing urban scales

This chapter discusses state spatial strategies that are constructing or redefining urban scales in India, with regard to economic and political activities, on the one hand, and to creating new state spaces, on the other. Building on arguments presented above, this chapter examines the modalities by which both the central state and regional States intervene in urban spaces, processes that have intensified since the 1990s. Indeed, after several decades of relative stability of its internal administrative arrangements, India is currently witnessing renewed interest for territorial reform, illustrated most remarkably by two constitutional amendments in the mid-1990s aimed at empowering local governments (rural and urban). Numerous other experiments are being carried out throughout the country, at various spatial scales. Contrasting examples of territorial reorganisation shall be examined here including one that involves the subdivision of municipal area and another that clubs together previously autonomous political units into one new territorial entity.

Devising specific regulatory frameworks for influencing socio-economic relations in spatially delineated urban spaces is another type of strategy that will be discussed, on the basis of an example of intentional industrial clustering. State spatial strategies also take the form of direct interventions in the urban built environment via public investments in infrastructure and through service provision, both of which increasingly involve partnerships with private sector actors.

These various types of state action can be analysed on several levels. They reconfigure the territorial organisation of the state, they aim to influence the geographies of economic activities, and they seek to regulate and reorganise the social and economic relations that define economic governance in a given context. It is useful to recall that state space can be conceptualised in two ways: (1) A 'narrow' definition refers to state territoriality, 'an ensemble of juridico-political institutions and regulatory capacities grounded in the territorialization of political power' (Brenner *et al.* 2003: 7). Devolution of power to a pre-existing political 'level' and creation of new territorial entities are examples of state rescaling in this narrow sense. Another conception of state spatiality (2), termed 'integral', designates 'the territory-, place-, and scale-specific ways in which state institutions are mobilized to regulate social relations and to

Table 6.1 Case studies engaging with two conceptions of state spatiality

'Narrow' sense	74th CAA – ward committees	Constitution of 'Greater Hyderabad'
'Integral' sense	New service delivery models (primary healthcare)	Special development area (HITEC City & Cyberabad Development Authority)

influence their locational geographies' (Brenner 2004: 78). These actions attempt, for instance, to reconfigure investment conditions within a given territorial jurisdiction or reorganise local delivery systems for public services.

In this chapter case material from Hyderabad is mobilised to examine four examples, which engage with these two conceptions of state space (see Table 6.1).[1] Many aspects of Andhra Pradesh's regional political economy have been discussed in previous chapters and will serve as a useful backdrop for the new material presented here.

The aim is to explore, on the basis of concrete examples, the extent to which state spatial strategies, whose modalities will be carefully analysed, are contributing to constructing new urban scales, alongside actions from other private actors, enterprises, but also residents' groups and civil society organisations. This involves questioning the consequences for the scope and scale of public action, as well as for other forms of collective action. Let us recall that scales are assumed to have social and political texture; they can be defined as arenas 'where sociospatial power relations are contested and compromises are negotiated and regulated' (Swyngedouw 1997: 140, cited by Brenner *et al.* 2003: 16). Although it is still early to draw conclusions about some of the case material presented, I will discuss the emerging patterns of these ongoing processes.

6.1 Entrepreneurialism and urban governance: engaging with the literature

Before examining the Indian case, it is useful to briefly recall some of the major trends emerging in urban studies scholarship in recent years. The literature on state rescaling, which has been a major source of inspiration for the conceptual framework used here, takes a special interest in urban scales, examining how states elaborate spatial strategies for adapting to economic conditions in a context of globalisation.

In the late 1980s, David Harvey proposed the term 'urban entrepreunialism' to refer to the broad shift observed among city governments from managerialism, a focus on providing urban services, to entrepreneurialism, a focus on the urban economy, including elaborating strategies to enhance growth (1989). This redefinition of functions and priorities was the result both of an objective situation – the economic slowdown of the 1970s had had negative local effects on growth and employment and led to reduced central government funding – and emerging norms about what *should* be the role of munici-palities in the economy. Indeed, there was a growing trend in Western Europe and North America for local governments to be more proactive, to take initiatives for improving the local economy. In Europe, a large body of literature highlighted the growing political and economic importance of cities throughout the 1990s, a phenomenon linked to globalisation and European integration,[2] and, fundamentally, to the restructuring of the nation-state. As discussed in Chapter 1, urban regions were becoming engines for their national economies and this conferred greater political legitimacy on cities as political actors. Following Neil Brenner: 'It is above all through their role in the mobilization of urban-regional territorial organization for purposes of accelerated global capital circulation that local and regional states, in particular, are acquiring increasing structural significance within each territorial state's internal administrative-organizational hierarchy' (1998: 16).[3]

A broad consensus transpires from the literature about the strategic importance of cities in conjunction with their growing economic might. The scope of their political mandates and their effective capacity for action in the economic realm remain, however, a subject of debate. The capacity of local government actions to influence socio-economic relations (e.g., wages, working conditions, social equity) beyond the immediate investment climate has been questioned, for instance, in the context of strong intercity competition. Com-pared to national states, local governments have limited capacity to influence or constrain economic actors (Jouve and Lefèvre 2004).

In the field of international political economy, the tendency has been to represent local urban scales as having relatively little agency, as discussed earlier: 'Cities are treated first and foremost as sites (...) outcomes of struc-tural processes rather than of both structure and local political agency' (Paul 2005: 5–6). In such representations, capital, global capital in particular, is seen as the main force driving economic outcomes at the local scale. That con-ceptualisation has been contested, as we discussed in Chapter 4, by those who underscore the importance of local scales for fixing capital in space, defining conditions for both land and labour, and as sites of political struggle.

In the urban governance literature too, the macro-structural view of local agency has been countered. Jefferey Sellers, for instance, considers that much contemporary urban theory, notably the 'global cities' thesis, assigns an overly central role to the influence of global capital and international business elites on policy-making within cities. He argues that the expansion of local initiatives 'often trace more to actors and interests within urban political economies than to pressures from without' (2002: 3). Using a rigorous comparative method of fifteen cities in France, Germany and the US, he shows that even cities within a given country, exposed to the same macroeconomic context, pursue fundamentally different governance patterns, with regard to the relative impor-tance given to social (employment, redistribution), economic (incentives for growth, evidence of a growth machine), environmental and neighbourhood issues.

Empirical research on decentralisation reforms in various cities of the South suggest that local mandates remain focused primarily on basic service delivery and do not extend to socio-economic development (Dubresson and Fauré 2005) or strategic planning (Scott 2001). In addition to their limited financial resources and scope for raising taxes, local governments in developing countries usually have to contend with centralised political institutions.[4] As Richard Stren reminds us, any approach to strategic planning 'cannot ignore the central reality of the inter-governmental structure and the support that poor cities must obtain from other levels of the political system' (2001: 210).

In order to critically discuss the Indian case in relation to this literature, its similarities and differences, local institutions are a necessary starting point. Indeed, given India's centralised political institutions, the issue of local agency must be questioned. Equally important is the the strategic importance given to cities in the national policy framework.

6.2 Policy neglect and the 'urban turn'

Cities have had an ambivalent status in India's overall development strategy since independence. As many scholars have pointed out, nationalist leaders identified the nation with the rural, and for Gandhi in particular, villages were considered to represent the 'real India' (Chatterjee 1993, cited by Prakash 2002). Even Nehru, who did not harbour the same ideological prejudices against the city as Gandhi, had a historicist view of the city; cities were symbols of modernisation, and urbanisation was a necessary phase in the nation's development (Prakash 2002).

As discussed in Chapter 2, development policies up until the 1990s were conceived at the national scale, calibrated on national boundaries that they intended to strengthen as part of the larger nation-building mission. In addition to those policies explicitly directed towards agriculture and rural development, numerous economic initiatives indirectly targeted rural areas, such as those promoting small-scale industries.

The ambivalence towards cities can be inferred from the general lack of attention given to urban issues in planning documents of the 1950s (the first two Five-Year Plans) and to the absence of an urban policy per se (Ramachandran 1989; Mahadevia 2003).[5] Urbanisation was generally seen in a negative light, and policies of decentralised industrialisation and urban dispersal were designed, *inter alia,* to discourage rural–urban migration (Dupont 1995). A gradual shift started occurring from the 1980s in relation to changes in the overall policy environment, and in 1985 a National Commission on Urbanisation was set up.

In 1989, Rajiv Gandhi's Congress government made a first attempt to undertake large-scale administrative reform to strengthen local government, but it was opposed on grounds that it bypassed State governments, many of which were governed by opposition parties. However, when the Congress came back to power in 1991, a new decentralisation initiative in the form of a constitutional amendment was proposed and passed by Parliament, the 74th Constitutional Amendment Act (CAA). The ostensible aim of this amendment was to decentralise functions and finances to urban local bodies thereby empowering them as a genuine 'third tier' of government (the second tier being the State level). Whereas the scope of most local bodies was limited to basic services (water supply, street lighting, solid waste management), the CAA proposed to expand their mandate to include planning for economic and social development and urban poverty alleviation.[6]

It is significant that this political reform, considered long overdue by proponents of decentralised democracy, was undertaken in the wider context of economic reforms. This supports the argument made in previous chapters that economic reforms have been largely instrumental in setting into motion rescaling processes in India. And as I have emphasised, the timing of those reforms reflected important political developments in the country, including the growing regionalisation of politics.

Although cities have not been politically empowered as a result of the CAA, as I shall discuss in the next section, they *have* started receiving more attention from policy-makers at all levels, as well as from academics, social activists and resident associations, and these processes are shaping governance. Urbanisation and especially metropolisation – the rapid increase in the number of large cities – are certainly one reason; metropolitan cities, those with a population of one million or more, have increased from 35 in 2001 to 53 in 2011, and they concentrate 42 per cent of the total urban population.[7]

Gyan Prakash considers that the 'urban turn', as he calls it, has come about partly as a result of a deepening of democracy, which has undermined the elitist political culture of the post-independence period. This has enabled the emergence of a 'new politics of urban space' that takes into account the *spatiality* of the city and which is illustrated, among others, by the assertion of urban-based political movements like the Shiv Sena in Mumbai, the organisation of slum dwellers, and the phenomenal growth of NGOs (Prakash 2002: 6). It is also critically linked, I will argue, to the growing strategic importance of cities in recent years in the economic sphere.

Indeed economic growth is increasingly concentrated in cities. Service sector activities are the most dynamic sectors of the economy and they tend to locate in urban areas. Between 1994 and 2004, the tertiary sector's contribution to growth exceeded 68 per cent at the all India level, ranging from 47 per cent for Bihar to 88 per cent for Kerala (Misra 2007: 36–8). The share of cities in GDP grew rapidly from 50 per cent in 1995 to 58 per cent in 2008 (and is projected to reach 70 per cent in 2030).[8] While linked in part to globalisation processes, e.g., for export-oriented business services, economic growth is also driven by the needs of the domestic economy and by the demands of a growing urban middle class e.g., for housing, schools, hospitals (Shaw 2012). Following economic liberalisation, metropolitan regions and industrial corridors have generally captured the largest share of new investments.[9] The most dynamic sectors are transport and communications and real estate development in residential and commercial ventures; investments in IT and IT-related services have been particularly important in the metropolitan regions of the South (Bengaluru, Chennai, Hyderabad) (Shaw 2012: 45). As I argued in Chapters 4 and 5, many State governments are actively promoting their largest cities through direct investments in infrastructure and through measures facilitating the entry of private capital. The central state's SEZ policy may have further contributed to the spatial concentration of economic infrastructure, since SEZ promoters have shown a clear preference for locating in urban areas (see maps in Appendix 5.9). Chakravorty and Lall have assessed in these terms the central state in the post-reform era: 'As far as regional development is concerned, the newly liberal state is both a reduced or spatially disengaged state (as far as the promotion of regional balance is concerned), and a more enlarged state in terms of promoting selected metropolitan regions for receiving investment, especially foreign direct investment' (2007: 20).

The Government of India explicitly recognised the importance of urban economies as drivers of national growth for the first time in 2005 with the announcement of a national urban renewal mission (NURM or JNNURM). The NURM policy statement recalls the contribution of urban areas to national revenue, estimated at 65 per cent of GDP, and the fact that productivity increases are dependent on the quality and quantity of urban infrastructure: 'such as power, telecom, roads, water supply and mass transportation, coupled with civic infrastructure, such as sanitation and solid waste management'.[10] This large-scale programme marks a significant policy rupture inasmuch as it specifically aims to benefit the country's largest cities, thereby announcing its intention to reverse decades of neglect. It involves a huge amount of resources (€15.4 billion for the entire programme), half of which is central government assistance; funds are tied to governance and other urban reforms.[11] Because of these conditionalities, as well as the project approval process and the oversight by central government officers, the programme is often perceived as an instrument for exercising central government control over subnational state scales.[12]

Decentralisation reforms, which coincided with the economic reforms of the 1990s, will be examined in the next section to explore to what degree they are effectively modifying state spatiality and creating new scales of collective action.

6.3 Decentralisation and territorial reorganisation

A first remark regarding basic institutional structure in India's metropolitan cities: the commissioner model as opposed to the mayoral model continues to dominate.[13] This colonial legacy places executive power in the hands of a high-ranking civil servant, the municipal commissioner, nominated by and answerable to the State government as opposed to an elected mayor, presumably answerable to the local constituency.

Although there is considerable variation among cities, even with regard to basic functions they dispense, most assessments agree that decentralisation reforms of the 1990s have *not* significantly empowered municipal governments, neither in terms of functions nor finances.[14] The devolution of functions has remained on paper for the most part (Ghosh and Tawa Lama-Rewal 2005; Pinto 2000), and the newly constituted autonomous State Finance Commissions, intended to ensure that transfers to local bodies are not solely dependent on the discretion of State governments, have not been effective. In practice, a State government can simply choose not to act on the Commission's recommendations.[15]

In analysing the implementation of the 74th CAA it is important to recall that State governments play a crucial role in the process because they are required to draft enabling legislation, in other words to translate the components of the CAA into law for application within their territorial boundaries, as well as to design the practical modalities. This illustrates intergovernmental articulation within India's federal system and is a reminder of the capacity of subnational states, as an institutional intermediary, to influence the outcomes of central state initiatives. The new legislation is shaped in each State by existing institutions, and the values they express. This explains the variations across States, including with regard to some of the basic components provided for in the constitutional amendment, such as the creation of ward committees at a sub-municipal scale, examined in further detail next.

Notwithstanding the overall failure of CAA to effectively devolve decision making to local governments and expand their mandates and resources,[16] the CAA includes at least three noteworthy features that have the potential to influence local political processes, if not immediately then in the medium to long term. At a very basic level, it guarantees the timely organisation of local elections; this seemingly mundane rule is enormously significant in light of the inordinately long lapses between elections in many towns and municipalities across the country, including large corporations. It would be naïve to imagine it will completely eliminate lapses, as a recent example attests,[17] but presumably it increases pressure on State governments to comply. A second important component is the compulsory creation of new categories of reserved seats in the municipal council for women (one-third of total), in addition to those already in place for scheduled castes and tribes. This provision would appear to hold potential, even though an early evaluation conducted in the metropolitan cities did not find any measurable difference in the content of local decision-making as a result of the increased participation of women councillors (see Ghosh and Tawa Lama-Rewal 2005). Lastly, the mandatory creation of ward committees is an innovative feature, providing for an additional sub-municipal layer of government by dividing municipal space into smaller jurisdictions. The stated aim is to devolve decision making and take local government closer to citizens. A critical examination of this territorial rescaling exercise on the part of subnational states provides a baseline for comparing other rescaling processes later in the chapter.

Subnational state rescaling: ward committees

Because local government comes under the constitutional jurisdiction of the States, it was up to the latter to decide how ward committees would be constituted in their respective territories, i.e., whether to form a committee for each electoral ward (constituency) or club several wards together in one committee.[18] The amendment does not specify the composition of wards committees, i.e., who participates, stipulating only that the elected representative shall be a member, so this too is at the discretion of State legislatures. In Mumbai the ward committees include representatives of civil society, a result of successful mobilisation on the part of voluntary organisations and activists, who led campaigns and filed court cases to achieve their end (Nainan 2005). In contrast, only elected representatives participate in the ward committees in Delhi, Kolkata and Hyderabad (see comparative data in Table 6.2). It is significant that in Hyderabad, the representatives in the State assembly (MLAs) elected from the city also take part, an expression of the State's centralised political culture (Kennedy 2008).

In comparing the institution of ward committees in four metro cities – Delhi, Hyderabad, Kolkata, Mumbai – it was seen that ward committees were formed by grouping together electoral wards. In the case of Hyderabad, the city's 100 electoral wards were grouped into 10 ward committees, comprising 10 wards each, in the run-up to the municipal elections in 2002, the first to be held since 1991.[19] Field research conducted in the mid-2000s indicated that ward committees were basically conceived as a tool for improving the efficiency of urban management by bringing elected representatives face to face with officials from the main departments of the municipality (public works, public health, town planning) to review work in progress.[20] In that respect, they probably *did* help improve municipal government, by favouring more regular communication between elected officials and administration, a finding corroborated in the other three cities.[21] However, they did not appear to function as a democratic arena, if indeed that was their intended purpose. Journalists were not allowed to attend meetings, except in Delhi, so little information about the proceedings actually circulates to the wider public. Even in Mumbai where civil society organisations were represented in the ward committees, and where there is generally a much stronger tradition of local government, they had quite limited effects with regard to promoting citizens' participation in local government (Pinto 2008). One study, which also examined other arrangements aimed at improving representation, found that ward committees did expand scope for particular constituencies, mainly low-income or vulnerable groups, to approach their elected representatives and make claims with regard to personal problems or their habitat (Baud and Nainan 2008). This was in contrast to arrangements aimed at middle-class residents e.g., the Advanced Locality Management scheme, which gave the latter direct access to the executive wing of the municipality, and also provided scope for collective organisation at the city-level across localities (ibid.).[22]

Table 6.2 Comparative data on ward committees (WC) in 2007

Municipal corporation	No. of elected councillors	No. of WCs	No. of electoral wards in each WC	Population of WC (approx.)	Membership, in addition to municipal officers	Press allowed in WC meetings
Delhi	134	12	4–16	1,100,000	MC	Yes
Hyderabad	100	10	10	363,000	MC, MLA	No
Kolkata	141	15[a]	7–11	305,370	MC	No
Mumbai	227	16[b]	8–19	745,000[c]	MC, 1–3 NGO/CBO per ward without voting rights	No

Sources: Kennedy (2009: 60), compiled from Ghosh and Basu (2007), Tawa Lama-Rewal (2007), Zérah (2007), Sivaramakrishnan (2004)

Notes

a: These indicate borough committees, which for all practical purposes resemble WCs in other cities.

b: In Mumbai 16 WCs have been formed out of a total of 24 administrative wards, according to the following breakdown: 9 administrative wards = 9 WCs; 3 small administrative wards in the island city = 1 WC 12 administrative wards = 6 WCs.

c: Varies from 450,000 to 1,000,000.

As this brief discussion suggests, in the first decade following the 74th CAA State governments without exception opted for an *a minima* mandate with regard to the creation of ward committees. It is an unambiguous indication of the unwillingness of the State governments to allow this constitutional amendment, perceived as being imposed by New Delhi, to upset the *status quo ante* by creating a new political space. Obstructing municipal empowerment was 'a deliberate course taken by many [S]tate governments' (Sivaramakrishnan 2011b: 161). In this context, it should be noted that other local practices, frequently observed, bear witness to this same reluctance to recognise the political dimension of the municipal tier of government. For instance the practice of allotting to each councillor a 'fund', a fixed amount to be spent discretionarily for works within her/his ward (mainly for small infrastructure projects and road improvement), reduced the need to collectively discuss, prioritise and build consensus on issues facing the city as a whole. This fragmentary approach to municipal government has favoured a technocratic style of rule, in effect leaving bureaucrats to run city government.

Compared to these examples of territorial reorganisation – decentralisation to local governments and creation of ward committees at sub-municipal level – the next section examines a very different type of reform. It too is an example of formal territorial restructuring, state space in the 'narrow' sense, but instead of subdividing municipal territory, this reform produced a new political entity by consolidating pre-existing units.

6.4 Metropolitan rescaling: the making of 'Greater Hyderabad'

In July 2005, the State government issued an Order stating its intention to create a new politico-administrative entity called the Greater Hyderabad Municipal Corporation.[23] It was formed by extending the borders of the municipality to encompass twelve other municipalities and eight villages (*gram panchayats*), increasing the total area of the municipality by more than four times (from 172 km^2 to 725 km^2).[24] The municipal council was not consulted about the merger (nor presumably were the other concerned towns and villages) and when it was put to a vote in 2005, *after* the official announcement, a majority of Hyderabad's municipal councillors rejected the proposal (75 against 15 in favour).[25] On the one hand, there was widespread resentment that the government did not consult the council or the public prior to taking the decision. On the other, local councillors were worried that the costs related to the merging municipalities and gram panchayats would fall on the exchequer of Hyderabad corporation, whose financial position was comparatively strong. Although opposition to the Greater Hyderabad project continued throughout 2006, the High Court quashed the petitions in January 2007 opening the way for elections, which were initially scheduled for early 2008, and finally held in November 2009.

The stated reason for this large-scale expansion was the need to meet the growing demand for services in an integrated manner through 'an appropriate civic management structure with proper planning, resource mobilisation, and technical capabilities'.[26] The idea then was to replace a series of independent administrative services with a rationalised organisational structure for coordinating city-level systems such as the road network, water supply, sewerage and drainage system networks, urban transport system, environment management system, etc. The rationale guiding this type of rescaling, observed in many countries, is to promote efficiency in the management of collective goods and services and to pool technical expertise and financial resources. Combining spaces with differential capacities for raising fiscal revenue can favour cross-subsidisation and increase scope for mobilising internal resources for infrastructure development. At present, the quality and quantity of basic services in Hyderabad City is vastly superior to that of the surrounding municipalities.[27]

In theory, a second justification for this kind of territorial strategy is to build political capacity at the metropolitan scale in order to face competition from other cities in India and throughout the world for productive investments. In discussing 'new regionalism' Allen J. Scott has underscored the tendency for metropolitan regions, or *global-city regions*, to engage in 'territorial and political amalgamation at the local scale' to construct inter-territorial bases of collective action (2001: 4).

Politically, as indicated earlier, India's large cities are not in a position to assert themselves within the territorial hierarchy, here *vis-à-vis* the State government, and it seems unlikely that the Greater Hyderabad Municipal Corporation will enjoy a broader mandate than before. The absence of consultation with local elected officials, civil society and other stakeholders prior to announcing the proposal can be considered a crude indicator of metropolitan governance, heavily dominated by the State government and by State-level institutions. As with other reforms initiated by the State government in the 1990s, the creation of Greater Hyderabad was conceived as a technical solution to urban problems, and did not seek to engage a political process (see Mooij 2003).

Although expanding municipal boundaries can be justified on grounds of scale economies and efficiency, the timing of the decision and the modalities of its implementation, i.e., in a top-down manner and without prior public debate, suggest that it may also conceal other political objectives. First, the expansion of municipal borders would erode the dominance of the Majlis-e-Ittehadul Muslimeen (MIM) party, whose constituency is based in Hyderabad City. This effectively happened in the first Greater Hyderabad Municipal Corporation election held in late 2009: MIM came in third behind Congress (52 seats) and TDP (45) with 43 seats. In the previous council it had 37 seats out of 100 total (against 21 seats each for TDP and Congress).[28] Incidentally, Congress was in power at the State level at the time of elections. A second political motivation is that Greater Hyderabad would have the critical mass (demographically, economically) to become a politically autonomous 'Union Territory', directly administered by New Delhi in the event that the territory of Andhra Pradesh is divided to create a new Telangana State. Pressure for the creation of Telangana has revived in recent years, and its formation is a distinct possibility. In such an event, the State government might lobby to transform Greater Hyderabad into a Union Territory, eventually to be shared between the newly formed States.[29] Economic interests would support such a move, and may be lobbying in that direction. However, Telangana territory encircles Hyderabad and such a move would be hotly contested by many of those demanding a new State.

Fundamentally, it appears that the State government's primary motivation for deploying this territorial rescaling tool is to better control resources within the metropolitan region, in order to leverage the city as an asset for promoting growth. In that respect, it can be seen as part of a larger strategy of state spatial rescaling aimed at enhancing economic advantage. Evidence for this claim is presented in Section 6.6. Unlike decentralisation, which was imposed from above, the creation of 'Greater Hyderabad' expresses an autonomous strategy of the State government.

It is still too early to evaluate whether metropolitan Hyderabad, encompassed within the enlarged municipal corporation, will become a significant scale, gradually building up social and political significance. However, it is noteworthy that the rules governing the constitution of Greater Hyderabad Municipal Corporation prescribe some radical institutional innovations, the ostensible aim of which is to get urban residents more involved in urban management. Especially notable in light of the previous discussion are the completely restructured ward committees and the creation of area sabhas;[30] in addition to the elected councillor of the ward, who serves as the chairperson, the committee consists of ten nominated members, drawn from different sections of 'civil society', e.g., office bearers of resident associations and NGOs. These committees, which are supposed to meet once in a month, have a range of new supervisory and inspection responsibilities including the power to withhold salaries in case the members are not satisfied with the execution of local services, e.g., garbage collection and street cleaning.[31] In addition to getting city residents involved in running the city, the new rules clearly intend to break the monopoly of political parties on local government and to reduce their discretionary powers. Particularly striking in this regard is the decision to include in the mandate of area sabhas the right to 'to identify the most eligible persons for beneficiary oriented schemes as per guidelines for the Government'; likewise, they are empowered 'to verify the eligibility of persons getting various kinds of welfare assistance from the Government'.[32] It is not surprising that there has been resistance on the part of political parties but also administrative personnel to relinquish their prerogatives; judging from press reports the new structures are experiencing serious problems getting off the ground, starting with the failure to organise regular meetings.[33]

In contrast to this example of the constitution of Greater Hyderabad, which illustrated state space in a narrow sense, the next case, dealing with changing modalities of service provision in the city, refers to state space in its integral sense.

6.5 Sub-municipal scales – new geographies of urban services

Urban governance in India's large cities has undergone important changes in recent years as a result of changes in economic governance in the wake of liberalisation. These are manifest in new forms of service delivery and the presence of new types of local actors (Baud and Dhanalakshmi 2007; Baud and Nainan 2008; Zérah 2009, 2011b). Compared to the previous cases analysed, based on territorial-based reorganisation, these changes are suggestive of other types of rescaling processes that modify established patterns of state spatial deployment and affect the geographies of municipal services and also their social dimension, i.e., the categories of residents served and the socio-economic relations involved in providing the services. These processes have consequences for collective action, which depend on the specific arrangements adopted and the political economic conditions of the localities where they are deployed.

In the process of administering their territory, municipalities have always relied on subdividing space into smaller units (circles, wards, units, etc.), but these spatial units came together under a common administrative framework. This is changing as new arrangements are put in place for service provision that involve public–private or public–community partnerships. In many cases, these arrangements were directly inspired by and implemented under the supervision of international development agencies, notably the World Bank and DFID for the Hyderabad case. They reflect new norms about urban service delivery derived from the new public management model and also the neo-liberal agenda, which advocates privatisation and public–private partnerships as more efficient modes of delivering services. These practices and arrangements are often legitimised in the name of greater citizen participation. There is a large body of literature, which looks critically at these processes, its logics and its consequences.[34]

In many respects, Hyderabad has been at the forefront of these experiments among India's large cities, outsourcing even core functions such as tax collection.[35] My earlier research on the reform of delivery systems and urban governance in Hyderabad focused on the new modalities and the actors involved (Kennedy 2008, 2009). Here I propose a critical review of that research using a state space lens to examine how the new modalities modify established patterns of state spatial deployment of municipal services and their social and spatial implications. Recent reform in providing primary healthcare will serve as an illustration.

A case study of reforms in primary healthcare services

In Andhra Pradesh public health (sanitation) is a statutory function for urban local government, but healthcare is not. This helps to explain why the municipal corporation of Hyderabad had a very limited mandate within the broad field of healthcare; it primarily dealt with primary out-patient care, preventive health, and family planning. Although the Constitution places health under the jurisdiction of the States, the central government plays a critical role both in shaping policy and in providing funds. Immunisation programmes, for instance, are mainly carried out within the framework of centrally-sponsored schemes, which follow a similar implementation pattern throughout the country (also called 'vertical programmes'). Curative healthcare in the city comes under the purview of the State government, which runs the secondary and tertiary hospitals. It should be noted that private healthcare facilities dominate the health field in Andhra Pradesh, for both out-patient and in-patient care. Although the privatisation of healthcare is a nationwide trend in both rural and urban areas that pre-dates the reforms of the 1990s, Andhra Pradesh is a somewhat extreme example. Already in the 1980s, the private sector provided about 70 per cent of in-patient care in the rural areas and 62 per cent in the urban areas, which was the highest proportion in the country (Narayana 2003: 342). Hyderabad's healthcare environment reflects these wider institutional trends; it hosts several large private for-profit hospitals, including 'corporate' hospitals,[36] and is one of the leading centres of medical tourism in India. As this suggests, policy frameworks elaborated at central and provincial state scales traverse local space and shape the context in which healthcare services are provided by the municipal corporation.

The most striking aspect about recent healthcare reforms in Hyderabad was the overwhelming influence of the World Bank sponsored Indian Population Programme (IPP-VIII). Implemented between 1994 and 2002, this programme advocated targeting municipal healthcare services specifically to the urban poor as opposed to the general population. In support of this, it funded the construction of new healthcare facilities (twenty-six urban health posts, UHPs, and five small maternity hospitals) in localities identified as 'slums'. In addition, it provided funds to renovate the thirty-six existing primary health centres. The target population of the UHPs is exclusively women and children, and the focus is on prevention of disease (via immunisation and outreach), pre- and post-natal care and family planning. For all of these, municipal personnel are expected to meet quantitative targets on a monthly basis.

The programme introduced new modalities of service provision based on partnerships with the private sector and with the NGO sector. For instance, NGOs were given the responsibility of running, on a contract basis, a certain number of UHPs. Under these contracts the municipality commits to fund a proportion of the total costs, with the remaining amount to be met through the NGO's own sources. The NGOs are given full responsibility for managing the clinics, including hiring the nurses and doctors from the 'market'. Under the IPP-VIII programme NGOs also played a critical role in identifying and training 'link volunteers', voluntary community health workers recruited among women living in slum areas, a central component of the programme. More than 5,500 in number, these women were in charge of informing slum residents about healthcare services and contraception and providing feedback to government staff. According to official statistics, the municipality worked with twenty-two NGOs in 662 slum localities in the city to implement this programme. Two additional components, intended to reduce costs, maintenance (cleaning) and security in the UHPs, were outsourced to private companies, and in some of these clinics medical personnel (nurses) were hired on a contract basis.

At the time of fieldwork in the mid-2000s, corporate sector actors were also undertaking initiatives in the field of primary and preventive healthcare in the city, as part of their 'social responsibility' mission. One such initiative, proposed by the IT firm Satyam involved using the existing UHP infrastructure to expand services by offering evening consultations and extending care to men and boys. The firm paid doctors a fixed amount for their services, which were free of charge for patients.

Fragmented local state space

The IPP-VIII programme effectively extended municipal healthcare services to more areas of the city, and was considered successful by the World Bank.[37] However, field surveys, which were conducted three years after the programme ended, underscored a number of weaknesses, starting with the limited scope of the programme in relation to the physical scale of the city. Even with a more focused approach on the urban poor, the geographical coverage of municipal services was grossly inadequate, with only 67 health posts for a slum population estimated at 1.4 million (39 per cent of the total population) living in 1,042 slums (Ghosh 2009: 216). Surveys and focus group discussions in different localities indicated that residents of informal settlements in newer areas of the cities had considerably less access to public services of all kinds compared to the core city, including primary healthcare. Here, people had to either travel long distances to reach a public facility or consult private doctors, including many unqualified 'registered medical practitioners' posing as doctors, who thrive in poor neighbourhoods.

The primary weakness of the programme, which was intended to be its strength, lies with the partnership arrangements. Of the two dimensions of the rationale that inspired the project, i.e., greater public involvement and cutting costs, only the latter seems to have been fully appropriated by the municipality. My field research suggests that the new partnerships are primarily seen by the municipal authorities as way to finance 'public' service delivery. For instance, the participation of the women volunteers, that gave the programme a base in the city's *bastis* (slums), has been allowed to lapse. Although basically volunteers, the IPP project provided the women with motivation through monetary and non-monetary means. The project afforded a structure, such as monthly meetings, and animation (training programmes), as well as a small sum of money (Rs. 150–300) each month to each of 662 slums to meet health or non-health needs of the community. When the project ended, neither the municipality nor the NGOs managed to keep up the momentum, casting doubt on the government's commitment to the institutionalisation of such community-based structures.[38]

The new modalities of service provision have had the effect of fragmenting local state space by putting in place a patchwork of service providers, with varying standards. NGOs in charge of running UHPs pay their medical staff, especially the nurses, at rates well below those prevailing in the public sector. Although in theory they are expected to contribute financially to running their clinics, in reality they rely on the funds contracted with the municipality, which according to interviews correspond to approximately half the amount of the cost of running 'public' clinics, i.e., those staffed with permanent employees. In this context, it is inevitable that service levels will vary from place to place, including the quality of healthcare, the availability of publicly subsidised medicines, etc., all of which contribute to a fragmented service.[39]

A serious problem identified with regard to the deployment of a partnership strategy was the seeming inability of municipal government to respect its contracts with its partners and to take on a regulatory role. NGOs on contract with the municipality to run UHPs complained that they did not receive the monthly funds on time, nor on a regular basis. Likewise, cleaning and security personnel in UHPs reported that their salaries were regularly late, sometimes by several months, because the labour contractors who employed them had not received payment from the municipality. In other words, the municipality put in place new partnership and sub-contracting arrangements, following the World Bank guidelines, but did not fully assume them in practice. In delegating responsibility to other actors, 'partners', the local state did not take seriously the need to ensure oversight, to regulate and inspect, and sanction if necessary.[40] In this context, the quality of public service, its effective reach, was dependent on the volition and commitment of private actors, who were largely left on their own to interpret their mission. Likewise, the sustainability of healthcare initiatives promoted by the corporate sector as part of their 'social responsibility' agenda, depend solely on the commitment of those private organisations and not on the local state. Yet residents cannot demand public accountability from private organisations, nor make claims for better service. Like in the Mumbai ALM example cited above, spatial differentiation contributes to creating or reinforcing a situation of differential rights. Moreover, because these services are targeted to the poor, the majority of urban residents are not directly concerned, which acts as an obstacle for mobilising opinion for making claims on the state through collective action.[41] On a territorial continuum, this example can be situated in the lower degrees, a form of delegation, which does not create the conditions for its own system of governance. This suggests a lessening hold of the local state over its territory, not because of contestation, but by its incapacity or unwillingness to fully integrate the implications of the new management practices that it had adopted.

The service delivery reforms discussed here modified local statehood by reconfiguring both state — society and state — market relations. The next section deals with state spatial strategies to influence the location of economic activities and enhance economic competitiveness.

6.6 Cyberabad Development Area – a spatial instrument[42]

In 2001, the Andhra Pradesh government created the Cyberabad Development Area (CDA) as a spatial support for its economic development strategies, which focused on developing high-tech industries, especially IT and business services.[43] In particular it was designed to complement one of the State's flagship industrial projects, 'HITEC City',[44] a large-scale IT park built in the late 1990s. HITEC City is a partnership venture between APIIC, the State government's industrial infrastructure agency, and a private promoter. The stated goal of CDA is to ensure the 'effective development of the areas around the HITEC City and surroundings' (CDA 2001: 5). Just near HITEC City to the west and south, the government set up other specialised enterprise parks on large tracts of land that are also included in CDA (see Map 6.1 in Appendix 6.8). HITEC City is located in Madhapur, outside Hyderabad's city limits at that time, but contiguous to the city's most affluent residential areas, Banjara Hills and Jubilee Hills, about 15 kilometres from the city centre. In this sense, CDA effectively contributed to expanding the built environment out towards the west. It covers 52 square kilometres, encompassing seventeen localities, most of which are located within the boundaries of Serilingampally Municipality.

CDA is regulated by a specific set of rules outlined in a Master Plan,[45] of which there are two main types: land use regulations[46] and special building rules. The building rules are intended to ensure the realisation of a particular type of urbanisation characterised by larger plot sizes in relation to floor space area and increased road widths compatible with building height, regulations intended to check densities of both population and built-up area. High-rise buildings are permitted, subject to rules and to payment of a 'premium' (surcharge), 'commensurate with the cost of higher infrastructure needed to support the higher densities' (CDA 2001: 34).The rationale was to finance the high standards of infrastructure and services in the enclave through internal sources, i.e., one-time external betterment charges and user fees. Indeed, in the HITEC City–Madhapur sector, firms enjoy uninterrupted electricity and excellent telecommunications, in addition to a relatively clean and well-maintained environment.

A bounded space, governed by a set of specific rules and regulations, CDA is an emblematic example of a spatialised instrument. It is one component of a broader strategy aimed to foster growth, which includes an 'aggressive' IT policy. This policy includes two main types of incentives, financial (e.g., rebate on power tariffs, tax exemptions, rebate on the cost of land) and regulatory (e.g., exemption from inspections under most labour laws in exchange for self-certification). It guarantees simplified rules and an accelerated application process for investors. This 'single window' operates via the APIIC, the agency in charge of guiding investors to specific location sites. In effect, the IT policy's 'business-friendly' incentives include concessions on land cost that are applicable to land in the government's possession, including in CDA. Hence, by providing a territorial fix for capital, the CDA instrument provides the crucial link between government strategy and private investors. It is specifically designed to influence locational strategies of firms and foster clustering.

In many respects, CDA is a textbook case of constructing territory for the purpose of enhancing the competitiveness of selected urban spaces. Using a place-specific regulatory framework the purpose is to augment the productive capacity of a delineated space by creating 'territorially rooted immobile assets' (Amin and Thrift, 1995: 10, cited by Brenner 1998: 15–16). Such assets take the form of 'world class' infrastructure and also iconic architecture in the form of state-of-the-art office buildings, e.g., Cyber Towers, Cyber Pearl, etc. It is a conscious effort then to concentrate enabling policies and capital investments in a particular place – here an enterprise park devoted to 'high-tech' activities – in order to attract investments and to foster growth and innovation.

Such initiatives of 'intentional clustering' are among the most important of the direct industrial policies at the disposal of subnational states (Chakraborty and Lall 2007: 143). Andhra Pradesh has been particularly proactive in mobilising this type of instrument, as we saw in the case of SEZs (Chapter 5). The creation of this high-tech cluster, Cyberabad Development Area, is part of a larger strategy of place-making for comparative economic advantage. It can be recalled that the TDP-ruled State government was openly competitive with other States in promoting its territory. As one policy document put it:

> To (its many) strengths, Andhra Pradesh will add speedy reform and capability building, giving it a significant competitive edge. Most Indian [S]tates and many countries are anticipating opportunities and moving to capture them. What will separate the winners from the losers will be the ability to move fast, reform government, create infrastructure and develop human resources. Andhra Pradesh will move quickly on all these fronts to ensure that it emerges a winner.
>
> (Government of Andhra Pradesh 1999: 10)

Consequences on the ground

The rules laid down in the CDA regulatory framework were not all strictly applied. For instance, the external betterment charges were replaced in 2003 by 'Value Addition Charges', which were about half the amount of the betterment charges, floor area ratios were also modified and surcharge rates were reduced. The reason given by the authorities was simply that the regulations had been drawn up by a consulting agency; when the government realised the rates did not correspond to ground realities, it decided to reduce them. As for user charges, field surveys in 2005 indicated they were not being applied. Regarding building rules too, CDA rules had not been followed to the letter, nor had they been applied to the entire area. In the first phase especially, there was a certain amount of leniency with regard to building rules and to levying betterment charges. Individuals building their own houses continued to follow the old rules and obtain permissions through the local municipality (Serilingampally).[47] Subsequently, they were required to submit their building plans to the CDA administration and conformity was enforced. More stringent building rules, higher fees and the betterment charges were all disincentives for builders, since it raised final costs. Buyers were unwilling to accept the higher rates charged within the CDA boundaries as long as land was available just outside the boundaries. Indeed, land contiguous to CDA witnessed a rapid increase in value.

Taken altogether, this evidence suggests that the core components of CDA regulatory framework, i.e., building rules and betterments charges, have only been systematically applied to a small portion of the CDA territory, namely the industrial area in Madhapur (including HITEC City: see Map 6.1 in Appendix 6.8). It is significant that jurisdiction over this sub-area was delegated to a government agency, again the APIIC, considered to be the 'deemed local authority'. In other words, the APIIC took charge of all the traditional functions of the local government: general maintenance of the area, new infrastructure development and tax collection. Field surveys conducted in 2006 indicated that revenue from property tax was partially shared (35 per cent of total) with the local municipality (Serilingampally), whereas the betterment charges were handed over to the the the metro planning authority, and the building fees were kept by the APIIC in a special account for the CDA.[48]

This partial application of the key regulations of CDA underscores the political and administrative difficulties that accompany this kind of strategy. It also raises questions about the strategic motivation of putting in place this spatial instrument. The unwillingness to apply the regulatory framework to the entire area contradicts the stated goal of transforming it into a 'model enclave' and suggests that the government is primarily concerned about creating and maintaining a favourable environment for the core part of the zone near HITEC City. It seems likely that the rationale for delineating such a large area was to give the government a wide margin for responding to future developments; it 'earmarked' land that could be developed progressively and over which the regulations could be gradually applied. The analysis underscores that the territorialisation process intended to create the CDA is incomplete, and that it is a contested process. Indeed, the partial implementation of certain components can be interpreted as a state response to opposition on the part of builders and individual homeowners to comply with the regulations. Perhaps the authorities realised that since the government is not able to provide even basic facilities to the entire area it is not realistic to expect homeowners or businesses to pay betterment charges or user fees. Conversely, since the government *did* meet its commitment to provide excellent quality infrastructure to the new industrial areas around HITEC City, it could legitimately apply the rules and regulations there.

Premium networked space

HITEC CITY corresponds to what Stephen Graham (2000) calls a 'premium networked space', wherein high performance infrastructures are superposed on the existing public utility networks. They are 'customized precisely to the needs of powerful users and spaces, whilst bypassing less powerful uses and spaces' (ibid.: 185). In Graham's analysis such spaces emerge as part of a strategy of economic restructuring and indicate a relative weakening of universal service norms and comprehensive urban planning. Such spaces are globally connected, but not necessarily integrated with the surrounding localities, spatially or economically.

Outside the perimeter of Madhapur–HITEC City basic services have not noticeably improved across the vast area of CDA. There is, however, increasing differentiation in service levels at the local scale; the very high standards of infrastructure and global connectivity in Madhapur contrast quite spectacularly with the under-serviced villages. Still, as noted, the creation of CDA does not appear to have put these localities in direct competition for public resources because the 'premium spaces' in the Madhapur–HITEC City area are administered by a distinct agency and the funds dedicated to equipping them come down a separate stream. Nonetheless, like the example of healthcare delivery, the existence of this separate and special administration has fragmented local space. In this case the risk is that voices from the villages falling outside this 'high performance' zone will be stifled. From the point of view of politicians and political organisations, removing the dynamic Madhapur zone from the local political space deprives them not only from accessing potentially abundant resources but from influencing future developments. 'Technocratic' management, in the form of a single-window for all requests and grievances, has in effect been substituted for democratic representation. Such fragmentation of local space acts as an obstacle to collective action.

With regard to the primary objectives driving this spatial strategy, i.e., the promotion of the IT industry and business services, the area around HITEC City enjoyed strong economic growth throughout most of the 2000s in IT-related activities and in financial and business services as well as commercial ventures and housing. Although it is difficult to measure precisely, it can be safely assumed that the advantages offered by the IT policy in conjunction with large-scale public investments in specialised infrastructure in and around HITEC City contributed to the high levels of private investment.[49]

6.7 Conclusion

With regard to the literature discussed at the beginning of the chapter, it can be seen that in some important respects processes under way in India's cities compare with international experiences, but there are also critical differences. As in other parts of the world, India's urban regions have become engines of growth. This has become remarkably more pronounced in recent years following liberalisation. There is a *mechanical* side to this development: tertiary activities are driving India's growth and these tend to concentrate in cities, especially those sectors such as IT and financial services that are linked to the global economy. Such developments feed in turn the transport, communications and real estate sectors. At the same time, there is a *strategic* side to the growth story, with which we have been concerned here: central and regional states are promoting urban space as part of their overall economic development strategies, rescaling their territories in favour of the metropolitan cities in particular. However, and this is an important distinction, municipal governments in India are *not* major actors of this evolution and city politics do not generally provide an arena for deliberation and agenda-setting about urban futures. To borrow Harvey's term (1989), Indian cities have remained focused on managerialism, whereas other state scales have shifted to entrepreneurialism. In this respect, India's experience with decentralisation appears more comparable to that of many other developing countries than that of Europe.[50] Urban governance has changed, inspired notably by international policy experts and their public management models, but local mandates remain limited; in particular, India's city governments do not elaborate economic development policies and State governments do not necessarily consult local governments before deploying their strategies in urban space.

A major divergence then with the European experience is with regard to political capacity at local scales. Although the 74th amendment was designed to rescale territorial organisation in favour of local government and create sub-municipal arenas for deliberation, State governments, responsible for implementation of this reform, have resisted devolving powers and finances. This is a compelling illustration of the contested nature of the local state scale; regional (provincial) states effectively thwarted the rescaling strategy of the central state. That has not prevented the central state from pursuing direct interventions, in the form of megaprojects, e.g., the metro in Delhi, or from launching the National Urban Renewal Mission, which effectively opens a parallel channel for funding specific infrastructure projects in the metropolitan cities.

The decision by the Andhra Pradesh government to form Greater Hyderabad Municipal Corporation gave expression to a State-level initiative of territorial reorganisation. In theory, this new territory has the potential to enhance the scope for collective action at the metropolitan scale in the medium term, although it will depend on the response of social actors (political parties, NGOs, residents' associations, community-based organisations, etc.), the degree to which they appropriate this space and transform it into an organisational frame of action.

Whereas these two examples (devolution and merger) both illustrate examples of state rescaling in the narrow sense, the other two cases mobilised state institutions in ways that reconfigured their rapport with territory and positioned them to regulate social relations in more significant ways.

Reforms in service delivery introduced in the last two decades have effectively rescaled local state space by introducing differentiation in spatial deployment of services, and modifying the social relations mobilised for providing the service, based increasingly on sub-contracting and co-production. Although the specialised literature documents cases where initiatives based on NGOs and community partnerships provided scope for collective action, this was not the case for the example of healthcare examined here from Hyderabad, which was characterised by spatial and functional fragmentation. By explicitly targeting the service to the urban poor and delegating implementation to various types of actors, the scope for mobilisation across income groups and localities was curtailed. The inability or unwillingness of the State government to assume the role of regulator, effectively monitoring the actions of non-state actors, as well as its failure to respect the terms of the partnerships, were analysed as indicators of the incomplete nature of the emerging post-reform policy framework at the local scale.

In the case of HITEC City and Cyberabad Development Authority (CDA), the State government mobilised spatial instruments in conjunction with an aggressive sectoral policy in order to pursue its economic growth strategy aimed at promoting the IT industry. In particular, HITEC City, a premium space in the form of an enterprise park, and CDA more generally, were conceived as spatial 'fixes' for the policy; a special regulatory framework was conceived to ensure that the fast emerging built environment would correspond to 'norms' inspired by international examples considered appropriate for a technology/business cluster. Via the policy, investors are channelled by state agencies either to HITEC City, where office space is available on lease, or to selected plots in Cyberabad, owned by the government. In these ways, the State government is effectively contributing to the creation of territorially rooted assets, the construction of new geographies of infrastructure, and economic activities. In a short period of time, a critical mass of built-up area in Madhapur, including HITEC City, has come to be identified with 'new economy' activities. The large-scale construction of apartments and commercial establishments, in addition to its economic specialisation in IT, have contributed to putting Madhapur on the map in IT circles nationally and globally.

Regarding spaces of statehood, the CDA is the expression of a technocratic governance structure, effectively removing local state territory from the realm of democracy to bureaucracy. It offers numerous advantages for businesses in the locality but the advantages for residents are less apparent, and for the surrounding localities still less. Although tax sharing arrangements allow local governments to avail of part of the fiscal receipts generated by the new activities, locally elected officials do not take part in decision making in these new spaces.

6.8 Appendix

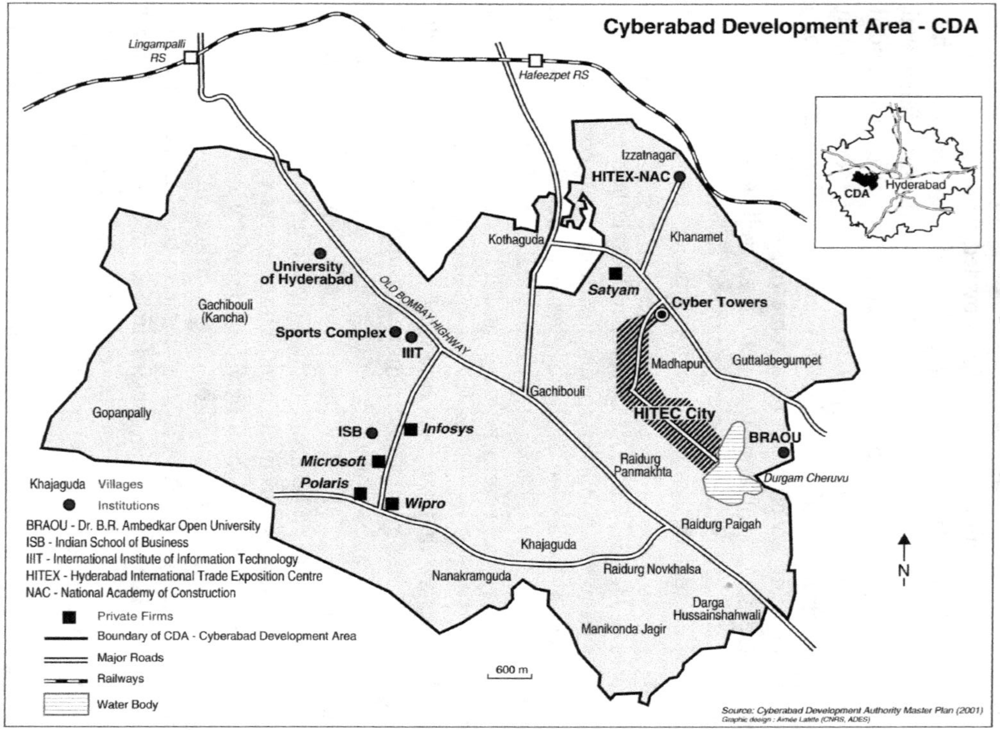

Map 6.1 Schema of Cyberabad Development Area, in relation to the metropolitan planning area, ca. 2005

Notes

1 These examples, which have been analysed where indicated in other publications, are revisited here using a spatially sensitive lens in order to understand the emerging patterns of territorial organisation of the Indian state.
2 For a revue of this literature see Le Galès (1995).
3 In a similar vein, Bernard Jouve and Christian Lefèvre noted: 'En investissant le champ du développement économique, les métropoles européennes ont, avec l'appui et le soutien des Etats, intégré dans leur champ de compétence un domaine d'action publique "noble", valorisant, répondant à une demande sociale très forte dans un contexte de crise économique très importante' (Jouve and Lefèvre 2004: 6).
4 For a discussion of the decentralisation experience of various countries in Africa and Latin America, see the special issue of *Revue Tiers Monde* (Dubresson and Fauré 2005). For an earlier assessment of four cases in South Asia (including Karnataka in India) and West Africa, see Crook and Manor (1998).
5 This brief policy review draws on Kennedy and Zérah (2008).
6 These are listed in the Twelfth Schedule, appended to article 243W of the 74th Amendment pertaining to the Powers, authority, and responsibilities of Municipalities.
7 The total urban population in 2011 was 377 million. See Shaw (2012).
8 Source estimates by McKinsey Global Institute 2010. Because the Indian government does not produce statistics on urban economies, various proxy indicators are used to make estimates.
9 Ahmedabad–Mumbai–Pune in western India emerge at the forefront followed by the metropolitan region of Delhi (Shaw 2012: 36).
10 See Mission overview on the website: jnnurm.nic.in, last consulted on 20 January 2012.
11 Among the mandatory reforms: abolition of rent control and the urban land ceiling and property tax reform.
12 As Partha Mukhopadhyay remarked about NURM, 'The relationship between the central government, state government and the ULB [Urban Local Body] is similar to that of a refinance institution, a lending institution and a borrower, rather than that of three levels of government working in tandem to provide services to urban citizens' (Mukhopadhyay 2006: 882). For an evaluation of the first phase of implementation, see Sivaramakrishnan (2011b).
13 Kolkata being a notable exception with its mayoral system.
14 Two recent comparative studies of urban governance in India's large cities analyse the implementation of the 74th CAA: Baud and de Wit (2008); Ruet and Tawa Lama-Rewal (2009). My own research was carried out largely in the frame-work of the latter research project, 'Urban Actors, Policies and Governance', coordinated by the Centre de Sciences Humaines, Delhi.
15 This was the conclusion of studies carried out in Maharashtra and Andhra Pradesh in the mid-2000s. See respectively Pethe and Lalvani (2007) and Sreedevi (2005).
16 Studies of decentralisation in rural areas suggest slightly better results, but evaluations vary tremendously across regions. See, for example, Kumar (2006).
17 Hyderabad Municipal council lapsed in 2007 and new elections for the greatly expanded Greater Hyderabad were not held until late 2009.
18 Article 243S outlines the basic provisions for the constitution and composition of Wards Committees: '(1) There shall be constituted Wards Committees, consisting of one or more wards, within the territorial area of a Municipality having a population of three lakhs [three hundred thousand] or more. (2) The Legislature of a State may, by law, make provision with respect to (a) the composition and the territorial area of a Wards Committee; (b) the manner in which the seats in a Wards Committee shall be filled. (3) A member of a Municipality representing a ward within the territorial area of the Wards Committee shall be a member of that Committee. (4)

Where a Wards Committee consists of (a) one ward, the member representing that ward in the Municipality; or (b) two or more wards, one of the members representing such wards in the Municipality elected by the members of the Wards Committee, shall be the Chairperson of that Committee.'

19 The previous gap had lasted even longer: from 1973 to 1986.

20 My fieldwork in Hyderabad was conducted in 2004 and 2005. I held interviews with twelve municipal councillors and several administrative officers in the municipal corporation, including Additional Commissioners in charge of line departments and the Municipal Commissioner.

21 For a comparative analysis of the functioning of wards committees in Delhi, Hyderabad, Kolkata and Mumbai, see Kennedy (2009, especially pp. 59–62).

22 Marie-Hélène Zérah (2009), who also analysed the ALM scheme in Mumbai, came to similar conclusions namely that such arrangements can confer different rights to different groups of residents, and in that respect lead to (or reinforce) double standards of citizenship. Stéphanie Tawa Lama-Rewal (2007), who studied the *bhagidari* scheme in Delhi, also reached a similar conclusion.

23 See GO Ms No. 704, Municipal Administration and Urban Development Department, Government of Andhra Pradesh, dated 20 July 2005.

24 The municipalities are L.B. Nagar, Gaddiannaram, Uppal Kalan, Kapra, Alwal, Qutubullapur, Malkajgiri, Kukatpally, Serlingampally, Rajendranagar, Patancheru and Ramachandrapuram. The Gram Panchyats are: Shamshabad, Mamidipalli, Satamarai, Jalapally, Mankhal, Tukkuguda, Sardarnagar and Ravarala.

25 See 'Majority corporators vote against Greater Hyderabad proposal', *The Hindu*, 5 August 2005, Hyderabad edition.

26 The reasons cited in the Government Order are the following: facilitating improved and high standard of civic services; providing better civic administrative mechanism; ensuring better planning and focused development of the Mega City; more equitable devolution of finances and utilisation of resources; ensuring uniform enforcement; to make the city internationally competitive with world-class infrastructure and services.

27 On water and drainage, see Huchon and Tricot (2008).

28 In percentage terms, MIM's seat share dropped from 37 per cent of the total to 28.7 per cent.

29 There is a precedent for such an arrangement in Chandigarh, the capital of both Punjab and Haryana, which separated in 1960.

30 1,081 area sabhas have been constituted in Hyderabad representing approximately 5,000 people, an average of 6–8 per ward. See the GHMC website, see www.ghmc.gov. in/Ward_Committee_ info.asp, last consulted 26 April 2013.

31 These include supervision of garbage collection, sweeping and street light maintenance as well as the authority to inspects public works. For an optimistic and laudatory description, which includes the theoretical inspiration for some aspects of the law and rules, see www.iuc2011.in/conference/mysore-conference/ institutionalising-area-sabhas-hyderabad-experience-and-challenges-sameer-sharma-mcp-phd, last accessed 26 April 2013.

32 Information collected from the GHMC website, see www.ghmc.gov.in/Ward_ Committee_info.asp, last consulted 26 April 2013.

33 See 'GHMC ward panel, area sabha members in quandary', *The Hindu*, 19 November 2011, and 'Corporators to meet public every month', *New Indian Express*, 5 March 2013.

34 For a discussion of the Indian case, see the introduction by Baud and de Wit (2008).

35 See also Zérah (2011) for an analysis of schemes for managing solid waste in Hyderabad.

36 As Bertrand Lefebvre points out, some of these are now listed on the Bombay Stock Exchange (2008: 88).

37 See for instance the study by Gill (1999).
38 Similarly other government sponsored community structures, such as the Community Development Societies (CDS) have not been encouraged. Archana Ghosh noted 'Once MCH [municipal corporation of Hyderabad] elections were held in 2002 (after a 14-year gap), the newly-elected council completely discouraged the functioning of CDSs. The elected councillors feared that the CDS would be a parallel institution at the local level, jeopardising their authority as people's representatives' (2009: 233).
39 This finding is broadly consistent with many studies critically examining new urban management tools and their social and spatial consequences, a full discussion of which is beyond the scope of this chapter. For a theoretical discussion and application to Sub-Saharan Africa, see Jaglin (2005).
40 Similar conclusions about the State government's unwillingness to regulate the private sector have been made in relation to primary education, see Mooij and Jalal (2009).
41 Again, similar problems of middle-class defection have been cited with regard to education. See Mooij and Jalal (2009).
42 The analysis in this section draws on Kennedy and Ramachandraiah (2006), and Kennedy (2007a).
43 CDA was created through a Government Order (GO) Ms No. 21 MA, dated 20 January 2001.
44 It stands for Hyderabad Information Technology Engineering Consultancy City.
45 The Master Plan for CDA was notified through GO Ms No. 538 dated 29 October 2001, with effect from 1 November 2001.
46 One key feature of the CDA Master Plan is to allow computer software units to set up in designated residential areas, subject to certain conditions (e.g., minimum plot size, minimum road width).
47 Author interview with J. Srinivasan, owner of Sri Venkteshwara Enclaves Pvt. Ltd, Hyderabad, 6 March 2006. This builder contended that most individuals, unable to adhere to the stringent rules, could not obtain approval for their plans although some built their houses anyway and hoped for ex post regularisation.
48 Interview with C. Balasubrahmanyam, Manager, APIIC, Hyderabad, 3 March 2006. Interestingly, the officials at Serilingampally municipality with whom I spoke did not express displeasure over losing jurisdiction, but rather pointed out their revenues had increased quite dramatically as a result of the economic boom around HITEC City.
49 Between 1995 and 2010 the State government was the source of 46 per cent of investments in Rangareddy District, where CDA is located (Shaw 2012: 42). In 2006–7, when operations at HITEC City were in full swing, exports in the IT sector grew at faster rates in Andhra Pradesh than the national average (48 per cent compared to 33 per cent).
50 This corroborates the conclusions of an international research programme that examined the links between decentralisation reforms and local development in cities of the South and found that a change in scale with regard to *governance* does not automatically lead to a change in the scale of economic regulation (Dubresson and Fauré 2005). The conclusions were based on research from studies in Mexico, Brazil, South Africa, Senegal and India.

7   Conclusion

The politics of economic and state restructuring in India

This study of India's political economy undertook to analyse how changes in state–market and state–society relations in the context of liberalisation have redefined economic governance and significantly reconfigured the Indian state's rapport with its territory, at all spatial scales. These processes of *state restructuring*, I argued, are crucial for comprehending emerging patterns of growth as well as uneven development. They emerge as a result of endogenous political strategies that accompany and respond to institutional change and the territorial reorganisation of economic activities within India and beyond. In that sense, the effective construction of new state spaces occurs as the consequence of largely uncoordinated actions on the part of various state and non-state actors, situated at various spatial scales, which distinguishes this process from more formal types of state-led reform such as decentralisation or (re-)centralisation.

One objective of this study was to provide a more fine-grained account of India's decision to pursue economic reforms and to show how the consequences of the new policy regime, which are playing out in space, are not simply the product of impersonal market forces. They reflect the strategies of India's political elites, in conjunction with initiatives of other types of actors, originating from subnational and supranational levels. The reform process has significantly reconfigured the conditions and modalities of *economic governance*, defined as the institutions and actors who shape the economic and political processes that coordinate economic activities. So rather than focus on the economic effects of reforms, the objective here was to understand the political effects, in the broad sense of both 'politics' and 'policies', on the conditions shaping economic development. My central thesis was that in India's reformed institutional context, where both state spaces *and* economic geographies are being rescaled, subnational scales now play a more critical role in coordinating socio-economic activities than in the past.

To recall, this study undertook to analyse three sets of interrelated processes: (1) the reconfiguration of state spatial scales; (2) economic policy-making at subnational scales; and (3) the interactions between rescaling and economic governance.

7.1 Institutions, social processes and space

To engage with these interdisciplinary research questions, which revolve around institutional change, political economy as well as space and territory, I built up a conceptual framework, discussed in Chapter 1, with elements from three main bodies of literature. To reiterate briefly, the foundation is an institutionalist understanding of socio-economic processes. It is assumed that economic behaviour like other types of behaviour is shaped by formal and informal institutions. Public policies are implemented through existing institutions at the same time that they contribute to modifying institutions through the incentive structures they put in place. To understand state action at various scales I used a qualitative political economy approach, a perspective that recognises the political influence of organised social groups while allowing for agency on the part of state actors. With regard to both economic and state actors, the theoretical framework is not based on utility maximising assumptions but rather on the *contingent rationality* of social actors, whose choices are always situated in an institutional context and motivated by an array of values (following Campbell *et al.* 1991). Lastly, I mobilised the concept of *rescaling* to analyse changing geographies of economic activities and the reconfiguration of state spaces in relation to both territory and traditional policy domains. With respect to territory, one classical conception of state space refers to the territorialisation of political power, and takes the nation-state as the starting point. In this more narrow conceptualisation, restructuring can take the form of *scaling up*, through the constitution of supranational trading blocs or multilateral agreements, for instance, or *scaling down*, by devolving responsibilities to local and regional territorial state institutions, which can include specialised agencies, or *ad hoc* bodies. State space is also conceptualised in abstract terms, where territoriality is one dimension among others, to designate the ways in which state institutions regulate socio-economic relations in space and influence locational geographies. The analysis of specific policies, mainly economic development policies, mobilised this 'integral' conception of state space (Brenner *et al.* 2003).

Although the rescaling concept has it origins in structural Marxism, it was seen that the foremost theoreticians working in this field today do not generally proceed on the assumption of the subordination of the political sphere to the economic sphere, and are careful to give attention to historically unique political societies and state formations. Nevertheless, the literature often contains a number of built-in assumptions arising from the specific context in which this theory emerged, i.e., the North Atlantic Fordist crisis, assumptions that this study of the Indian case helps bring to light.

To argue my thesis, I mobilised a large body of empirical case material, constituted over two decades of research in India. This research, built up from both fieldwork and secondary sources, concerns primarily four States: Kerala, Tamil Nadu, Andhra Pradesh and Haryana. This case material was 'revisited' here, using a spatially sensitive lens, and the research questions were analysed through the conceptual framework elaborated in the first three chapters. For each of the Chapters 4, 5 and 6 the approach consisted in discussing a specific research question, in relation to the literature, on the one hand, and to the case material, on the other, usually bringing in data and analysis from several different examples.

A multiscalar approach was used for examining the processes of economic reforms and the restructuring that has accompanied them, with a focus on national and subnational processes taking place within India's federal democracy. Interactions with the global sphere were considered to be beyond the scope of this study, except for the discussion in Chapter 3, where it was of vital importance for engaging with the claim that economic liberalisation was imposed on the Indian government from the outside. I argued that although various external factors did influence the decision to adopt reforms, endogenous factors were the main drivers.

7.2 Reconfiguration of state spatial scales

In order to examine how economic reforms are contributing to rescaling state spaces with regard to economic development policies, it was necessary to have a baseline, as well as background about the institutional context. Chapter 2 briefly outlined India's federal arrangements, with attention to the division of responsibilities between the Union and the regional States. It was seen that in the first period following independence, *grosso modo* 1950–80, India's development policies were largely calibrated on the national scale, a strategy consistent with the broader political objective of nation-building, which included grounding and legitimising the national state. The policy framework was fundamentally linked to the objective of constructing a national economy based on a single market, through the integration of disparate socio-economic spaces. These political and economic goals were mutually reinforced through national policies, e.g., freight equalisation, and national-scale institutions. In the governance structure that emerged, the central state occupied the commanding heights of the economy, and markets for many goods and services were highly regulated. Elaborate instruments were put in place to channel private industrial investments to the sectors and spaces considered most beneficial to national interests. This system, the licence-permit raj, generated its own incentives and economic and social actors situated at different scales mobilised skills and resources to 'work' the system and try to influence outcomes.

This institutional framework put regional States in a subordinate position *vis-à-vis* New Delhi with regard to policy-making, especially for industrial policies. Despite that, concrete examples from case studies illustrated how regional politicians manoeuvred and adapted central government programmes to their own conditions. *In fine*, their political capacity, and scope for strategic engagement with the central government were seen to be dependent on socio-political factors situated at subnational scales, within their territorial jurisdiction, and not on formal power-sharing arrangements. Nevertheless,

I argued that the State governments' contribution to defining the country's overall economic policy was limited, and that generalising on the basis of industrially developed States such as Gujarat or Maharashtra would over-estimate the agency of States during the licence-permit raj era. The central state purposefully pursued its agenda with a degree of autonomy and mobilised powerful instruments to shape economic governance. This position qualifies to some extent Aseema Sinha's thesis that national economic policy was 'the aggregate product of regional political strategies and institutions given a certain set of centrally imposed constraints' (2005: 115).

Following on this discussion, I proposed to explore the theoretical proposition that that not all subnational state territories are equally salient *as a frame of reference for organising social and economic activities*, despite their identical status in the formal territorial architecture of India's federal polity. This is because territorialisation processes are not contingent on political boundaries; rather, they emerge from spatial patterns of social organisation. India's widely divergent patterns of socio-economic relations bear testimony to these diverse processes and help explain in turn the variable geometry of federal governance.

Re-examining my doctoral research in Kerala, conducted in the early 1990s, I argued that regional patterns of social mobilisation, by shaping political objectives, were key determinants of the manner in which State governments responded to the centralised institutions for economic policy-making and planning. In other words, the incentive structure, resulting from a combination of central government institutions and policies, did not elicit a uniform response from States because their political objectives with regard to growth and development differed substantially. Social mobilisation was in turn contingent on local institutions, which reflect inherited social and economic structures. This approach suggests that caution is needed when comparing institutional variables in isolation from their contexts.

It can be recalled that scales, as they are defined here, correspond to spatial patterns of social organisation; they emerge from unique territorialisation processes and do not necessarily 'fit' with formal political boundaries. It follows that subnational states exhibit unique internal scalar hierarchies, reflecting variegated patterns of collective action, a hypothesis that was mobilised throughout the remainder of the study.

7.3 Scalar effects of economic reforms and post-reform strategies

The economic reforms adopted in the early 1990s, which followed the broad outlines of a structural adjustment formula, deregulated industrial investments and took steps to liberalise trade and investment. One of the immediate consequences was to dismantle the complex apparatus constructed to enable the centralised management of the national economy. Industrial investors were no longer required to obtain authorisation from the central government ministries and could choose the geographical location for their projects. This, and other forms of deregulation, had the significant effect of delinking the national development strategy, based on industrialisation, from national territory, a frame of reference that had been carefully built up in the immediate post-independence period. Combined with other structural changes that redefined the state's participation in the economy, such as control over credit institutions, these reforms significantly reconfigured economic governance, including its scalar dimensions.

Reforms had important implications for federal financial relations, cumulatively resulting in an increase in the responsibilities to be borne by the States. Because of fiscal consolidation measures, central transfers to the States decreased initially, and States were expected to generate a greater proportion of their revenue even though their formal fiscal powers were not enhanced. Under pressure to get the country's public finances in order for its own borrowing status in international circles, the central government adopted fiscal responsibility measures and devised incentives to induce State governments to do the same, progressively revising long-established practices of a hands-off approach to States' budget exercises. Central transfers became increasingly the object of negotiation, an evolution that put less financially independent States at a disadvantage compared to those with greater fiscal scope (Chapter 4). This example underscored the continued relevance of the national frame of reference for certain types of state action and demonstrated that the central government has capacity to implement structural reforms when committed to do so. The deployment of new instruments to elicit compliance from the States and changing norms in the way that transfers are negotiated suggested a more coercive approach than in the past. This was an important reminder that although the broad trend involves scaling economic regulation down to subnational States, national state power is *not* contracting as a result; rescaling is not a one directional movement, and always involves contestation, here between different state spatial scales.

In other policy areas too, the central state manifested its determination to remain a key player by reorganising national territory with implications for both state space and economic geographies. The 74th constitutional amendment, aimed to empower municipal bodies, was an initiative sponsored by the central government to rescale state space, via the devolution of powers and financial resources to urban local bodies. However, as the case material on four large metropolitan cities showed, State governments effectively resisted the strategy of transforming urban local governments into relevant political economic scales and refused to implement most of the core elements of that reform. This example, too, illustrated that state rescaling is a highly contested political process. This resistance to devolve power to local government is not new, but it takes on renewed significance in light of the growing contribution of cities to national revenue (estimated at 65 per cent of GDP). It is a reminder that effective changes in governance emerge as a result of struggles over the strategic control of socio-economic relations.

7.4 Economic policy-making at subnational scales

Economic reforms, by provoking institutional changes that reconfigure both state–market and state–society relations, contributed in rescaling the regulation of socio-economic activities to subnational scales. I detailed the various ways that this occurred, starting with the withdrawal of licence-permit raj and the deregulation of trade and investment. It was seen that rather quickly, by the late 1990s, most of India's major States had adopted similar 'promotional policies' for promoting industrial development, based on the simplification and streamlining of investment procedures, fiscal incentives and project finance. Specific examples indicated the broad range of instruments at their disposal, and the scope of their discretionary powers in dealing with private sector actors. Providing land for industrial projects, in particular, was seen to be a powerful lever used by State governments and many have directed or allowed their semi-autonomous industrial development agencies to use the power of eminent domain to expropriate landowners to build up 'land banks' or establish industrial estates in attractive locations. Tamil Nadu's policy with regard to industrial estates provided a forceful illustration of how spatial logics have changed in the last twenty years from a focus on the region's *internal industrial geographies*, with a view to promote more balanced regional development through industrial dispersal, to *a global frame of reference*, the aim of which is to create internationally competitive spaces. The political jurisdiction based on the State's territorial boundaries is unchanged, but the scalar frame of reference for political action has shifted. This reconfigured rapport with the territorial dimension of state space, which can be observed at the national scale also, is a key characteristic of state restructuring.

A significant point emerging from the analysis was that changes occurring in multilevel policy-making in India were neither automatic nor one-directional. Processes of scaling up and scaling down were both observed. The enhanced policy space enjoyed by State governments with regard to economic development policies did not result from a devolution of powers, but rather a reconfigured institutional environment to which subnational state actors responded in varying ways. The comparison of Odisha and Andhra Pradesh (Chapter 4) indicated that the reception of reforms was conditioned in part by the relative 'fiscal scope' of State governments, i.e., the manoeuvring room in a government's budget for committing resources to priority areas, without jeopardising overall economic stability. But I concluded that regional socio-political factors, like the social bases of the ruling parties, the degree of proximity between political and economic actors and the position of regional political elites in national politics were ultimately more decisive for explaining interstate differences than fiscal scope.

This qualitative political economy approach yielded insights for explaining State-level industrial development strategies, such as the Haryana government's recent policy decisions in favour of landowners, i.e., guaranteed floor pieces for acquired land and equity shares in development projects in the form of annuity (Chapter 5), which went against the immediate interests of investors. The 'social compromise' expressed by these policies reflects the evolution of Haryana's political economy in the last decades notably the fact that landowners, an important political force, have diversified their economic activities beyond agriculture. This is occurring in a context of rapid urbanisation, especially in proximity to the National Capital Region, the largest urban agglomeration in the country.

I submit that such an approach, which puts subnational political economies at the heart of the analysis, is necessary not only for understanding interstate variations in policy, but for gaining a broader understanding of India's development trajectory. Whether subnational political elites are inclined to negotiate in the medium or long-term interests of society or whether they are fixated on short-term gains depends fundamentally on the regional political system, the degree of mobilisation of subaltern groups, and on governance institutions, which influence the capacity of various local groups to pressure political leadership and influence outcomes.

At the same time, a multiscalar perspective is imperative. In comparing and contrasting the political response of India's States to reforms, the research showed that the support of the governing coalition in New Delhi was an additional factor that enhanced the political capacity of regional political elites in Haryana (in the 2000s) and in Andhra Pradesh (in the 1990s). Like their economies, which are contingent on India's macroeconomic policy regime, subnational politics are played out, to a degree, within a larger, multiscalar political game. The regionalisation of politics, a significant trend in India today, has engendered contradictory processes. On one hand, an increasing number of regional-based parties are contesting power and forming governments in the States, which both reflect and contribute to a territorialisation of political processes and greater salience of subnational scales as a spatial frame for collective action. On the other hand, the increasing participation of regional parties in national ruling coalitions has favoured the interpenetration of regional and national political arenas. As argued, these political developments are critically important for explaining both the manner in which the economic reform process has played out, and the emergence of subnational scales as key sites of economic governance.

As the examples analysed here suggest, rescaling processes generate a constant tension between the central state and the regional States, which are indicative of their overlapping territorial jurisdictions as well as their distinct political strategies aimed at territorial economic development. The central government tries to obtain 'compliance' and 'cooperation' from State governments through various means in order to extend its state space and encompass them within it. The latter respond in a differing fashion, in ways that express agency and that integrate at the same time constraints. It can be in a State's interest to allow the central state to dictate its terms. At other times, in response to internal political compulsions, it asserts its prerogatives and claims its pre-eminence over its (subnational) state space.

7.5 Interactions between rescaling and economic governance

Chapters 4, 5 and 6 were dedicated to analysing state restructuring at different spatial scales and discussing the implications for economic governance. For instance, the SEZ policy, considerably reinforced and voted into law in 2005, created a special regulatory framework for industrial investments. Aimed at boosting exports and creating productive capacity, the SEZ governance structure effectively imposes an overarching framework intended to supersede the various regulatory regimes in place in India's States. Although the SEZ law applies to national territory, the special regulatory regime it creates is only applicable to spatially delineated enclaves – it parcels national territory and removes these special spaces from the territorial jurisdiction of the subnational States and localities. Beyond shaping conditions for capital investment, the SEZ regulatory framework attempts to impose conditions on collective action, e.g., labour organisations, and exert pressure on State governments to revise social and environmental legislation. States have responded differently, both to implementing the SEZ policy and to the reactions it provoked within their territories. Protests were dealt with in fundamentally different ways, as the examples from Goa and West Bengal indicated. Andhra Pradesh stood out for its proactive approach – it has the largest number of notified SEZs in the country – and for its strategy of directly promoting SEZ projects and assisting private promoters through joint ventures or equity share in the form of land.

The focus here was not on the economic outcomes of the SEZ policy but on how it has reconfigured state space, which includes the spatial effects of the policy. The vast majority of zones are located in just a few States and the SEZ projects proposed in the IT industry in particular have concentrated in the country's largest metropolitan regions. In contrast to earlier policies that sought to shape economic geographies to meet national goals of market integration and balanced regional development, the SEZ policy offers favourable investment conditions to SEZ promoters wherever they choose to locate their zone in the country. But as the case material indicated, the location of these zones does not express the spatial preferences of market forces only but also political strategies of State governments. Interstate comparisons illustrated the variegated response to the national SEZ policy, by both elected officials and organised groups within society, and underscored the fact that policies are mediated through territorially rooted institutions. The SEZ policy's objective to 'normalise' economic regulation across national territory through a centralised policy tool remains a modernist fantasy; local institutions and localised social mobilisation opposing the policy continue to shape outcomes.

In Chapter 6, the focus turned explicitly to urban spaces to examine to what extent rescaling processes were occurring and the implications for urban governance. Metropolitan regions, which have emerged as major sites of economic growth, are the object of national and subnational state spatial strategies. Designed to produce spatially based competitive advantage, these strategies involve both territorial reorganisation and non-territorial instruments, e.g., sectoral policies. At the same time, in contrast to the experience of European and North American cities, the mandates of urban local governments in India remain extremely limited; in particular their jurisdictions do not extend to economic development policies. This pointed to a major divergence with respect to much of the international literature that emphasised the increased political significance of metropolitan cities. India is a compelling case in which economic activities are being rescaled to urban areas *without* a concomitant rescaling of territorial organisation. This has important implications for urban governance and for accountability in particular: decision making that directly affects urban spaces is not connected to the local political arena. This includes virtually all large-scale infrastructure and development projects (transport, housing, renovation of informal settlements or industrial areas). Local political representatives are not involved in decision making, and residents are rarely consulted, which reduces scope for collective action. One of the few outlets for the expression of public opinion is through protest, most of which remains localised.

The explicit aim behind the strategy to create Greater Hyderabad, examined in Chapter 6, was to build technical competency at the metropolitan scale and thereby upgrade the quality of basic services within a vast region. On one level, the strategy conforms to international trends observed with regard to global city-regions, i.e., territorial regrouping to build capability for competing internationally. However, the new territory – four times larger than the pre-existing municipality – was imposed in a top-down manner, with little regard for local political representatives. As for the recent creation of ward committees and area sabhas, constituted with non-elected representatives of 'civil society', it is too early to assess whether they will usher in an era of greater citizen participation.

Nevertheless, there *have* been important changes in urban governance across India's cities as a result of economic reforms and the neoliberal ideology that has accompanied them. Experiments with new models of delivery systems are taking place, usually introduced by international policy experts in the framework of externally funded programmes. In the example of healthcare reform in Hyderabad, the municipality delegated primary healthcare to NGOs and privatised core and non-core operations. The research showed that that the new delivery arrangements resulted in greater differentiation of services within municipal boundaries – both in their spatial deployment and in their quality. Local state space became more fragmented and its relation to the public was redefined as a result of the partnerships and the sub-contracting relations with private sector firms and individuals. The local state lacked the capacity to ensure effective oversight of the new arrangements, to regulate private actors and to meet its contractual agreements.

7.6 Theoretical insights from the Indian case

This study engaged explicitly with the literature on state spatial rescaling and argued in favour of its conceptual relevance for analysing the Indian case.

This rich field of inquiry provided a powerful interpretative framework for developments currently unfolding in India. In turn, the analyses of the Indian case generated a number of theoretical insights for expanding the theory of state rescaling, which have been discussed in the chapter conclusions and in the previous section. In particular, by examining a large emerging economy, with federal political institutions, this study has contributed to the contextual and conjunctural dimensions of investigation within this theory.

Evidence was mobilised to demonstrate that national and subnational state restructuring is occurring in India, reconfiguring the 'intermediary architectures' between local and supra-local economic processes. These include for instance procedures for investment, supply of infrastructure and local regulatory frameworks. Indian States were seen to exercise conditional autonomy over their territories and under certain conditions, they demonstrated the capacity to elaborate endogenous economic development policies. On the basis of several empirical case studies, I argued that subnational scales are significantly contributing to determining the conditions for capital accumulation and circulation, thereby corroborating findings based on North American case studies (Paul 2005). My analysis of the Indian case emphasised that subnational states' policies remained hierarchically subordinate to national economic regulation, which limit their capacity to influence the rules of the game at the global scale. Yet, subnational States *do* influence the terms and conditions in which socio-economic actors interact within their territories including in their interactions with global players; they have conditional agency, composing with other organised interests, to shape economic governance. Moreover, they are contributing in a more significant way than in the past in aggregately shaping India's overall economic trajectory, for instance, through the industrial specialisations that they promote (IT industry, automobile manufacturing, mining). Further substantiating and theorising the modalities of this aggregation process is an objective for future research.

The Indian state adopted rescaling strategies in fundamentally different conditions than those prevailing in Europe in the 1980s and 1990s. State spatial restructuring in Europe is associated with the crisis of 'North Atlantic Fordism', economic stagnation and high unemployment, and the 'rolling back of the welfare state'. In this context, restructuring is interpreted as a *defensive* strategy for maintaining a competitive edge in international markets, on which advanced industrial economies rely. It has involved sacrificing social gains obtained through political struggles in the post-war period and consolidated in the context of strong economic growth over three decades. In India, rescaling strategies became increasingly apparent in the 1990s and are linked to the liberalisation of the national economy. Hence they are associated with major restructuring of a state-led model of economic development and, fundamentally, with a period of stronger growth. Even before market reforms were adopted in the early 1990s, a first round of deregulation in the 1980s contributed to redefining economic governance and stimulated industrial growth. The subsequent strong growth of the Indian economy, especially in the 2000s, has given tremendous scope to the Indian state for developing policies in both economic and social domains, and has raised India's aspirations to participate more prominently in international fora. In this context, rescaling appears primarily as an *offensive* strategy, deployed at different spatial scales both national and subnational, for engaging with the global economy, bringing in investment for developing new capacity in industrial activities, and enhancing productive capacity of Indian firms to better compete in world markets.

If, as this suggests, state rescaling strategies have an independent existence, and are not intrinsically linked to a particular economic context, i.e., crisis, or a particular phase of capitalist development then they can in theory be combined with other types of policies than those being adopted in Europe. Indeed it could conceivably coexist with the expansion of social welfare policies. Whether in Europe or India, state rescaling and reterritorialisation strategies introduce significant changes in economic governance, but the consequences, e.g., for collective action, are not predetermined and remain contingent on the overall political economy context. Certainly, state–market relations have been radically reconfigured in India in the context of liberalisation and the state is increasingly delegating to the private sector (not without contestation) services that it was earlier expected to provide. But herein lies a major difference with the European experience: although the Indian state embraced a model of universal service based on national territory, in practice it did not provide a uniform level of basic services across national space, and the process of integrating the domestic economy, e.g., in terms of prices, taxes and labour markets remains incomplete. In this context, and given current rates of high growth and access to external capital, the Indian state can more easily pursue economic development strategies of various types, without necessarily being seen as retrenching, or compromising on its commitment to broad social goals. A number of large-scale social programmes have been launched in recent years, most notably the employment guarantee scheme (NREGS), which are intended as a social safety net for the most vulnerable groups, those who in many cases have been the most adversely affected by liberalisation. However, it should be noted that these are largely top-down initiatives, and are only partially emerging from socio-political struggles. Notwithstanding, struggles are being played out across India's vast territory, and are largely focused on the state, with a purpose of negotiating a new social contract that would redefine the state's role *vis-à-vis* society and *vis-à-vis* the economy.

In this context, it is not irrelevant to ask whether India is becoming a 'competition state'. There can be little doubt that it has taken on at least two of the characteristics associated with this term: (1) prioritising the pursuit of strategies to create or reinforce the competitive advantage of its territory; and (2) increased marketisation of economic activities, which are typically not commodified in a welfare state regime, e.g., education and health.[1] We examined here specific examples of policies, such as SEZs and reforms in urban healthcare service delivery systems, which bear striking similarity in their form to broad trends identified in the literature on competition states in Europe.

However, both types of processes can still be considered experimental in India. The SEZ policy in particular is highly contested and the state could still reverse course.[2] Moreover, it is important to recall that India has a large domestic economy and is relatively less dependent on trade than Europe, making it less vulnerable to the vagaries of the global economy. Although India has moved closer to a market economy model, it is not a 'liberal' market regime and passionate debates continue within India about which path to follow, which mix of 'public' and 'private' is appropriate. Democratic politics explains the gradual sequencing of reforms, as well as the occasional backtracking, and leaves room for hope that political mobilisation will effectively contribute to the emergence of a socially sustainable future path.

Notes

1 These are presented by Neil Brenner as key perspectives on the post-Keynesian competition state (see Jessop 2002: 96; Cerny 1997: 259, cited by Brenner 2004: 173).
2 As mentioned, there was disagreement within the Indian state, between the Ministry of Finance and the Ministry of Commerce over whether the SEZ policy was justified in light of the notional tax revenues that would be lost. In 2011 the Ministry of Finance announced that a minimum alternative tax of 18.5 per cent would be imposed on SEZs, thereby backtracking on the total tax exemption initially offered.

References

Adeney, Katharine. 2005. 'Hindu nationalists and federal structures in an era of regionalism.' In Katharine Adeney and Lawrence Sáez, eds, *Coalition Politics and Hindu Nationalism*. London: Routledge, pp. 97–115.

Aggarwal, Aradhna. 2006. 'Special economic zones: revisiting the policy debate.' *Economic and Political Weekly* 41(43–4): 4533–6.

——2012. *Social and Economic Impact of SEZs in India*. Delhi: Oxford University Press.

Agnew, John A. and Stuart Corbridge. 1995. *Mastering Space: Hegemony, Territory and International Political Economy*. London; New York: Routledge.

Ahluwalia, Montek S. 2002. 'Economic reforms in India since 1991: has gradualism worked?' *Journal of Economic Perspectives* 16(3): 67–88.

——2004. 'Understanding India's reform trajectory: past trends and future challenges.' In Rob Jenkins and Sunil Khilnani, eds, *The Politics of India's Next Generation of Economic, India Review* 3(4).

Amable, Bruno. 2003. *The Diversity of Modern Capitalism*. Oxford and New York: Oxford University Press.

Amable, Bruno and Stefano Palombarini. 2005. *L'économie politique n'est pas une science morale*. Paris: Raisons d'agir.

Arora, Balveer. 2007. 'Adaptation and innovation in Indian federalism: institutional responses to socio-economic change.' Indo-French seminar, Rediscovery of India, Maison des Sciences de l'Homme, Paris, 31 May–1 June.

Austin, Granville. 1999. *The Indian Constitution: Cornerstone of a Nation*. Oxford and New York: Oxford University Press.

Bach, Jonathan. 2011. 'Modernity and the urban imagination in economic zones.' *Theory, Culture & Society* 28(5) (September 2011).

Bagchi, Amaresh. 2003. 'Rethinking federalism: changing power relations between the Center and the States.' *Publius* 33(4), Emerging Federal Process in India (autumn, 2003), 21–42.

Bajpai, N. and J. D. Sachs. 1999. 'The progress of policy reform and variations in performance at the sub-national level in India.' Development Discussion Paper 730, Harvard Institute for International Development, Cambridge, MA: Harvard University.

Banerjee-Guha, Swapna, ed. 2010. *Accumulation by Dispossession. Transformative Cities in the New Global Order*. New Delhi: Sage.

Banerjee, Partha Sarathi. Forthcoming. 'Orissa and West Bengal: of parties and protest' In Rob Jenkins, Loraine Kennedy and Partha Mukhopadhyay, eds, *Power, Policy, and Protest: The Politics of India's Special Economic Zones*. New Delhi: Oxford University Press.

Baru, Sanjaya. 2000. 'Economic policy and the development of capitalism in India: the role of regional capitalists and political parties.' In Francine R. Frankel, ed., *Transforming India: Social and Political Dynamics of Democracy*. New Delhi and New York: Oxford University Press.

Baud, Isa and R. Dhanalakshmi. 2007. 'Governance in urban environmental management: comparing accountability and performance in multi-stakeholder arrangements in South India.' *Cities* 24(2): 133–47.

Baud, I. S. A. and Joop de Wit, eds. 2008. *New Forms of Urban Governance in India. Shifts, Models, Networks and Contestations*. New Delhi: Sage.

Baud, Isa and Navtej Nainan. 2008. 'Negotiated spaces for representation in Mumbai: ward committees, advanced locality management and the politics of middle-class activism.' *Environment and Urbanization* 20(2): 483–99.

Bayart, Jean-François. 2004. *Le gouvernement du monde: une critique politique de la globalisation*. Paris: Fayard.

Benbabaali, Dalel. 2009. 'Importing new cultures into the city: the role of Kamma migrants in the development of Andhra culture in Hyderabad.' In Geetha Reddy Anant, ed., *Emerging Urban Transformations: Multilayered Cities and Urban Systems*. Proceedings of the International Geographical Union, Urban Geography Commission, Hyderabad.

Benjamin, S., R. Bhuvaneswari and P. Manjunatha. 2007. 'Bhoomi: 'E-governance', or, an anti-politics machine necessary to globalize Bangalore?' In CASUM-m Working Paper. Bangalore, India: Collaborative for the Advancement of Studies in Urbanism through Mixed-Media (CASUM-m).

Benko, Georges and Alain Lipietz, eds. 1992. *Les Régions qui gagnent. Districts et réseaux: les nouveaux paradigmes de la géographie économique*. Paris: Presses Universitaires de France.

Best, Michael H. 1990. *The New Competition. Institutions of Industrial Restructuring*. Cambridge, MA: Harvard University Press.

Bhagwati, Jagdish N. 2004. *In Defense of Globalization*. New York: Oxford University Press.

Boyer, Robert. 1990. *The Regulation School: A Critical Introduction*. New York: Columbia University Press.

Boyer, Robert and Yves Saillard. 2002. *Regulation Theory: The State of the Art*. London and New York: Routledge.

Brass, Paul. 2000. 'The strong state and the fear of disorder.' In Francine R. Frankel, Hasan Zoya, Bhargava Rajeev and Balveer Arora, eds, *Transforming India: Social and Political Dynamics of Democracy*. New Delhi and New York: Oxford University Press.

Brenner, Neil. 1998. 'Global cities, glocal states: global city formation and state territorial restructuring in contemporary Europe.' *Review of International Political Economy* 5(1): 1–37.

——2001. 'State theory in the political conjuncture: Henri Lefebvre's "Comments on a New State Form".' *Antipode* 33(5): 783–808.

——2004. *New State Spaces: Urban Governance and the Rescaling of Statehood*. New York: Oxford University Press.

——2009. 'Open questions on state rescaling.' *Cambridge Journal of Regions, Economy and Society* 2(1): 123–39.

Brenner, Neil, Bob Jessop, Martin Jones and Gordon MacLeod, eds. 2003. *State/ Space: A Reader*. Malden, MA and Oxford: Blackwell.

Brusco, Sebastiano. 1982. 'The Emilian model: productive decentralisation and social integration.' *Cambridge Journal of Economics* 6(2): 167–84.

Cadène, Philippe and Mark Holmström, eds. 1998. *Decentralized Production in India. Industrial Districts, Flexible Specialization and Employment*. Pondicherry: French Institute of Pondicherry and New Delhi: Sage.

Campbell, John L., J. Rogers Hollingsworth and Leon N. Lindberg. 1991. *Governance of the American Economy*. Cambridge; New York: Cambridge University Press.

Caseley, Jonathan. 2004. 'Public sector reform and corruption: CARD façade in Andhra Pradesh.' *Economic and Political Weekly* 39(11).

CDA, Cyberabad Development Area. 2001. *Cyberabad Master Plan*. Government of Andhra Pradesh.

Chakraborty, Pinaki, Anit N. Mukherjee and H. K. Amarnath. 2009. 'Macro policy reform and sub-national finance: why is the Fiscal space of the states shrinking?' *Economic and Political Weekly* 44(14): 38–44.

Chakraborty, Pinaki. 2000. 'How does structural reform affect regional development? Resolving contradictory theory with evidence from India.' *Economic Geography* 76(4): 367–94.

Chakravorty, Sanjoy and Somik V. Lall. 2007. *Made in India: The Economic Geography and Political Economy of Industrialization*. New Delhi and New York: Oxford University Press.

Chelliah, Raja J. 2005. 'Malady of Continuing Fiscal Imbalance.' *Economic and Political Weekly* 40(31): 3399–3404.

Cornwall, Andrea. 2002. 'Making spaces, changing places: situating participation in development.' *IDS Working Paper* 170.

Crook, Richard C. and James Manor. 1998. *Democracy and Decentralisation in South Asia and West Africa: Participation, Accountability, and Performance*. Cambridge and New York: Cambridge University Press.

Crouch, C., W. Streeck, R. Boyer, B. Amable, P. A. Hall and G. Jackson. 2005. 'Dialogue on "institutional complementarity and political economy".' *Socio-Economic Review* 3(2), 359–82.

CSDS team with Suri K. C. 1999. 'A triumph of alliance arithmetic.' *Frontline*, 16(23): 6–19 (November 1999).

Cunyi, Yin, Tang Zhilin and Tak-Wing Ngo. 2012. 'Rent seeking and spatial politics in China's Development Zones.' In *State Restructuring and Economic Development in India and China. Subnational Scales in Comparative Perspective*. Workshop, organised at the Centre for South Asian Studies (CEIAS, CNRS-EHESS), Paris, 4 May 2012.

Da Silva, Solano. Forthcoming. 'Goa: the dynamics of reversal.' In Rob Jenkins, Loraine Kennedy, Partha Mukhopadhyay, eds, *Power, Policy, and Protest: The Politics of India's Special Economic Zones*. New Delhi: Oxford University Press.

Das, Keshab, ed. 2005. *Indian Industrial Clusters*. Burlington, VT: Ashgate.

De Haan, Arjan. 2004. 'Disparities within India's poorest regions: why do the same institutions work differently in different places?' Background paper for the World Bank World Development Report 2006.

Denis, Eric. 2010. 'The land question in India, in relation to a city-centric growth strategy.' *Background paper for the India Country Report: Chance2Sustain Project* (FP7, European Commission). See www.chance2sustain.eu

Dubresson, Alain and Sylvy Jaglin. 2005. 'Gouvernance, régulation et territorialisation des espaces urbanisés Approches et méthode.' In Benoît Antheaume and Frédéric Giraut, eds, *Le territoire est mort. Vive les territoires!* Paris: IRD Editions.

Dubresson, Alain and Yves-André Fauré. 2005. 'Décentralisation et développement local: un lien à repenser.' *Revue Tiers-Monde* 46(181): 7–20.

Dupont, Véronique. 1995. *Decentralized Industrialization and Urban Dynamics. The Case of Jetpur in West India.* New Delhi: Sage.

Durand-Dastès, François. 1995. 'Monde indien.' In R. Brunet, ed., *Géographie Universelle.* Belin: Reclus.

Echeverri-Gent. 2004. 'Financial globalization and India's equity market reforms.' In Rob Jenkins and Sunil Khilnani, eds, *The Politics of India's Next Generation of Economic, India Review* 3(4).

EPCES. 2008. *Guide: A Comprehensive Compilation of Notifications and Circulars,* 5th edn. New Delhi: Export Promotion Council for EOUs and SEZs.

Ghosh, Archana and A. M. Basu. 2007. 'Urban governance in Kolkata: actors, policies and reforms.' In paper presented at the seminar on Urban Actors, Policies and Governance in Four Metropolitan Cities, India International Centre and CSH, New Delhi, 23–24 January.

Ghosh, Archana. 2009. 'Participatory urban governance and slum development in Hyderabad and Kolkata.' In Joel Ruet and Stéphanie Tawa Lama-Rewal, eds, *Governing India's Metropolises.* New Delhi: Routledge.

Ghosh, Archana and Stéphanie Tawa Lama-Rewal. 2005. *Democratization in Progress. Women and Local Politics in Urban India.* New Delhi: Tulika.

Gill, K. 1999. *If We Walk Together. Communities, NGOs, and Government in Partnership for Health – The IPP VIII Hyderabad Experience.* Washington, DC: World Bank.

Gill, Sucha Singh, ed. 2001. *Land reforms in India, Volume 6: Intervention for agrarian capitalist transformation in Punjab and Haryana.* New Delhi: Sage.

Gilly, Jean-Pierre and André Torre. 2000. *Dynamiques de proximité.* Paris: Harmattan.

GoAP, Government of Andhra Pradesh. 1999. *Andhra Pradesh: Vision 2020.* Hyderabad: Government of Andhra Pradesh.

GoH, Government of Haryana. 2007. 'Policy for rehabilitation and resettlement of landowners – land acquisition oustees.' Chandigarh: Notification dated 7 December 2007, Revenue and Disaster Management Department.

——2010. 'Revision of minimum floor rates and the Policy for Rehabilitation and Resettlement of Land Owners–Land Acquisition Oustees.' Chandigarh: Notification dated 9 November 2010, Revenue and Disaster Management Department.

GoI, Government of India. 1987. *Commission on Centre–State Relations: Report.* Volume II.

——1988. *Commission on Centre–State Relations: Report.* Volume I.

——2005. *The Special Economic Zones Act, 2005.* New Delhi: Gazette of India.

——2010, 2011. *Land Titling Bill (Revised).* Available at: www.prsindia.org (last consulted 21 January 2012).

——2010. *Commission on Centre–State Relations Report. Volume I. Evolution of Centre–State Relations in India.* New Delhi: Government of India.

——n.d. [2011]. 'Discussion Paper to Facilitate Stakeholder Consultation on Potential Reform of the SEZ Policy and Operating Framework.' Department of Commerce SEZ Division, sezindia.nic.in/writereaddata/updates/sez_review.pdf (consulted 22 November 2011).

Government of Orissa. 2009. *Economic Survey of Orissa, 2008–9*. Bhubaneswar.

Govinda Rao, M. and Nirvikar Singh. (2003). 'The political economy of Center–State fiscal transfers in India.' In John McLaren, ed., *Institutional Elements of Tax Design and Reform*. Washington, DC: World Bank, pp. 69–101.

Graham, Stephen. 2000. 'Constructing premium network spaces: reflections on infrastructure networks and contemporary urban development.' *International Journal of Urban and Regional Research* 24(1): 183–200.

Grant, R. and J. Nijman. 2004. 'The rescaling of uneven development in Ghana and India.' *Tijdschrift voor Economische en Sociale Geografie* 95(5): 467–81.

Grasset, Jérémy and Frédéric Landy. 2007. 'Les zones franches de l'Inde, entre ouverture à l'international et spéculation immobilière.' *Annales de géographie* 658: 608–27.

Gupta, Akhil and K. Sivaramakrishnan, eds. 2011. *The State in India after Liberalization*. London and New York: Routledge.

Hall, Peter A. 1986. *Governing the Economy: The Politics of State Intervention in Britain and France*. New York: Oxford University Press.

Harriss, John. 1999. 'Comparing political regimes across Indian States.' *Economic and Political Weekly* 34(48) (27 November).

Harriss-White, Barbara. 2007. *Rural Commercial Capital. Agricultural Markets in West Bengal*. New Delhi: Oxford University Press.

Harvey, David. 1989. 'From managerialism to entrepreneurialism: the transformation in urban governance in late capitalism.' *Geografiska Annaler. Series B* 71(1): 3–17.

Heller, Patrick. 1995. 'From class struggle to class compromise: redistribution and growth in a South Indian State.' *Journal of Development Studies* 31(5): 645–72.

Heller, Peter. 2005. 'Back to basics – fiscal space: what it is and how to get it.' In *Finance & Development*: www.imf.org/external/pubs/ft/fandd/2005/06/basics.htm.

Hibou, Béatrice, ed. 2004. *Privatizing the State*. New York: Columbia University Press (published in France in 1999 as *La Privatisation des États*, Paris: Karthala).

Hochraich, Diana. 2002. *Mondialisation contre développement: le cas des pays asiatiques*. Paris: Syllepse.

Holmström, Mark. 1998. 'Introduction: industrial districts and flexible specialization, the outlook for smaller firms in India'. In Ph. Cadène and M. Holmström, eds, *Decentralized Production in India*. New Delhi: Institut Français de Pondichéry and Sage, pp. 7–41.

Huchet, Jean-François and Joel Ruet, eds. 2006. *Globalisation and Opening Markets in Developing Countries and Impacts on National Firms and Public Governance. The Case of India*. New Delhi: Report CSH-LSE-NCAER-ORF-Cerna.

Huchet, Jean-François. 2010. 'Le rôle de l'Etat dans le décollage industriel de la Chine depuis 1978.' Rennes: Habilitation à diriger des recherches, Université Rennes 2.

Huchon, Agnès and Guillaume Tricot. 2008. 'Between citizens and institutions: the dynamics of the integration of water supply and sanitation services in Hyderabad.' New Delhi: Occasional Paper No. 22, Centre de Sciences Humaines, New Delhi, www.csh-delhi.com/ops.php?idop=22.

Jaffrelot, Christophe. 2003. *India's Silent Revolution: The Rise of the Lower Castes in North India*. New York: Columbia University Press.

Jaglin, Sylvy. 2005. *Services d'eau en Afrique subsaharienne. La fragmentation urbaine en question*. Paris: CNRS Editions.

Jenkins, Rob. 1999. *Democratic Politics and Economic Reform in India*. New York: Cambridge University Press.

——2004. 'Introduction.' In Rob Jenkins and Sunil Khilnani, eds, *The Politics of India's Next Generation of Economic, India Review* 3(4).

——2011. 'The politics of India's special economic zones.' In S. Ruparelia, S. Reddy, J. Harriss and S. Corbridge, eds, *Understanding India's New Political Economy.* London and New York: Routledge, pp. 49–65.

Jenkins, Rob, Loraine Kennedy, Partha Mukhopadhyay, eds. Forthcoming. *Power, Policy, and Protest: The Politics of India's Special Economic Zones.* Delhi: Oxford University Press.

Jodhka, Surinder S. 1999. 'Haryana. Change of government and beyond.' *Economic and Political Weekly* 34(32): 2217–18.

Jodhka, Surinder S. and Murli Dhar. 2003. 'Cow, caste and communal politics: Dalit killings in Jhajjar.' *Economic and Political Weekly* 38(3): 174–6.

Jones, M. 2001. 'The rise of the regional state in economic governance: "partnerships for prosperity" or new scales of state power?' *Environment and Planning A* 33(7): 1185–1211.

Joshi, Dhananjai and Praveen Rai. 2009. 'Haryana. A verdict beyond anti-incumbency.' In S. Shastri, Suri, K. C., Yadav, Y., eds, *Electoral Politics in Indian States.* New Delhi: Oxford University Press.

Jouve, Bernard. 2005. 'Réétalonnage polique et régime urbain: le cas de Montréal.' In Congrès de l'association française de science politique, 14–16 septembre, Université Lyon II.

——2007. 'Le "political rescaling" pour théoriser l'état et la compétition territoriale en Europe.' In Alain Faure, Jean-Philippe Leresche, Pierre Muller and Stéphane Nahrath, eds, *Action publique et changements d'échelles: Les nouvelles focales du politique.* Paris: L'Harmattan.

Jouve, B. and Christian Lefevre, eds. 2004. *Horizons Métropolitains.* Lausanne: Presses polytechniques et universitaires romandes.

Kapur, Devesh. 2004. 'Ideas and economic reforms in India: the role of international migration and the Indian diaspora.' In Rob Jenkins and Sunil Khilnani, eds, *The Politics of India's Next Generation of Economic, India Review* 3(4).

Kennedy, Loraine. 1994. 'Articulation des espaces de développement en Inde: les industries traditionnelles au Kerala.' Paris: doctorat de l'École des Hautes Études en Sciences Sociales (spécialité: socio-économie du développement).

——1996. 'La crise de l'État-Providence au Kérala (Inde).' *Revue Tiers Monde* 37(148): 897–918.

——1999. 'Cooperating for survival: tannery pollution and joint action in the Palar Valley (India).' *World Development* 27(9): 1673–91.

——2004a. 'The political determinants of reform packaging: contrasting responses to economic liberalization in Andhra Pradesh and Tamil Nadu.' In Rob Jenkins, ed., *Regional Reflections: Comparing Politics Across India's States.* New Delhi: Oxford University Press.

——2004b. 'Mobilizing regional identity in pursuit of Swarna Andhra. Strategies to foster growth and engage with globalization in Andhra Pradesh.' Paper presented at the symposium Regions and Regional Consciousness in India, Arizona State University, 7–9 March.

——2004c. 'Endogenous development and globalisation. An industrial district in Tamil Nadu.' In F. Landy and B. Chaudhuri, eds, *Examining the Spatial Dimension: From Globalisation to Local Development in India.* New Delhi: Manohar, pp. 83–6.

——2007a. 'Regional industrial policies driving peri-urban dynamics in Hyderabad, India.' *Cities* 24(2): 95–109.

——2007b. 'Shaping economic space in Chennai and Hyderabad. The assertion of State-level policies in the post-reform era.' *Purusartha* (special issue on cities in South Asia), Éditions EHESS, Paris, pp. 315–51.

——2008. 'New forms of governance in Hyderabad: how urban reforms are redefining actors in the city.' In I. Baud and J. de Wit, eds, *New Forms of Urban Governance in India. Shifts, Models, Networks and Contestations*. New Delhi: Sage, pp. 253–87.

——2009. 'New patterns of participation shaping urban governance.' In Joel Ruet and Stéphanie Tawa Lama-Rewal, eds, *Governing India's Metropolises*. New Delhi: Routledge.

——2011. 'Indian federalism: moving towards a more balanced system.' In Christophe Jaffrelot, ed., *India Since 1950. Society, Politics, Economy and Culture*. New Delhi: Yatra Books India.

——Forthcoming. 'Haryana. Beyond the rural–urban divide.' In Rob Jenkins, Loraine Kennedy and Partha Mukhopadhyay, eds, *Power, Policy, and Protest: The Politics of India's Special Economic Zones*. New Delhi: Oxford University Press.

Kennedy, Loraine and Chigurupati Ramachandraiah. 2006. 'Logiques spatiales d'une stratégie régionale "high-tech". L'exemple de HITEC City à Hyderabad (Inde).' *Flux* 2006 1–2 (63–4) (Dossier: 'Innovations et territoires'): 54–70.

Kennedy, Loraine and Marie-Hélène Zérah. 2008. 'The shift to city-centric growth strategies: perspectives from Hyderabad and Mumbai.' *Economic and Political Weekly* 43(39): 110–17.

Kennedy, Loraine, Kim Robin and Diego Zamuner. 2013. 'Comparing State-level policy responses to economic reforms in India.' *Revue de la Régulation*, online journal, 13/spring 2013, 24 June 2013, http://regulation.revues.org/10247.

Kennedy, Loraine and M. Vijayabaskar. 2011. 'Emerging institutional arrangements in India's land market.' Paper presented at the International Symposium entitled Institutional Voids and the Governance of Developing Economies. International Institute of Asian Studies, Rotterdam, the Netherlands, 16 May.

Khemani, Stuti. 2003. 'Partisan politics and intergovernmental transfers in India.' In SSRN eLibrary. Washington, DC: World Bank Policy Research Working Paper No. 3016.

Knorringa, Peter. 1999. 'Agra: an old cluster facing the new competition.' *World Development* 27(9): 1587–604.

Kohli, Atul. 1987. *The State and Poverty in India: The Politics of Reform*. Cambridge; New York: Cambridge University Press.

——1989. 'Politics of economic liberalization in India.' *World Development* 17(3): 305–28.

——2012. *Poverty Amid Plenty in the New India*. Cambridge and New York: Cambridge University Press.

Kumar, Girish. 2006. *Local Democracy in India. Interpreting Decentralization*. New Delhi: Sage.

Kumar, Sanjay. 2004. 'Janata regionalized: contrasting bases of electoral support in Bihar and Orissa.' In Rob Jenkins, ed., *Regional Reflections: Comparing Politics across India's States*. New Delhi: Oxford University Press.

Landy, Frédéric. 2006. *Un milliard à nourrir: grain, territoire et politiques en Inde*. Paris: Belin.

——2009. *Feeding India. The Spatial Parameters of Food Grain Policy*. Delhi: Manohar Publishers and Centre de Sciences Humaines.

Landy, Frédéric, ed. 2010. *Dictionnaire de l'Inde contemporaine*. Paris: Armand Colin.

Lefebvre, Bertrand. 2008. 'The Indian corporate hospitals: touching middle class lives.' In Christophe Jaffrelot and Peter van der Veer, eds, *Patterns of Middle Class Consumption in India and China*. New Delhi: Sage.

Le Galès, Patrick. 1995. 'Du gouvernement des villes à la gouvernance urbaine.' *Revue française de science politique* 45(1): 57–95.

Lobo, Albert and Suresh Balakrishnan. 2002. 'Report card on service of Bhoomi Kiosks: An assessment of benefits by users of the computerized land records system in Karnataka.' Bangalore: Public Affairs Centre.

Mahadevia, Darshini. 2003. 'Policies towards globalizing cities.' In Darshini Mahadevia, ed., *Globalisation Urban Reforms and Metropolitan Response*. New Delhi India: Manak.

Mawdsley, Emma. 2002. 'Redrawing the body politic: federalism, regionalism and the creation of new States in India.' *Commonwealth & Comparative Politics* 40(3): 34–54.

Melchior, Arne. 2010. 'Globalisation, domestic market integration, and the regional disparities of India.' In NUPI Working Paper 780: Norwegian Institute of International Affairs, Oslo, Norway.

Menon, S. Narayan and Soumya Kanti Mitra. 2009. 'Special economic zones. The rationale.' New Delhi: Centre for Policy Research, No. 16.

Mishra, Banikanta. 2010. 'Agriculture, industry and mining in Orissa in the post-liberalisation era: an inter-district and inter-state panel analysis.' In *Economic and Political Weekly* 45, 15: May, 49–68.

Misra, Biswa Swarup. 2007. *Regional Growth Dynamics in India in the Post-Economic Reform Period*. New York: Palgrave Macmillan.

Mitra, Subrata K. 2007. 'Federalism's success.' In Sumit Ganguly, Larry Jay Diamond and Marc F. Plattner, eds, *The State of India's Democracy*. Baltimore, MD: Johns Hopkins University Press.

Mody, Anjali. 2010. 'Special economic zones: a briefing note.' Delhi: IndiaSEZPolitics.org.

Moisio, Sami. 2011. 'Political geographies of the state and scale.' *Political Geography* 30(3): 173–4.

Molotch, Harvey. 1976. 'The city as a growth machine: toward a political economy of place.' *American Journal of Sociology* 82(2): 309–32.

Mooij, Jos E. 2003. 'Smart governance? Politics in the policy process in Andhra Pradesh, India.' In ODI Working Paper No. 228. London: Overseas Development Institute.

——2005. 'Introduction.' In Jos E. Mooij, ed., *The Politics of Economic Reforms in India*. New Delhi and Thousand Oaks, CA: Sage.

——2007. 'Hype, skill and class: the politics of reform in Andhra Pradesh, India.' *Commonwealth & Comparative Politics* 45(1), 34–56.

Mooij, Jos E. and Jennifer Jalal. 2009. 'Primary education in Delhi, Hyderabad and Kolkata: governance by resignation, privatisation by default.' In Joel Ruet and Stéphanie Tawa Lama-Rewal, eds, *Governing India's Metropolises*. New Delhi: Routledge.

Mukherji, Rahul, ed. 2007. *India's Economic Transition: The Politics of Reforms*. Oxford and New York: Oxford University Press.

Mukhopadhyay, Partha. 2006. 'Whither urban renewal?' *Economic and Political Weekly* 41(10): 879–84.

Nadvi, Khalid and Hubert Schmitz, eds. 1999. 'Industrial clusters in developing countries.' Special Issue, *World Development* 27(9): 1503–1734.

Nagaraj, R. 2008. 'India's recent economic growth: a closer look.' *Economic and Political Weekly* 4(15): 55–61.

Naidu, N. Chandrababu and Sevanti Ninan. 2000. *Plain Speaking*. New Delhi: Viking.

Nainan, Navtej. 2005. 'Ward committees of Mumbai – functions, finances and practices.' Paper presented at the Indo-Dutch conference on New Forms of Urban Governance in Indian Mega-Cities, Jawaharlal Nehru University, New Delhi, 10–11 January 2005.

Narayana, K. V. 2003. 'Size and nature of healthcare system.' In C. H. Hanumantha Rao and S. Mahendra Dev, eds, *Andhra Pradesh Development. Economic Reforms and Challenges Ahead*. Hyderabad: Centre for Economic and Social Studies (dist. Manohar New Delhi).

Nayar, Baldev Raj. 2005. *The Geopolitics of Globalization: The Consequences for Development*. New Delhi: Oxford University Press.

Nehru, Jawaharlal. 1968. *Jawaharlal Nehru's Speeches*. New Delhi: Government of India Publications (5 vols).

Nooruddin, Irfan and Pradeep Chhibber. 2008. 'Unstable politics: fiscal space and electoral volatility in the Indian States.' *Comparative Political Studies* 41(8).

North, Douglass Cecil. 1990. *Institutions, Institutional Change, and Economic Performance*. Cambridge and New York: Cambridge University Press.

Ohmae, Kenichi. 1996. *The End of the Nation State. The Rise of Regional Economies*. New York: Free Press Paperbacks (Simon & Schuster).

Ong, Aihwa. 2006. *Neoliberalism as Exception: Mutations in Citizenship and Sovereignty*. Durham, NC: Duke University Press.

Painter, J. and M. Goodwin. 1995. 'Local governance and concrete research: investigating the uneven development of regulation.' *Economy and Society* 24(3): 334–56.

Paul, Darel E. 2002. 'Re-scaling IPE: subnational states and the regulation of the global political economy.' *Review of International Political Economy* 9(3): 465–89.

——2005. *Rescaling International Political Economy: Subnational States and the Regulation of the Global Political Economy*. New York: Routledge.

Pecqueur, Bernard and Jean-Benoît Zimmermann. 2004. *Économie de proximités*. Hermès Lavoisier.

Pecqueur, Bernard. 2001. 'Gouvernance et régulation.' *Géographie, Économie, Société* 3(2): 229–45.

Pethe, A. and M. Lalvani. 2007. 'Analyze this: deciphering the code of "Mumbai" budgets'. Paper presented at the seminar on Urban Actors, Policies and Governance in Four Metropolitan Cities, India International Centre and CSH, New Delhi, 23–24 January 2007.

Pinto, Marina R. 2000. *Metropolitan City Governance in India*. New Delhi: Sage.

——2008. 'Urban governance in India – spotlight on Mumbai.' In Isa Baud and Joop de Wit, eds, *New Forms of Urban Governance in India. Shifts, Models, Networks and Contestations*. New Delhi: Sage.

Piore, Michael J. and Charles F. Sabel. 1984. *The Second Industrial Divide: Possibilities for Prosperity*. New York: Basic Books.

Prakash, Gyan. 2002. 'The urban turn.' In Ravi Vasudevan *et al.*, eds, *The Cities of Everyday Life*. Delhi: Centre for the Study of Developing Societies.

Purohit, Mahesh. 2008. 'Harmonizing taxation of interstate trade under a subnational VAT: lessons from international experience.' In Anwar Shah, ed., *Macro Federalism and Local Finance*. Washington, DC: World Bank.

Racine, Jean-Luc. 2003. 'L'Inde et l'ordre du monde.' *Hérodote* 108: 91–112.

——2008. 'Quête de puissance, multipolarité et multilatéralisme' In Christophe Jaffrelot, ed., *New Delhi et le monde*. Paris: Autrement.

Ramachandran, R. 1989. *Urbanization and Urban Systems in India*. New Delhi: Oxford University Press.

Reddy, D. Narasimha, ed. 1999. *Vision 2020: Myths and Realities*. Hyderabad: Sundarayya Vignana Kendram.

Robin, Kim. 2009. *A Study on Fiscal Space*. New Delhi: Centre de Sciences Humaines [published in 2013 as a CSH Working Paper; www.csh-deihi.com/index.php?option= com_flexicontent&view=category&cid=100&Itemid=493&lang=en (last consulted 30 October 2013)]

——2010. 'Why are people poor? A study of the determinants of poverty in rural India.' Master's thesis, SciencesPo, Paris.

Rodrik, Dani and Arvind Subramanian. 2004. *From 'Hindu Growth' to Productivity Surge: The Mystery of the Indian Growth Transition*. Cambridge, MA: National Bureau of Economic Research.

Rodrik, Dani, ed. 2003. *In Search of Prosperity: Analytic Narratives on Economic Growth*. Princeton, NJ: Princeton University Press.

——2007. *One Economics, Many Recipes: Globalization, Institutions, and Economic Growth*. Princeton, NJ: Princeton University Press.

Rodrik, Dani, Arvind Subramanian and Francesco Trebbi. 2002. 'Institutions rule: the primacy of institutions over integration and geography in economic development.' Washington, DC: IMF Working Paper WP/02/189.

Rosen, George. 1988. *Industrial Change in India 1970–2000*. Riverdale, MD: Riverdale Company.

Ruet, Joel and Stéphanie Tawa Lama-Rewal, eds. 2009. *Governing India's Metropolises*. New Delhi: Routledge.

Sack, Robert David. 1986. *Human Territoriality: Its Theory and History*. Cambridge and New York: Cambridge University Press.

Sáez, Lawrence. 2002. *Federalism without a Center: The Impact of Political and Economic Reform on India's Federal System*. New Delhi and Thousand Oaks, CA: Sage.

Sarangi, Prakash. 2005. 'Economic reforms and changes in the party system.' In Jos E. Mooij, ed., *The Politics of Economic Reforms in India*. New Delhi and Thousand Oaks, CA: Sage.

Sassen, Saskia. 1991. *The Global City: New York, London, Tokyo*. Princeton, NJ: Princeton University Press.

Schmitz, Hubert. 1995. 'Collective efficiency: growth path for small scale industry.' *Journal of Development Studies* 31(4).

Scott, Allen J. 2001. 'Introduction.' In Allen J. Scott, ed., *Global City-Regions: Trends, Theory, Policy*. Oxford and New York: Oxford University Press.

Scott, Allen John. 1998. *Regions and the World Economy: The Coming Shape of Global Production, Competition, and Political Order*. Oxford and New York: Oxford University Press.

Sellers, Jeffrey M. 2002. *Governing from Below: Urban Regions and the Global Economy*. Cambridge and New York: Cambridge University Press.

Shaw, Annapurna. 2012. *Indian Cities*. New Delhi: Oxford University Press.

Shaw, Annapurna and M. K. Satish. 2007. 'Metropolitan restructuring in post-liberalized India: separating the global and the local.' *Cities* 24(2): 148–63.

Singh, Mahendra P. and Douglas V. Verney. 2003. 'Challenges to India's centralized parliamentary federalism.' *Publius* 33(4), Emerging Federal Process in India (autumn, 2003), 1–20.

Sinha, Aseema. 2005. *The Regional Roots of Developmental Politics in India: A Divided Leviathan*. Bloomington, IN: Indiana University Press.

——2011. 'An institutional perspective on the post-liberalization state in India.' In Akhil Gupta and K. Sivaramakrishnan, eds, *The State in India after Liberalization*. London and New York: Routledge, pp. 49–68.

Sivaramakrishnan, K. C. 2004. 'Municipal and metropolitan governance. Are they relevant to the urban poor?' In *Forum on Urban Infrastructure and Public Service Delivery for the Urban Poor, Regional Asia*. New Delhi: Woodrow Wilson International Centre for Scholars and the National Institute of Urban Affairs.

——2009. 'Special economic zones. Issues of urban growth and management.' Centre for Policy Research, Occasional Paper No. 19: Centre for Policy Research.

——2011a. 'Urban development and metro governance.' *Economic and Political Weekly* 46(31): 49–55.

——2011b. *Re-Visioning Indian Cities. The Urban Renewal Mission*. New Delhi: Sage.

Smith, Neil. 2003. 'Remaking scale: competition and cooperation in pre-national and post-national Europe.' In Neil Brenner, Bob Jessop, Martin Jones and Gordon MacLeod, eds, *State/Space. A Reader*. Oxford: Blackwell.

Sreedevi, N. 2005. 'Finances of the Municipal Corporation of Hyderabad.' Paper presented at workshop entitled Actors, Policies and Urban Governance in Hyderabad, 20 September 2005, ASCI–CME, Hyderabad.

Srinivasulu, K. 2003. 'Party competition and strategies of mobilisation: an analysis of social coalitions in Andhra Pradesh.' In P. Wallace and R. Roy, eds, *India's 1999 Elections and 20th Century Politics*. New Delhi: Sage.

——2004. 'Political articulation and policy discourse in elections. Andhra Pradesh 2004.' *Economic and Political Weekly* 39(34).

Stone, Diane. 2004. 'Transfer agents and global networks in the "transnationalization" of policy.' *Journal of European Public Policy* 11(3): 545–66.

Stren, Richard E. 2001. 'Local governance and social diversity in the developing world: new challenges for globalizing city-regions.' In Allen J. Scott, ed., *Global City-Regions: Trends, Theory, Policy*. Oxford and New York: Oxford University Press.

Subramanian, T. S. 1996. 'Seeing the fiesta through.' *Frontline*, 20 September, 82–8.

Swyngedouw, Erik. 1992. 'The mammon quest: "glocalisation", interspatial competition and the monetary order – the construction of new scales.' In M. Dunford and G. Kafkalas, eds, *Cities and Regions in the New Europe*. London: Belhaven Press.

——1996. 'Reconstructing citizenship, the re-scaling of the state and the new authoritarianism: closing the Belgian mines.' *Urban Studies* 33(8): 1499–1521.

Swyngedouw, Erik, Frank Moulaert and Arantxa Rodriguez. 2002. 'Neoliberal urbanization in Europe: large-scale urban development projects and the new urban policy.' In Neil Brenner and Nik Theodore, eds, *Spaces of Neoliberalism: Urban Restructuring in North America and Western Europe*. Malden, MA and Oxford: Blackwell.

Tawa Lama-Rewal, Stéphanie. 2007. 'Neighborhood associations and local democracy: Delhi municipal elections 2007.' *Economic and Political Weekly* 42(47): 51–60.

Tewari, Meenu. 1999. 'Successful adjustment in Indian industry: the case of Ludhiana's woollen knitwear cluster.' *World Development* 27(9): 1651–71.

Therwath, Ingrid. 2008. 'La diaspora indienne aux Etats-Unis comme acteur international.' In Christophe Jaffrelot, ed., *New Delhi et le monde*. Paris: Autrement.

Trigilia, Carlo. 1986. 'Small-firm development and political subcultures in Italy.' *European Sociological Review* 2(3): 161–75.

Varshney, Ashutosh. 1999. 'Mass politics or elite politics? India's economic reforms in comparative perspective.' In Jeffrey Sachs, Ashutosh Varshney and Nirupam Bajpai, eds, *India in the Era of Economic Reforms*. New Delhi: Oxford University Press.

Vaugier-Chatterjee, Anne. 2009. 'Two dominant castes: the socio-political system in Andhra Pradesh.' In Christophe Jaffrelot and Sanjay Kumar, eds, *Rise of the Plebeians? The Changing Face of Indian Legislative Assemblies*. New Delhi: Routledge.

Veltz, Pierre. 1996. *Mondialisation, villes et territoires: une économie d'archipel*. Paris: PUF.

Verniers, Gilles. 2005. 'La montée des partis régionaux en Inde.' Institut d'Etudes Politiques de Paris, unpublished Master's thesis.

Vithal, B. P. R. and M. L. Sastry. 2001. *Fiscal Federalism in India*. New Delhi: Oxford University Press.

Warf, Barney and Santa Arias. 2009. *The Spatial Turn: Interdisciplinary Perspectives*. London and New York: Routledge.

World Bank. 2005. *State Fiscal Reforms in India: Progress and Prospects: A World Bank Report*. New Delhi: Macmillan India.

——2008. *Orissa in Transition*. Report No 44612–IN. Washington, DC: World Bank Document.

Wyatt, Andrew. 2009. *Party System Change in South India: Political Entrepreneurs, Patterns and Processes*. London: Routledge.

Zérah, Marie-Hélène. 2007. 'Middle class neighbourhood associations as political players in Mumbai.' *Economic and Political Weekly* 42(47): 61–8.

——2009. 'Participatory governance in urban management and the shifting geometry of power in Mumbai.' *Development and Change* 40(5): 853–77.

——2011. 'Le rôle des associations de résidants dans la gestion des services urbains à Hyderabad.' *Métropoles* [online], September 2011, mis en ligne le 29 novembre 2011, last consulted 27 January 2012. http: //metropoles.revues.org/4481.

Index

For Product Safety Concerns and Information please contact our EU
representative GPSR@taylorandfrancis.com
Taylor & Francis Verlag GmbH, Kaufingerstraße 24, 80331 München, Germany

www.ingramcontent.com/pod-product-compliance
Lightning Source LLC
Chambersburg PA
CBHW050512280326
41932CB00014B/2290